Lecture Notes in Computer Science 7757

Commenced Publication in 1973
Founding and Former Series Editors:
Gerhard Goos, Juris Hartmanis, and Jan van Leeuwen

Maristella Agosti   Nicola Ferro   Pamela Forner
Henning Müller   Giuseppe Santucci (Eds.)

Information Retrieval Meets Information Visualization

PROMISE Winter School 2012
Zinal, Switzerland, January 23-27, 2012
Revised Tutorial Lectures

 Springer

Volume Editors

Maristella Agosti
Nicola Ferro
University of Padua
Department of Information Engineering
Via Gradenigo 6/a, 35131 Padua, Italy
E-mail: maristella.agosti@unipd.it, ferro@dei.unipd.it

Pamela Forner
Center for the Evaluation of Language
and Communication Technologies (CELCT)
Via alla Cascata 56/c, 38123 Povo, TN, Italy
E-mail: forner@celct.it

Henning Müller
University of Applied Sciences Western Switzerland
TechnoArk 3, 3960 Sierre, Switzerland
E-mail: henning.mueller@hevs.ch

Giuseppe Santucci
Sapienza University of Rome
Department of Computer, Control
and Management Engineering Antonio Ruberti
Via Ariosto 25, 00185 Rome, Italy
E-mail: santucci@dis.uniroma1.it

ISSN 0302-9743   e-ISSN 1611-3349
ISBN 978-3-642-36414-3   e-ISBN 978-3-642-36415-0
DOI 10.1007/978-3-642-36415-0
Springer Heidelberg Dordrecht London New York

Library of Congress Control Number: 2013930306

CR Subject Classification (1998): H.3.1, H.3.3-5, H.3.7, H.4.1, H.5.1-3

LNCS Sublibrary: SL 3 – Information Systems and Application, incl. Internet/Web
and HCI

© Springer-Verlag Berlin Heidelberg 2013

Typesetting: Camera-ready by author, data conversion by Scientific Publishing Services, Chennai, India

Printed on acid-free paper

Springer is part of Springer Science+Business Media (www.springer.com)

Preface

In the context of the European Union (EU)-funded research project PROMISE (Participative Research labOratory for Multimedia and Multilingual Information Systems Evaluation), a winter school was organized in the small ski resort of Zinal, Valais, Switzerland during January 23-27, 2012[1].

PROMISE aims at advancing the experimental evaluation of complex multimedia and multilingual information systems in order to support individuals, commercial entities, and communities who design, develop, employ, and improve such complex systems. The overall goal of PROMISE is to deliver a unified environment collecting data, knowledge, tools, methodologies, and to help the user community which is involved in the experimental evaluation.

The title of the winter school was *From Information Retrieval to Information Visualization* and the goal was to bring together these two research domains that are currently quite separated but have an important potential to help each other in advancing the fields. Indeed, the school was attended by participants who came from one domain or the other and offered them the possibility of starting to acquire cross-disciplinary competencies. Interestingly enough, the school turned out to be a brainstorming and discussion opportunity also for the lecturers, since they had the chance to meet colleagues from a quite different field with their own perspectives on a ground of shared topics and issues, such as how to envision models and design systems around user needs, how to consider the user interaction and context, how to conduct evaluation, and so on.

In all, 17 high-quality lecturers from academia and industry were invited to speak on a large variety of topics from introduction talks to hot topics such as crowd sourcing and social media; 62 participants from 25 countries and four organizers followed the courses and helped to create lively discussions and an open atmosphere with many questions. Most of the speakers stayed for the entire week and enriched the discussions as well.

All participants had the possibility to present their own work with a poster during the first day of the winter school at the evening welcome reception that started many discussions among the participants. An evaluation and selection of the posters was performed and a symbolic best poster award – a bottle of excellent Swiss wine – was given to the three best posters.

The fact that the participants remained close together during the five days of the winter school and had many possibilities to meet with the other participants and the lecturers gave rise to many discussions and to a stimulating environment for both the participants and the lecturers.

---

[1] http://www.promise-noe.eu/events/winter-school-2012/

Altogether the PROMISE winter school can be seen as a great success in connecting two research domains and allowing a large number of participants to get in contact with high-quality lecturers and give them hopefully a better view of the research domains and also on the ways in which they can evaluate their own research and profit from tools of visualization that are available. Most participants gave very positive feedback, and hopefully the proceedings of the winter school will also help to record the main outcomes of the winter school for the future and for those persons who could unfortunately not participate.

An analysis of the evaluation forms after the winter school highlighted that most students very much enjoyed (more than 90% of the participants) the winter school and the atmosphere among the participants and the lecturers. Most presentations were enjoyed (about 90% of the participants); but sometimes the introductory presentations were regarded as too simple for a majority of PhD students. The students were generally interested in the different topics offered by the school (about 90% of the participants). The setting in a remote alpine valley was very much appreciated but the lack of a professional conference room and of limited infrastructures such as for lunch time were also regarded as problematic. Lectures of 90 minutes were regarded as too long, and perhaps short breaks after 45 minutes would have been a better option.

Acknowledgement

We would like to thank all the lecturers and participants to the PROMISE Winter School who gave an extremely valuable contribution and made the school a success.

We would like to thank those institutions and individuals who have made this school possible: University of Applied Sciences Western Switzerland and Conférence Universitaire de Suisse Occidentale (CUSO).

The PROMISE Winter School has been supported by: the PROMISE[2] network of excellence (contract n. 258191), the Khresmoi[3] (contract n. 257528) and CULTURA[4] (contract n. 269973) projects, as part of the 7th Framework Program of the European Commission, and by the ELIAS[5] research networking programme of the European Science Foundation.

December 2012   Maristella Agosti
                                                          Nicola Ferro
                                                          Pamela Forner
                                                          Henning Müller
                                                          Giuseppe Santucci

---

[2] http://www.promise-noe.eu/
[3] http://www.khresmoi.eu/
[4] http://www.cultura-strep.eu/
[5] http://www.elias-network.eu/

Organization

The 2012 PROMISE Winter School was organized by the University of Applied Sciences Western Switzerland, Sierre (HES-SO), together with Sapienza, University of Rome, Italy, and the University of Padua, Italy.

General Chair

Tiziana Catarci   Sapienza, University of Rome, Italy

Program Committee

Maristella Agosti	University of Padua, Italy
Nicola Ferro	University of Padua, Italy
Henning Müller	University of Applied Sciences Western Switzerland, Switzerland
Giuseppe Santucci	Sapienza, University of Rome, Italy

Local Organizing Committee

Alexandre Cotting	University of Applied Sciences Western Switzerland, Switzerland
Henning Müller	University of Applied Sciences Western Switzerland, Switzerland

Publicity Committee

Pamela Forner	Centre for the Evaluation of Language and Communication Technologies (CELCT), Italy
Hélène Mazo	Evaluations and Language resources Distribution Agency (ELDA), France

Table of Contents

Introduction to Information Visualisation

Alan Dix[1,2]

[1] Talis, 43 Temple Row, Birmingham, B2 5LS, UK
[2] University of Birmingham, School of Computer Science, Birmingham, UK
alan@hcibook.com
http://alandix.com/academic/teaching/Promise2012/

Abstract. This is a short introduction to information visualisation, which is increasingly important in many fields as information expands faster than our ability to comprehend it. Visualisation makes data easier to understand through direct sensory experience (usually visual), as opposed to more linguistic/logical reasoning. This chapter examines reasons for using information visualisation both for professional data analysts and also end-users. It will also look at some of the history of visualisation (going back 4,500 years), classic examples of information visualisations, and some current challenges for visualisation research and practice. Design of effective visualisation requires an appreciation of human perceptual, cognitive and also organisational and social factors, and the chapter discusses some of these factors and the design issues and principles arising from them.

Keywords: information visualisation, human–computer interaction, HCI, visual analytics.

1   Introduction

Information assails us in business, in science, in government and in day-to-day life, from the processing of massive scientific streams at CERN to sentiment analysis of millions of Twitter messages to gauge the popularity of a party, or to locate power outages. Information retrieval is about selecting out of this morass of data, relevant documents, images, and audio. Visualisation is about helping people make sense of either the original data sources or the subsets of data obtained through information retrieval. Both can operate independently, but also they have great power together.

This chapter is a short introduction to information visualisation. In it we will look at a number of areas. First, in the next section, we will look at the definition and scope of visualisation in general and information visualisation in particular. Most critically, despite the term being '*visual*isation', it may in fact involve other senses and is centrally about the use of these *senses* to *make sense* of data. Visualisation has various purposes and users; section 3 considers these, in particular the different ways in which information visualisation is used by data analysts compared with data consumers (whether a company CEO or newspaper reader).

While visualisation seems like a modern phenomenon, and indeed interactive computer visualisation is comparatively recent, in fact the roots of static visualisation

M. Agosti et al. (Eds.): PROMISE Winter School 2012, LNCS 7757, pp. 1–27, 2013.

can be traced back at least 4500 years. Section 4 presents a brief history of visualisation from Mesopotamian financial tables and 10th century line graphs to current spreadsheet graphics, data journalism and visual analytics. This is followed in section 5, by an overview of some of the kinds of visualisation that might be particularly useful in the context of information retrieval.

The chapter concludes with a discussion of some of the human-centred design principles that can be applied to visualisation choice and creation. We will consider detailed design issues; in particular the way interaction can soften the trade-offs that are inherent in making (static) visualisation choices. However, we will also consider the way visualisation (and for that matter information retrieval) fits into a larger social and organisational context.

2   What Is (Information) Visualisation

Defining Visualisation

Visualisation is perhaps easier to recognise than define. In his textbook "Information Visualisation" [1], Bob Spence refers to the dictionary definition:

> *visualize: to form a mental mode or mental image of something [1]*

He emphasises that visualisation is critically about *in*sight, what happens in your head, not a computer. Often the most powerful mental images are formed from words alone, but that would not correspond to the common notion of visualisation, which is often about the design of media (computer, paper) to help people.

So, for this chapter we shall adopt a slightly different definition of (information) visualisation:

> *making data easier to understand using direct sensory experience*

Note this is still about insight and understanding, but also about the perception ('sensory experience') and deliberate design ('making').

Note also that this definition says 'sensory', not simply 'visual', as the inner visualisation that makes you say "I see" can also be engendered by other senses. Although less common, you can have aural and tactile 'visualisation' – think of the click of a Geiger counter – faster clicks mean more radiation. These non-visual forms are particularly valuable for those with visual disability, but also in contexts when the eyes need to be elsewhere, for example while flying a plane. This all said, the vast majority of visualisation is, as the name suggests, visual. The visual cortex accounts for around 50% of our brain, and so it makes sense to use it.

Also note that the word 'direct' is in the definition to exclude *purely* rich textual descriptions, no matter how sharply they focus the mind. Although you use your eyes to read words or even tables of numbers, they are processed linguistically and logically, rather than the more instant feeling you get when you see a rising graph.

With many caveats to beware of pseudo-science, you can think of this as a form of left brain / right brain distinction. Not that one is better than the other. In statistics, one is taught never to start by calculating means, t-tests, etc., but instead always to start off by drawing graphs, trying to get a feel for the data (very right brain). Things are often obvious by simply glancing at a graph. However, having got an idea of what one thinks is true of the data, one does not trust that intuition, but then starts to calculate the statistics (very left brain) to verify the insight. The two work together.

Visualising Numbers

This does not mean that text and numbers are not an integral part of visualisation. Good layout can create direct visual (or other sensory) impressions. Look at the two columns of numbers in Figure 1. In each column try to see, as quickly as possible, which is the biggest number. This is harder in the left-hand column than the right-hand one. This is because the numbers in the right-hand column have their decimal points aligned, so the biggest numbers are also the ones that stick out furthest to the left of the decimal point. Effectively the line of figures acts like a miniature bar graph.

532.56	627.865
179.3	1.005763
256.317	382.583
15	2502.56
73.948	432.935
1035	2.0175
3.142	652.87
497.6256	56.34

Fig. 1. Visualising in numbers

Of course one may not care about the biggest numbers, in which case the alignment doesn't matter. As a first heuristic for information visualisation: "*think purpose*" – work out what you want the viewer to be able to do with the visualisation and use that to determine the form.

A more complex form of visualisation, where the numbers are still central, can be found in Table Lens [2]. This is like a spreadsheet except that columns and rows can be collapsed down to a few pixels each. Where a cell is not collapsed the numbers can be read (and will be aligned properly!). However, when the height of the cell becomes too small to show the number it is reduced to a line of pixels so that the column ends up a sort of mini-histogram. By sorting the middle column, it is immediately obvious that the column to the left is correlated to some extent with it, but that the right hand column far less so. When the column width is collapsed the histogram becomes even more miniature (columns 2 and 3 in figure 2), giving less detail, but still allowing an at a glance view of the tiny columns.

This is also an example of a general visualisation technique called 'focus+context' or fisheye view [3]. The expanded cells allow one to look at certain values in detail (the focus), whilst the collapsed cells allow one to get an idea of how that fits into the big picture (the context).

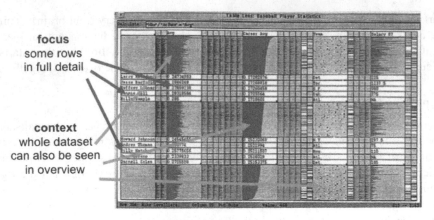

focus
some rows
in full detail

context
whole dataset
can also be seen
in overview

Fig. 2. Table Lens [2]

Information Visualisation

The term 'information' visualisation, as opposed to 'visualisation' in general, is usually used to contrast it with 'scientific' visualisation. In science there are many phenomena that have a direct connection to the physical world, but are in some way invisible, for example the airflow around an aircraft wing. This scientific data is often in the form of fields of numbers of vectors defined continuously over a 2D or 3D space.

In contrast, information visualisation is often concerned with data sometimes more complex structurally, but almost always discrete: hierarchies, tables, point data. Furthermore, the data of information visualisation often includes categorical data (e.g. gender male/female) as well as continuous data (e.g. height).

The two are not entirely distinct, for example, geographical information systems (GIS) involve data over 2D maps. Methods used to display regional petrol consumption for marketing purposes will not be so different from those showing average temperature patterns for climate modelling, and of course one might want to use both these data sets to understand patterns of global warming.

3   Why Use Visualisation and Who Is It for?

When creating visualisations there are two kinds of target audience.

First there is the data analyst, whose job it is to sift through data whether the academic interpreting experimental results, the forensic accountant looking for anomalies in a bank's accounts, the city planner working out the best route for a new cycleway, or the intelligence officer piecing together emails, tweets and passport data to prevent a terrorist attack.

The other group is the eventual data consumer, the client, audience, newspaper reader, or the CEO. These may range from a time-strapped manager to an illiterate peasant, but have in common that they are not experts at data analysis, and may not even be highly numerate beyond what they recall of basic school mathematics.

Given you are reading this book, it is likely that you have more in common with the first group, the scientist, statistician or professional, than the second. This means you need to work harder to design visualisations for the data-consumer, as you will not have as intuitive a grasp of what is good.

For each of these two groups we'll look at reasons why you may want to use visualisations.

For the Data Consumer

For the data consumer, the focus usually needs to be on simple, well understood, representations, that can be grasped at first time of looking. Sometimes, for example, when using a visualisation as part of a presentation, it is possible to introduce an audience to a more complex graphic, but often the visualisation has to work at first glance or not at all.

There are two main reasons for providing visualisations to the data consumer: *understanding* and *rhetoric*.

understanding – This is when we want to help others see what the analyst has already seen. For example, as part of teaching a course on mobile internet, you may want a graph to show the number of people accessing the internet via a mobile plotted against time. For the general public, graphs are often augmented with text and graphics to form 'infographics'. This is partly to make the visualisations more visually appealing (if the readers do not look at the visualisation they will learn nothing), and partly to point out particular features. For example, the page in figure 3, from the Guardian Datablog [4], shows the UK budget deficit from 1979 (the start of the Thatcher administration) until 2011. The colours denote the dominant party in power (blue=Conservative, red=Labour), the pictures at the top are the various Chancellors of the Exchequer at the time and actual numbers included in the figure.

Fig. 3. UK Deficit and Borrowing [4]

rhetoric – Visualisation can also be used to persuade readers of a particular point, whether valid or not. For example, every business plan includes a 'hockey stick' graph (see Fig 4.), that plots projected users / income over time, starting slow, but eventually taking off, showing the potential investor that this is a good business in which to invest. When we see graphs it is easy to be impressed, whether or not they are comprehensible. They seem professional, scientific, and, sadly, often the less comprehensible they are, the more people are impressed (if they are difficult they must be clever!). Rhetorical use of numbers or graphs can be misleading[1], or can be used to convince others of the truth, whether in an academic paper, newspaper, party political pamphlet, or PhD thesis.

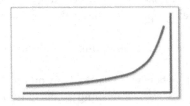

Fig. 4. A 'hockey stick' graph, as found in most business plans

It would be nice to say that the answer to rhetoric is facts, but sadly the world is not like that. The good guys have to tell as good a story as the bad guys! However, data certainly helps. Note that as well as infographics, the Guardian Datablog allows the download of the raw data behind the visualisations; a part of the practice called 'data journalism'. This means that a more experienced reader can download the data and manipulate or visualise it in any way that they wish, crucial for informed debate and democracy in an age where information is power.

Often small changes in a diagram can make a big difference to the lesson people take away. Consider figure 5, this shows UK deficit again (up means deficit, so bad, in this graph). However, unlike figure 3, this has been corrected for GDP (figures also obtained from the Guardian Datablog [4, 6]), so that deficit is shown relative to the size of the economy and hence its affordability (like looking at your credit card bill relative to your income.) In both figures it is clear that the deficit shot up in 2009 with the world credit crisis. Figure 3 also shows that with successive governments deficits have risen and fallen, with even the occasional foray into surplus. However, the graph also suggests a tendency for it to increase with time. Correcting for GDP, makes it clear that the overall level in real terms has remained pretty steady, with the last administration actually substantially lower than the long term average (2% GDP compared with 3%), counter to the popular narrative of all political parties.

---

[1] As Winston Churchill said, "*the only statistics you can trust are those you falsified yourself*", or as has been attributed to Disraeli and others "*there are three kinds of lies: lies, damned lies, and statistics*" [5].

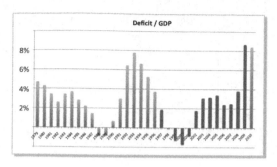

Fig. 5. UK Deficit relative to GDP (data from [4, 6])

For the Data Analyst

While many of the same lessons are true for the experienced data analyst, there is also the opportunity for training, or growing experience, so visualisations can afford to be more complex and powerful, potentially including novel techniques. Visualisation must still in a sense be 'first glance', as the purpose is to use the power of our sensory perception; if you have to spend too long figuring out what a visualisation means, then probably you are better looking straight at the numbers. However, this can be a 'first glance' *after* you have extensive experience and training. For example, engineers have many specialised graphs used to understand fluid flows, electric circuits or cybernetic systems. Some take several years of training during undergraduate study to master, but *once mastered* offer an instant overview.

For the data analyst we can also consider two kinds of purpose: *understanding* and *exploration*.

understanding – Like the data consumer, the analyst may in a sense 'know something' at least in abstract terms, but wish to make it salient to themselves. For example, we may be expecting a power law, so plot points on a log-log scale. For the academic, the graphics used to help oneself understand may well be similar to those published in an article as the audiences (oneself and other scientists) are similar. For example, figure 6 shows a box plot from the famous neutrinos faster than light paper [7]. For publication purposes the aim is to help others see (or convince others to believe) what you have seen in the paper. For the scientist who performed the experiment, the purpose is to confirm/disconfirm hypotheses, highlight exceptions or outliers.

exploration – The other purpose for the data analyst is to find new things that haven't even been considered before. This may be a scientist encountering a new kind of data or new phenomenon, or an intelligence officer seeking patterns amongst the chaos of billions of intercepted emails. In the previous cases, the design or selection of visualisation is driven by the desire to expose and clarify a previously known pattern. Here the aim is to seek the *unknown*, indeed maybe deliberately try to design visualisations that avoid the obvious, exploring new angles (maybe literally in a multidimensional plot!). Typically this may involve flipping between different kinds of visualisation, each of which may emphasise one aspect of the data, but hide others, or maybe present several visualisations at once (see Figure. 7).

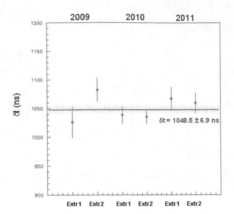

Fig. 6. Box plot of Neutrino transit times [7]

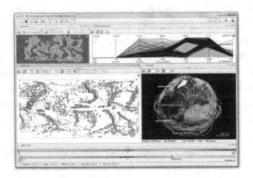

Fig. 7. Multiple parallel visualisations [8]

The human sensory system is tuned to find patterns, and this is exploited to the full in visualisation for data analysis, especially exploratory. However, we may also see patterns where there are none. The more different ways you look at something, the more likely one will appear to have a pattern, purely by chance. Visualisations, particularly those for exploratory analysis, therefore need to help the analyst distinguish happenstance from real underlying patterns.

4   A (Very) Brief History of Visualisation

4.1   Static Visualisation (From 2500 BC to 1990 AD)

The computer-driven visualisations shown so far are comparatively recent, but visualisations of various forms date back many millennia. The Mesopotamian clay tablet in Figure 8 is around 4500 years old, and contains a table of administrative information. We may think bureaucracy is new, but the vast majority of early clay tablet writing is of an administrative / financial nature, often including simple tables of numbers.

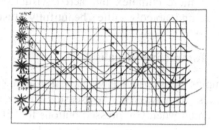

Fig. 8. Mesopotamian table on a clay tablet   **Fig. 9.** 10th Century time line

Moving on 3500 years, Figure 9 shows an early line graph of solar, lunar and planetary movements. The x-axis is days in the month and the lines track each heavenly body, where the y-axis is their height in the sky. Figure 10 skips forward to the 19th century and shows a visualisation of the Paris–Lyon train timetable, with the x-axis hours of the day (from 6am to 6am the next day) and the y-axis showing the distance along the route (Paris at the top Lyon at the bottom). Fast trains stand out clearly as the steeper lines.

These early visualisations were created painstakingly by hand, but with the advent of computing it became possible to create the same visualisations more quickly or easily, or to create new ones that would have been impossible before. In the early days this was done using very slow x-y pen plotters or character-graphics on a line printer, but now it is simply a matter of selecting a few options in Excel and pressing print!

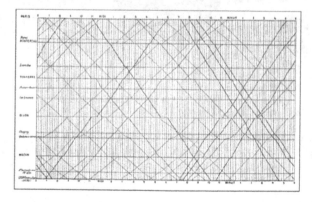

Fig. 10. 1855 Paris-Lyon train timetable

This use of computers to create fixed visualisations whether on screen, on a web page or PDF, or printed in a newspaper, is in many ways similar to the older hand-drawn illustrations. These static visualisations are still of great importance, particularly when communicating with others. Furthermore, understanding the effective design and qualities of *static* visualisations is an essential first step to creating more complex interactive visualisations. For static visualisation, the core texts are undoubtedly Tufte's beautifully illustrated books [9–11].

4.2   Interactive Visualisation

Examples of *interactive* visualisation can be traced back to early scanning vector graphics displays, or the seaside information boards where tiny lights were illuminated when you pressed buttons for different kinds of features. However, it was in the early 1990s when growing graphics power made it possible, for the first time, to create rich 3D graphics, complex visualisations and real-time interaction. This led to a blossoming of information visualisation (and other graphics) research notably in the groups at Xerox PARC and University of Maryland. Not all the ideas were good, just like with gloriously multi-fonted documents during the desktop publication revolution in the 1980s, there were many examples of gratuitous 3D, most of which are deservedly forgotten. However, despite this, most of the core kinds of visualisations in use today were introduced at that time (see selection in Figure 11), several of which will be discussed in the next section.

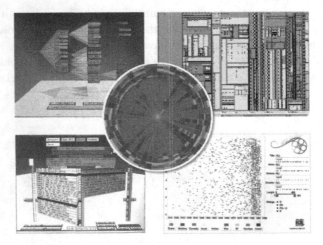

Fig. 11. Interactive Visualisations from the early 1990s: clockwise from top left: Cone Trees [12], TreeMaps [13], FilmFinder [14], Buttefly Browser [15], and Pixel Plotting [16] in centre (note how use of 3D distorts text in Butterfly Browser)

4.3   Current Directions

We have already seen examples of data journalism where rich, but simple to understand, infographics have made their way into mainstream media. Furthermore the web has increased the public expectations of high quality, often interactive, visualisations. These web visualisations are sometimes 'authored', that is created by the individual or institution responsible for the article or blog. However, there are also a number of data sharing and analysis sites that make it easy to upload and visualise your own data; figure 12 shows one example, IBM's "Many Eyes" [17]. Furthermore open data initiatives by governments and corporations across the world are making data on many aspects of life available to all from the environment to employment, crime to concert venues. Often this comes with an invitation to mashup and visualise the data in citizens' own interfaces.

Fig. 12. IBM Many Eyes [17]

Various factors including eScience and the web itself have led to an increase in the volume of available data, from the scientific data streams of ozone monitoring stations, to the trivia of Twitter streams. Analysing this data has become big business and a major challenge. Happily, in parallel with the rise in big data there has been a rise in processing power, both on the desktop and also in the cloud where it is now relatively easy to spin up significant computational power as needed and computational frameworks, notably MapReduce [18], for dealing with distributed computation on massive data.

Where this computation meets visualisation, the nascent field of visual analytics is growing [19, 20] (see the chapter later in this volume). This combines machine learning and other data processing algorithms with interactive visualisation to enable interactive problem solving.

5   Classic Visualisations for Information Retreival

There are at least as many kinds of visualisation as there are kinds of data. In this section we will look at a few classes that are particularly relevant for information retrieval.

5.1   Hierarchical Data

Trees, taxonomies and hierarchies are perhaps the most ubiquitous form of data structure after the humble table; we all encounter trees whether organisation charts, biological taxonomies, (parts of) formal ontologies, XML data, or file system hierarchies. After file browser/outliner style textual layouts, the most common form of tree visualisation is some sort of box and line 'organisation' chart as in Figure 13.

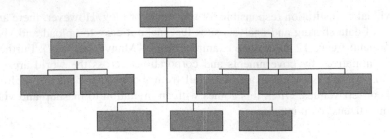

Fig. 13. Simple tree visualisation

However, these simple visualisations tend to breakdown as trees get bigger. Figure 14 shows a relatively small tree (part of a task structure), but even on this small tree, we can see a number of problems of scale. The boxes are labelled, but it is often hard to fit the labels in the boxes without them overlapping. Furthermore, as one looks at lower levels of the tree, the width grows very rapidly leading to extensive horizontal scrolling, and consequent loss of context. One option is to use 3D, and figure 15 shows the Cone Tree [12], which lays out the tree nodes in rings vertically or horizontally (Cam Tree) connected to their parents, creating 'cones'. When a user selects a node the relevant ring swings round so that the selected node is in the centre of attention.

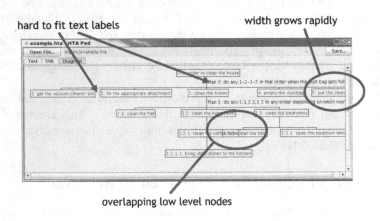

Fig. 14. Simple tree visualisation

While the use of 3D apparently increases the amount of space available we still view these in 2D, so the occlusion is still there, just more acceptable as we view it as the natural essence of the 3D world. Note how the shadows are used to help make sense of the trees in figure 15. The vertical layout on the left of Figure 15 had particular problems with text labels, solved partially by the horizontal layout on the right – small differences matter in visualisation.

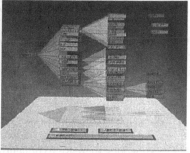

Fig. 15. Using 3D: the Cone Tree, vertical and horizontal variants [12]

Another approach is TreeMaps, which dissect and fill 2D space [13]. TreeMaps are particularly suitable for trees where there is some notion of size or volume (e.g. disk utilisation in a file system, staffing or spending in organisational units). The TreeMap divides the space horizontally and vertically on successive steps, using the 'size' of the subtree to determine the space allocated. In the end each smallest level has area proportional to its size (see Fig. 16).

```
x
    x/a  – 4
    x/b  – 2
y
    y/c  – 1
    y/d  – 1
    y/e  – 1
```

Fig. 16. TreeMap of two level hierarchical data: data on the left, TreeMap on the right

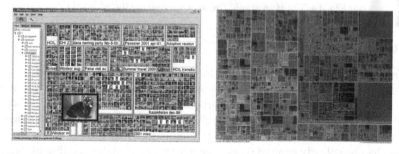

Fig. 17. TreeMap variants for images at leaves and large numbers of nodes [13]

Early versions of TreeMaps applied the simple alternating horizontal/vertical layout algorithm. However, later variants have divided space differently to avoid artefacts such as many thin rectangles when a node has a large number of children, particularly important when displaying images in the leaf nodes (Figure 17, left). The TreeMap is in many ways quite simple, but is one of the more heavily used 'complex' visualisations, proving itself able to manage vast trees (Figure 17, right) and yet still be relatively comprehensible.

Finally for here, although not the end of the visualisation of hierarchical data by any means, are methods that distort space in order to show a tree. The most well known (but not most well used or understood) of these is the Hyperbolic Browser [21]. This began with the failure of simple circular layouts to deal with larger trees. If a tree has a constant branching factor, say on average 3 nodes per parent, then the number of subnodes increase exponentially at each level down: 3, 9, 27, 81, 243, 729, ... However, when we layout in a circle, then the circumference of successively larger circles only grows linearly – there is never enough space!

Mathematicians deal with a kind of curved space called hyperbolic geometry. This had theoretical beginnings, but now turns out to have applications in cosmological physics. The important feature of hyperbolic space is that the circumference of 'circles' in this (rather odd) geometry increases exponentially with the diameter of the circle – perfect for trees. Unfortunately we do not see in hyperbolic geometry, so this is then projected back down into 2D (see Fig. 18) leading to an effect rather like earlier Fish Eye visualisations [3].

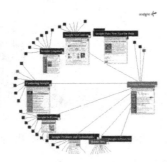

Fig. 18. The Hyperbolic Browser visualising the web [21]

5.2   Clustered Data

Quite frequently in information retrieval there is no fixed structure, instead, we have large sets of search results, with common attributes, but no given hierarchical structure. Although there is no given structure, sometimes a form of structure is induced using clustering, whether at a single level to give groups of related nodes, or at multiple levels with clusters of clusters leading to tree structure.

Hierarchies are clearly centred on our linguistic/logical understanding of the world, and to some extent need to be made more immediate to our sensory perception. In contrast, clusters correspond closely to human perception, we see a group of sheep and, without consciously thinking, "they are all similar" they become a flock in our minds. However, the fuzzier concept has its own challenges.

Where the data is numeric and can be shown on some sort of scatter plot, there are obvious ways to show a cluster. Figure 19.a shows a group of elements that have been identified as a cluster. This might have been done by an automatic algorithm, or maybe by the user choosing or encircling elements interactively. If they are being visualised on a 2D plane like this, then we may visualise the cluster by showing its extent, perhaps by drawing a border around the cluster (Fig. 19.a) or shading the area included in the cluster (Fig. 19.b, shading). This is particularly appropriate when there is an obvious region, for example, if the user has lassoed the elements, or the clustering algorithm creates a segmentation of space. Of course this may not be an ellipse as in Fig. 19, but perhaps an area delimited by lines, or a more complex shape, and if there is not an obvious region we might just use the convex hull of the points.

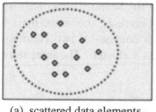 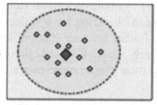

(a) scattered data elements   (b) show average or extent

Fig. 19. Visualising numeric clusters

The other obvious way to show a cluster is using some form of average position. The large point in Figure 19.b is not one of the original points, but an average of all the points. Using an average like this is an advantage if we want to reduce the clutter of the display [22], reducing the number of points displayed by just showing the centre point of each cluster. Of course, this can be odd for some sorts of data, for example, the (in)famous average of "2.2 children" per family in the 1970s. However, numbers at least admit this form of representation.

Things get far more difficult when the clusters represent non-numeric data, images, text, or even categorical data such as gender – 0.2 of a child is at least more easily comprehensible than 55% female. Sometimes this kind of data is mapped into 2D space, for example with multi-dimensional scaling, in which case this derived numeric data can be used to display in the same way as numeric data. However, the average value of such derived statistics is likely to become increasingly hard to interpret, and you are still left with the problem of what details to show if the user selects the 'average' element.

Where the data is categorical there may be some attributes that are common to most or all of the cluster, in which case these may be used, but for rich media: text, images, sound, rather than trying to compute some form of average, or generated archetype, it is often better to give one or more real examples.

These examples may be deliberately chosen to be 'typical' using some measure (Fig. 20.a). For example, with text one may compute similarity measures based on co-occurrence of words and then use examples that are central based on this.

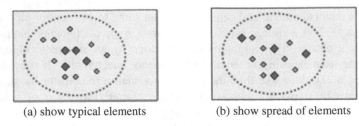

(a) show typical elements   (b) show spread of elements

Fig. 20. Visualising non-numeric clusters

Alternatively one may deliberately look for examples that are spread widely over the elements in the cluster (Fig. 20.b). When there is no systematic way of choosing these, one can simply randomly choose a number of examples.

This use of example data points can be seen in the Scatter-Gather browser, a classic visualisation of clustering for text documents. Figure 21 shows the main window of the Scatter–Gather browser (bottom left), which consists of two columns with five regions in each. Each of these regions represents a cluster. The inset shows a close-up of one of these cluster representations.

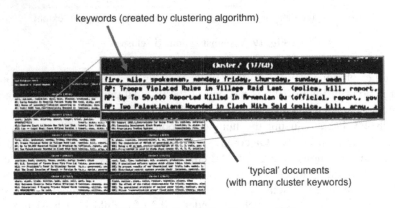

keywords (created by clustering algorithm)

'typical' documents
(with many cluster keywords)

Fig. 21. The Scatter–Gather Browser [23]

The Scatter–Gather browser is designed to help users find documents based on hard to state or 'recognised when seen' criteria. The system starts with some collection of documents, perhaps the entire library or perhaps the results of a keyword search. It then uses an automatic algorithm to cluster the documents into 10 clusters. The users selects one or more clusters that look interesting, the system gathers these into a new set, and then repeats the process clustering the chosen document set into 10 new clusters. Eventually, when the clusters are small enough, the user can swop to a more conventional view for final selection.

The problem here is that the original library may consist of many thousands or millions of documents so that the early clusters themselves consist of very large sets. In the inset image in Figure 21 there are two main regions. On the top are a number of keywords. These are commonly occurring words in the cluster – a form of the 'common attribute' visualisation. Below that area are three individual documents represented by a short title or snippet; that is, a form of visualisation by choosing typical elements.

5.3   Multi-attribute Data

Data items have many attributes, for example a bibliographic record may have title, authors, date and place of publication, number of pages, references, citations, keywords and taxonomic classification.

The earliest approach to such data was some form of boolean query using a command-line interface (Fig. 22). This form of querying is still possible both for traditional SQL databases and more recent databases such as RDF data using SPARQL or noSQL databases such as MongoDB's command line mode [24].

```
> new query
> type='journal' and keyword='visualisation'
query processing complete - 2175 results
list all (Y/N)
> N
```

Fig. 22. Boolean queries at a command line

Of course ordinary users are not expected to use this form of query language, however, the most common interfaces are really only one step beyond, giving some sort of search form allowing target values to be entered against different fields. For example, Figure 23 is the Gmail advanced search form. Boolean queries dressed up!

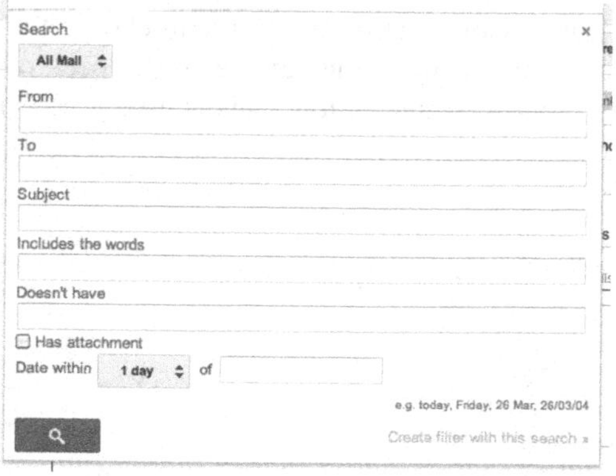

Fig. 23. Google Gmail search form (http://mail.google.com/)

More sophisticated interfaces allow faceted browsing. This is where several selection attributes are shown simultaneously then, as one makes selections against one, the options on others are narrowed correspondingly. For example, Figure 24 shows three document attributes: keywords, author and document type. The user has selected 'interaction' and 'visualisation' from the keywords and 'journal' as the document type. The count '173' shows the total number of documents satisfying both – effectively documents where:

```
(  "interaction"  IN  keywords  OR  "visualisation"  IN  keywords  )
    AND type = "journal"
```

Note that against each author and keyword is a count. This shows the number of selected documents that also include the relevant attribute. Note that in the keywords list 39+157>173 as there are 23 documents with both keywords.

keywords		authors		types	
▸ digital libraries		▾ all	173	▾ all	173
▾ HCI	173	catarci	53	book	
formal models		dix	9	conference	
interaction	157	jones	17	journal	173
task analysis		shneiderman	153	other	
visualisation	39	smith	0		
web		wilson	22		

Fig. 24. Faceted browsing, similar to HiBrowse [25]

There are many examples of faceted browsing, both for conventional tabular data and also alternative data including Semantic Web data [26]. The images above are based on one of the earliest, HiBrowse [25], which was used for various applications including large document repositories and hotel selection.

The dynamic counts are a critical feature of the HiBrowse. With early command line query interfaces it was easy to refine a search and then find it ended up with no results. In Figure 24 it is obvious that if you decide to choose the author 'smith', then you will have no results – that is the counts give a sort of peek over the horizon as to what will happen *after* your next interaction. This is a very powerful, but underused, visual interaction heuristic.

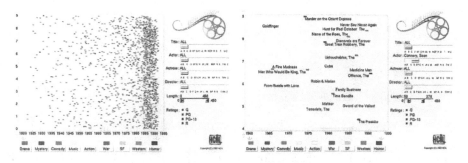

Fig. 25. Dynamic filtering in FilmFinder [14]

In the above example, the interactions were discrete, selections of attributes leading to updated values. However, sometimes interactions can be made more rapid and continuous. Figure 25 shows two screenshots of FilmFinder [14], another early faceted browsing interface. Within each screen there is a larger area to the left which shows a scatter plot of films, coloured by genre and plotted against date (x-axis) and popularity (y-axis). On the right are a number of sliders, which allow the setting of maximum and minimum values for various attributes. As the user moves these sliders, the points on the scatter graph are filtered in real time giving instant feedback. Note that in the right-hand screen shot the filtering has reduced the number of points and so the titles of the films are also shown.

Another example of faceted browsing is the Influence Explorer [27, 28]. This was designed to allow exploration of complex engineering problems including simulations. An example problem was light bulb design choices. There are various input parameters that can be chosen (e.g. material, thickness and length of filament), and various output measures (e.g. cost, lifetime). Large numbers of simulations are run to create a large set of multi-dimensional data points, each corresponding to a single simulation run. The engineer can then use dynamic sliders to either select 'input parameter' ranges (e.g. choose range of thicknesses), or 'output' parameters (e.g. maximum cost). So far, this is like the FilmFinder interface, except above each slider is a small histogram showing the way the currently selected items (simulation runs) are distributed over the relevant values. This is effectively like the counts in HiBrowse making it possible to see whether the sliders are hovering near critical values.

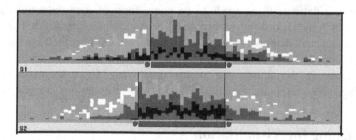

Fig. 26. 'Peek over the horizon' histograms in Influence Explorer [27, 28]

5.4   Big Data

One of the trends noted in section 4.3 is the vast data sets that now need to be analysed. Many visualisations fail when dealing with large data. Some problems are computational, simply too many points to perform calculations on, especially for real time interactive visualisation. Some problems are more intrinsic to the visualisation, for example if there are too many points on a scatter plot it becomes unreadable, just solid colour.

One approach is to simply use less space to visualise each item. Figure 27 shows VisD, an example of *pixel plotting* [16], which uses a single pixel for each data point and then packs these densely filling the available space. In Figure 27 the pixels are plotted in circles starting in the centre and then spiralling outwards. Similar techniques are also used for filling square areas. The colour represents a single attribute of the data, and some other attribute is used to order the plotting. For example, if the data is ordered by time then trends in the data would appear as changes in the average colour between centre and periphery, and periodicity would show up as segments or swirling patterns.

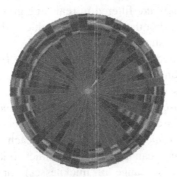

Fig. 27. Pixel plotting [16]

Pixel plotting allows 100s of thousands or millions of data points to be plotted on an ordinary display, but still this does not help with many current datasets, for example the tens of billions of web pages on a typical crawl.

For these vast datasets there needs to be some form of data reduction. This may take the form of some sort of pre-programmed or emergent aggregation. For example, detecting clusters and displaying the cluster averages, as described earlier – that is visualising groups not individual elements. Example data points can also be used, effectively reducing the number of points displayed. These examples might be selected using some systematic technique, or simply using random sampling [29].

6   Designing for Visualisation

6.1   Perception and Purpose

As we have seen there are many different forms of visualisation. When choosing a visualisation or designing a new one there are several factors to take into account:

visual 'affordances' – what we can see – Our eyes are better at some things than others. For example, they are much better at discriminating levels of darkness, than hues of colour, and are much better comparing lengths of lines when the lines share a common base.

objectives, goals and tasks – what we need to see – Recall the lists of numbers in Figure 1, if the purpose is to compare sizes or find the biggest/smallest, then aligning the decimal points helps you to do this. If you can understand the purpose of a visualisation, you are in a better position to ensure that the visual affordances make this purpose achievable.

aesthetics – what we like to see – Sometimes visualisations simply need to be functional, but often they also need to be attractive. This is certainly true of the infographics intended for public consumption. However, it is also true of professional systems as we all work better when things are pleasant to look at.

These different visualisation factors often conflict. For example, business reports often use 3D charts as they look impressive, even though it is usually harder to make visual discrimination of (static) 3D images. Particularly common, and problematic are 3D pie charts. Pie charts are difficult anyway as our eyes are not good at comparing angles, but when the pie chart is put in perspective it becomes nearly impossible to compare the resulting differently shaped segments.

For some purposes the functional aspects, the fit between perception and purpose, is most important. For others, including the persuasive use of visualisation, the aesthetics may be as or even more important. Furthermore there may be several intended purposes, which may each be optimally suited for different visualisations. As in all design the art is in choosing an appropriate trade-off between these conflicting goals.

6.2   Interaction

One of the advantages of interaction is that it can relax some of the trade-offs intrinsic in visualisation by allowing some choices to be altered dynamically. This can be used in complex visualisations, for example, the FilmFinder allowed the setting of parameter ranges for filtering which would have to be chosen beforehand and fixed in a static visualisation. However, very simple visualisations can be made surprisingly powerful by just a little interaction.

As an example, let's consider the simple stacked histogram of fruit sales in Figure 28. This representation is quite good at giving one a sense of the overall trend of the total over time (the overall height of the bars) and of the breakdown of fruits within overall sales. It is also easy to see the trend over time of apple sales, as they are the bottom category. However it is very hard to see the trends of other fruits, for example, are the sales of bananas increasing or decreasing? With a static stacked histogram, not all fruits can be equally easy to visually analyse and so the designer needs to make choices and trade-offs.

Fruit Sales 1992-1997

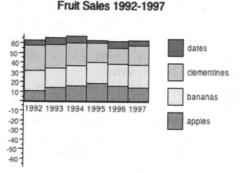

Fig. 28. Stacked Histogram

However, if the histogram is augmented with interaction, this trade-off can be relaxed. Figure 29 shows (a static screen shot of) interactive stacked histograms (also called 'dancing histograms') [30]. Two very small interactive additions have been made. Figure 29.a shows how the area at the bottom right changes to show details of a given cell of the histogram as the user floats their mouse over it. Figure 29.b shows how selecting a particular fruit makes the histogram bars drop so it is possible to see trends in the chosen fruit. We can now answer the question; in fact banana sales have a slight, but steady increasing trend.

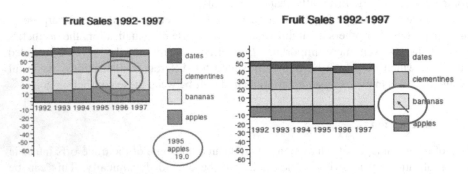

Fig. 29. Interactive Stacked Histogram [30] (a) counts for individual cells (b) changing the base

You can probably think of other simple interactive modifications to a chart like this, perhaps allow the user to re-order the fruits by dragging the labels in the key, maybe completely swopping the visualisation to show side-by-side bars.

There are various different kinds of interaction, most of which we have seen in previous examples:

highlighting and focus – In the Cone Tree in figure 15, the user has selected one of the nodes causing it and its parents to be highlighted and also rotated to the front of the view. This highlighting is useful even for simple elements, but more so for examples such as this, when the focus is not just a single point, but in some way spread across the visualisation, as in this case with the node and its parents, or highlighting a line in a chart such as the Paris–Lyon timetable in Figure 10.

drill down and hyperlinks – In the TreeMap of images in Figure 17, the image of the cat has been selected and expanded so that we can see more details. Sometimes items of interest are expanded in place, as in this case, or an outliner or file chooser when a folder is opened. Alternatively drilling into an element may open a fresh window or page, so being more like a hyperlink.

overview and context – As well as seeing details it is often important to get an overview of all the data. The TreeMaps in Figure 17 do this showing an entire photo collection (on the left) or file system (on the right). When we are seeing details, we may have to hide or reduce this overview, but having some idea of the context of what we are looking at is important. This is sometimes achieved by having a separate high-level view, for example, when you zoom in to a part of a picture, image editors often show a thumbnail of the whole image with the currently selected portion marked.

Alternatively the surrounding data may be shown in a compressed way, as in the TableLens in Figure 2 or the Hyperbolic Browser in Figure 18; this is called a FishEye view [3], as the effect can be similar to looking through a FishEye camera lens.

changing parameters – As noted, when making a static visualisation, one has to make choices including choosing the values of critical parameters. By making these modifiable by the user some of the trade-offs can be softened. We saw this in the dynamic sliders in FilmFinder (Figure 25) and Influence Explorer (Figure 26). The Dancing Histograms (Figure 29) are also an example of this, in this case the parameter being the data row on the baseline.

changing representations – Another simple form of interaction is to allow the user to swop entirely the kind of visualisation. For example we might allow users to swop between histogram and pie chart. This should not be used as a 'cop out', avoiding making the design decision by passing it to the user; only certain visualisations are meaningful or helpful. However, where there are several forms of visualisation, each of which may be good for seeing different things in the data, then it is reasonable to allow the user to choose which is most appropriate at a particular moment.

temporal fusion – Rather than swopping between visualisations, we may have more than one visualisation present at the same time. Sometimes these represent views so different that they are simply alternatives. However, often there are points of connection, maybe literally points representing the same data item. We can often make these connections more apparent through interactions that have parallel effects of several visualisations (hence *temporal fusion* bringing them together through things happening at the same time). For example, selecting a data item in one view might highlight it in the other. Figure 30 shows another example of temporal fusion, the PieTree [30, 31]. On the left is a view of the screen with an ordinary Pie chart on the left and the corresponding table of data on the right. However, the data has an hierarchical structure (regions and counties), and when the outliner view on the right is opened to view the region in more details, the corresponding Pie chart segment on the left 'explodes' with each thin segment representing one of the constituent counties.

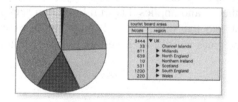 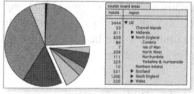

Fig. 30. PieTree [30, 31] (a) Pie chart on left and table of data on the right (b) Pie segment explodes as outliner is expanded

Ben Shneiderman brought several of these methods of interaction together in what is often referred to as his visualisation mantra [32]:

- *overview first,*
- *zoom and filter,*
- *then details on demand*

Figure 31 shows these as they apply to FilmFinder. First one is presented with a StarField display of dots representing films (*overview first*). The dynamic sliders allow one to zoom into particular parts of this, both spatially looking at particular date ranges, and also in terms of filtering out unwanted films by some criteria such as genre (*zoom and filter*). Finally, if one of the dots is selected details of the chosen film appears in a pop-up (*details on demand*).

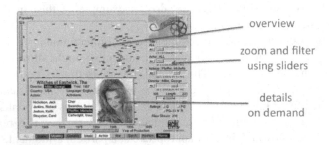

Fig. 31. Shneiderman's visualisation mantra on FilmFinder [14]

6.3   Information Scent

With the FilmFinder you can zoom into areas, look at particular films, all following the visualisation mantra; but how do you know which film to click? You might just explore using trial and error, simply clicking things until you found something useful. In fact, FilmFinder does give a little more than this, in the screen shot on the right in Figure 25, as the user filtered down the results to a small enough number the titles appear. Even if you don't know a film the title would give you some idea of whether it was worth looking in more detail. This is rather like the 'looking over the horizon' effect we saw in HiBrowse counts or the Influence Explorer's miniature histograms.

Pirolli calls these clues as to where to go next Information Scent [33]. He likens finding information to a wild animal seeking food and borrows the analysis techniques and mathematics of biological foraging theory and applies this to information seeking giving *information foraging theory*. Just like the smell of fresh grass might give a sheep hints as to the best way to go, these clues act like scent telling us where to look next for information.

6.4   The Wider Context

It is important to remember that visualisation takes place within a wider human and organisational context. In figure 32, the lower portion shows aspects of the visualisation process that are perhaps most obviously core. There is first data, which is typically processed in some way, perhaps using information retrieval methods, and then visualised. The segment on the bottom is where the user is interacting directly with the visualisation and maybe also, especially in the case of visual analytics, interacting with the processing.

However, this is neither the beginning nor the end of the story. Originally the data came from the world, it was collected for a reason, maybe selected based on criteria before it ever enters the visualisation system. Furthermore, one visualises data for a reason. It will in some way influence one's own future decisions and actions, or those of the organisation of which one is a part.

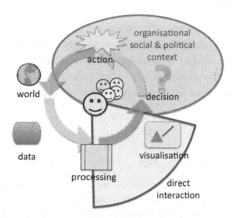

Fig. 32. The big picture – visualisation in context (from [34])

When designing or using visualisation systems this often needs to be taken into account. For example, recalling the different purposes and audiences described in section 1, one might start off with a visualisation system focused on the professional data analyst, maybe engaged in some form of exploratory analysis. However, once the analyst has found some interesting pattern, it will need to be presented to a decision maker, maybe a senior manager in a company, that is a move from exploratory analysis to end-user understanding and/or persuasion. It is sadly rare to find a visualisation system which takes this into account.

Of course, the decisions and actions one makes based on visualisation have an effect on the world yielding more data, that may need to be visualised in order to assess the impact of one's actions.

7   Summary

Information visualisation can involve different senses, not just vision; visual representations are most common and often most powerful because of the overwhelming proportion of our brains dedicated to visual processing. Visualisation can be used to aid understanding or to persuade (or even mislead). However, most challenging is the design of visualisation for exploratory analysis, as by definition we don't know what we are looking for and hence what to emphasise visually.

We have considered examples of many kinds of visualisation, both static visualisations (ancient and modern) and, most importantly, interactive information visualisation. We looked at ways to visualise three main kinds of data structure:

hierarchies, clusters and multi-attribute data. However, these are just common examples and there are as many kinds of visualisation as there are data, including, *inter alia*, temporal data, geographic data, and multi-media.

We have also seen that designing visualisations requires an understanding of the human visual (or other sensory) system, the objective/goals that the visualisation is to aid, and aesthetics (especially for persuasive graphics). Choosing an appropriate representation typically requires choices and trade-offs between factors, but interactive visualisation can soften these trade-offs, allowing choices to be remade by the user as they interact with the system. However, it is also important to remember that visualisation takes place within a broader context where the data being visualised comes from the world, the visualisation helps individuals or organisations to make decisions, and these decisions lead to actions, which change the world and thus the data being visualised.

References

1. Spence, B.: Information visualization: design for interaction. Prentice Hall (2007)
2. Pirolli, P., Rao, R.: Table lens as a tool for making sense of data. In: Proceedings of the Workshop on Advanced Visual Interfaces, pp. 67–80. ACM, New York (1996)
3. Furnas, G.W.: Generalized fisheye views. In: Proceedings of the SIGCHI Conference on Human Factors in Computing Systems, pp. 16–23. ACM, New York (1986)
4. Deficit, national debt and government borrowing - how has it changed since (1946), http://www.guardian.co.uk/news/datablog/2010/oct/18/deficit-debt-government-borrowing-data
5. Lee, P.: Lies, Damned Lies and Statistics. part of Materials for the History of Statistics (2012), http://www.york.ac.uk/depts/maths/histstat/lies.htm
6. UK GDP since (1948), http://www.guardian.co.uk/news/datablog+business/economicgrowth.
7. Adam, T., Agafonova, N., Aleksandrov, A., et al.: Measurement of the neutrino velocity with the OPERA detector in the CNGS beam. Arxiv (November 17, 2011)
8. Tominski, C., Abello, J., Schumann, H.: CGV–An interactive graph visualization system. Computers & Graphics 33, 660–678 (2009)
9. Tufte, E.: The Visual Display of Quantitative Information. Graphics Press, Cheshire (1983)
10. Tufte, E.: Envisioning Information. Graphics Press, Cheshire (1990)
11. Tufte, E.: Visual Explanations. Graphics Press, Cheshire (1997)
12. Robertson, G.G., Mackinlay, J.D., Card, S.K.: Cone Trees: animated 3D visualizations of hierarchical information. In: Proc. CHI 1991, pp. 189–194. ACM Press, New Orleans (1991)
13. 2D space filling visualisation for hierarchical data
14. Ahlberg, C., Shneiderman, B.: Visual information seeking: tight coupling of dynamic query filters with starfield displays. In: Proceedings of the SIGCHI Conference on Human factors in Computing Systems: Celebrating Interdependence, pp. 313–317. ACM Press, New York (1994)
15. Mackinlay, J.D., Rao, R., Card, S.K.: An organic user interface for searching citation links. In: Proceedings of the SIGCHI Conference on Human Factors in Computing Systems, pp. 67–73. ACM Press/Addison-Wesley Publishing Co., New York (1995)

16. Keim, D.A., Hao, M.C., Dayal, U., Hsu, M.: Pixel Bar Charts: A Visualization Technique for Very Large Multi-Attribute Data Sets. Information Visualization Journal 1 (2002)
17. IBM Many Eyes, http://www-958.ibm.com/software/data/cognos/manyeyes/.
18. Dean, J., Ghemawat, S.: MapReduce: simplified data processing on large clusters. Commun. ACM 51, 107–113 (2008)
19. Thomas, J.J., Cook, K.A.: Illuminating the Path: The Research and Development Agenda for Visual Analytics. IEEE Press (2005)
20. Keim, D., Kohlhammer, J., Ellis, G., Mansmann, F.: Mastering the Information Age Solving Problems with Visual Analytics. Eurographics Association (2011)
21. Lamping, J., Rao, R., Pirolli, P.: A focus+context technique based on hyperbolic geometry for visualizing large hierarchies. In: Proc. ACM CHI 1995 Conference (1995)
22. Ellis, G., Dix, A.: A Taxonomy of Clutter Reduction for Information Visualisation. IEEE Transactions on Visualization and Computer Graphics 13, 1216–1223 (2007)
23. Pirolli, P., Schank, P., Hearst, M., Diehl, C.: Scatter/Gather browsing communicates the topic structure of a very large text collection. In: Proc. CHI 1996, pp. 213–220. ACM Press, Vancouver (1996)
24. Mongo - The Interactive Shell (2012), http://www.mongodb.org/display/DOCS/mongo+-+The+Interactive+Shell
25. Pollitt, A.S., Ellis, G.P., Smith, M.P.: HIBROWSE for bibliographic database. J. Inf. Sci. 20, 413–426 (1994)
26. Schraefel, m.c, Karam, M., Zhao, S.: mSpace: interaction design for user-determined, adaptable domain exploration in hypermedia. In: Workshop on Adaptive Hypermedia and Adaptive Web Based Systems, pp. 217–235 (2003)
27. Tweedie, L., Spence, R., Dawkes, H., Su, H.: The Influence Explorer. In: Proc. ACM CHI 1995 (1996)
28. Tweedie, L., Spence, R., Dawkes, H., Su, H.: The Influence Explorer (video) - a tool for design. In: Proc. ACM CHI 1996 (1996)
29. Dix, A., Ellis, G.: By Chance - enhancing interaction with large data sets through statistical sampling. In: Proceedings of the Working Conference on Advanced Visual Interfaces, pp. 167–176. ACM, New York (2002)
30. Dix, A., Ellis, G.: Starting Simple - adding value to static visualisation through simple interaction. Presented at the Proceedings of Advanced Visual Interfaces, AVI 1998, L'Aquila, Italy (1998)
31. O'Donnell, R., Dix, A., Ball, L.: Exploring the PieTree for Representing Numerical Hierarchical Data. Presented at the Proceedings of Proceedings of HCI 2006, People and Conputers XX - Engage (2006)
32. Shneiderman, B., Plaisant, C.: Designing the User Interface: Strategies for Effective Human-Computer Interaction, 4th edn. Pearson Addison Wesley (2004)
33. Pirolli, P.: Information foraging theory: adaptive interaction with information. Oxford University Press, Oxford (2007)
34. Dix, A., Pohl, M., Ellis, G.: Perception and Cognitive Aspects. In: Mastering the Information Age Solving Problems with Visual Analytics, pp. 109–130. Eurographics Association (2011)

Principles for Human-Centred Design of IR Interfaces

Maria Francesca Costabile and Paolo Buono

Dipartimento di Informatica, Università degli Studi di Bari Aldo Moro
Via Orabona 4, Bari, Italy
{buono,costabile}@di.uniba.it

Abstract. Since the '80s, Human-Computer Interaction (HCI) researchers have performed a lot of work to identify principles, techniques, and methodologies that can support design, evaluation and implementation of interactive systems that fulfill needs and expectations of their users. This chapter discusses concepts, such as usability and user experience, which are of great importance for the success of interactive systems, illustrating how Human-Centred Design is fundamental to create successful user interfaces. Principles proposed by the HCI community to support interface design are presented, analyzing the principles that have a major impact on IR interfaces.

Keywords: user interfaces, usability, user experience (UX), design principles.

1   Introduction

Before the advent of the web, Information Retrieval (IR) systems were used almost exclusively by librarians and information professionals, such as paralegals and journalists. They were frequent and expert users, who, after an initial training phase, somehow tolerated the complexity of a command-line interface. Today the rapid increase of web-based accesses to IR systems has completely changed the use scenario. Also users have completely changed, since now almost every person accessing the web uses a search engine. According to a survey, made by Pew Internet & American Life Project, in February 2012 the web was accessed by the 80% of American adults population [1] and about 90% of them used online search engines [2]. Before the Web, a search for a document consisted in accessing the IR system where only data about the source of the document were available; such data allowed to get the physical copy of the document in order to get the full text. By exploiting the advance of technology, from networked database systems to graphical displays, the Web provides an enormous amount of content of different types, which includes not only traditional unstructured documents but also multimedia information (images, audio, video) about people, companies, organizations, etc. Moreover, it can be searched by directly asking questions such as: "What is the amount of water vapor in the air?".

This new scenario has pushed towards a completely new way of designing the IR system user interface that, as for any interactive system, is a critical component because it has a great impact on the users' performance and satisfaction. This chapter describes Human-Centred Design as the approach for creating successful interfaces,

M. Agosti et al. (Eds.): PROMISE Winter School 2012, LNCS 7757, pp. 28–47, 2013.
© Springer-Verlag Berlin Heidelberg 2013

able to generate a positive User Experience (UX), and illustrates principles that support interface design, analyzing the principles that have a major impact on IR systems.

2   Usability of Interactive Systems

It is widely acknowledged that *usability* is a crucial factor of the overall quality of any interactive system. One of the first and most representative definitions is proposed by J. Nielsen within a model of the acceptability of the system by its end users, which reflects whether the system is good enough to satisfy different needs and requirements of the users [3]. In Nielsen's model, one of the *system acceptability* characteristics is its *usefulness*, decomposed in *utility* and *usability* (see Fig. 1). Specifically, utility considers if the functionality of the system can do what users need, while usability considers how well users can use that functionality. Usability is itself a multi-dimensional characteristic, and the following five dimensions are considered by Nielsen (see Fig. 1): *learnability*, i.e., the ease of learning the functionality and the behavior of the system; *efficiency*, i.e., the level of attainable productivity, once the user has learned the system; *memorability*, i.e., the ease of remembering the system functionality, so that the occasional user can return to the system after a period of non-use, without needing to learn again how to use it; *errors*, i.e., the capability of the system to support users in making less errors during the use of the system and, in case they make errors, to let them easily recover; *satisfaction*, i.e., the measure of how much the users like the system. The latter dimension must not be underestimated, since a system pleasant to use increases users' productivity.

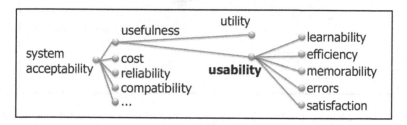

Fig. 1. Nielsen's definition of usability as decomposed into five sub-characteristics (adapted from [3])

Despite all the work carried out by HCI researchers in defining methods for ensuring usability of interactive systems, the many problems that people still encounter in interacting with various systems show that usability has been so far very much neglected by software developers. Actually, usability was already mentioned in the original definition of the standard for software product quality. In a more recent formulation, the standard ISO/IEC 9126-1 (Information Technology - Software Product Quality) emphasizes the importance of designing for quality, focusing on intrinsic system features which can help to create products which are effective, efficient and satisfying for the intended users [4]. The overall quality of a software product is given by its internal and external capability to support the achievement of the goals of users and their organizations, thus improving productivity and human health. The standard describes a model for software product quality, which includes internal quality, external quality and quality in use, each one decomposed in a number of characteristics that should be properly measured (Fig. 2). Usability is one of the six characteristics of external quality and it is defined as "the capability of the software product to be understood, learned, used and attractive to the user, when used under specified conditions". Specifically, it is further subdivided into five sub-characteristics: *understandability*, i.e., the intrinsic capability of the software product of showing to the users its appropriateness to the tasks to be accomplished and to the context of use; *learnability*, i.e., the intrinsic capability of the software product to help users to easily learn its functionality; *operability*, i.e., the intrinsic capability of the software product to make possible for the users the execution and the control of its functionality; *attractiveness*, i.e., the intrinsic capability of the software product to be pleasant for users; *compliance*, i.e., the capability of the software product to adhere to standards, conventions, style guides about usability.

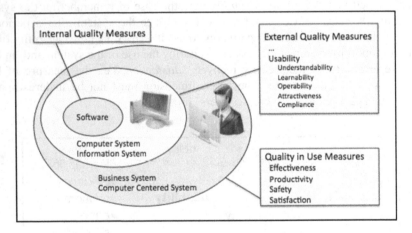

Fig. 2. Software qualities in ISO 9126. Usability is one of the six characteristics of external quality and it is further decomposed into five sub-characteristics.

The ISO 9126 standard introduces the concept of *quality in use* to address the interaction between user and software product, which is measurable only in the context of a real and observable task, also taking into consideration different relevant internal attributes, such as usability. Quality in use is defined in terms of characteristics that represent the user's view of the software quality, i.e., *effectiveness*, *productivity*, *safety* and *satisfaction*. These characteristics are very much related to those defining usability in another standard, the ISO 9241 (Ergonomic Requirements for Office Work with VDTs) [5], which is the standard of reference of the HCI community. In part 11 (Guidance on Usability) of the ISO 9241, the following definition is provided:

usability is the extent to which a product can be used by specified users to achieve specified goals with *effectiveness, efficiency and satisfaction* in a specified context of use.

Effectiveness is the accuracy and the completeness with which specified users achieve specified goals in particular environments. *Efficiency* refers to the resources expended in relation to the accuracy and completeness of goals achieved. *Satisfaction* is defined as the comfort and the acceptability of the system for its users and other people affected by its use. Usability is therefore intended as a high level goal of system design. We may conclude that both concepts of quality in use and usability, as defined in ISO 9241, incorporate the most significant characteristics generally associated to usability by the HCI community.

All usability definitions remark that usability is strictly dependent on the particular circumstances in which a product is used, i.e., the nature of the users, the tasks they perform, and the physical and social environments in which they operate. Therefore, the designer has to carefully analyze those circumstances in order to reach a good degree of usability of the developed product.

3   Human–Centred Design

Having a clear understanding of what usability means, the very problem is "how to obtain usability" or, in other words, how to design systems that users find usable. One of the reasons why many high-tech products, including computer-based systems as well as electronic equipment and everyday appliances, are so hard to use is that during the development of a product, the emphasis and focus have been on the system, not on the people who will be the ultimate end user. Developers counted on the fact that humans are flexible and adaptable, they can better adapt to the machine rather than vice versa. Human needs have been neglected in the past also because engineers were developing products for end users who were very much like themselves, since there was not yet the explosion of different types of end users we have today or, like in the case of IR systems, end users were people who used the system very frequently so that, after an initial training, they became somehow able to cope with systems difficult to use. With the large spreading of computers everywhere, the target audience has changed dramatically and keeps changing every day. One of the main requirements of the information technology society is to design for universal access, i.e., computer systems must be accessible by any kind of users. What has been done in the past does not work for today's users and technology. Designers must allow the human users to focus on the task at hand and not on the means for doing that task. Thus, methods and techniques to help designers change the way they view and design products, methods that work from the users' needs and abilities, have been developed.

The approach that has already proven as a key factor for leading towards the development of successful interfaces is Human-Centred Design, also called User-Centred Design (UCD) [6], [7]; it implies that final users are involved from the very beginning of the planning stage, and identifying user requirements becomes a crucial phase. Early involvement of users has the potential for preventing serious mistakes when designing innovative systems. Indeed, it compels designers to think in terms of utility and usability of the system they are going to develop. Benefits of UCD are mainly related to completeness of system functionality, repair effort saving, as well as user satisfaction. Involving users from early stages allows basing the system core on what is effectively needed. Poor or inadequate requirements specifications can determine interaction difficulties, including lack of facilities and usability problems. Even if late evaluations are useful to assess the usability of final systems, it is unrealistic to expect that these results cause a complete redesign.

The basic principles of UCD are: 1) analyze the users, the tasks they perform and the context in which they operate; 2) design and implement the system iteratively through prototypes of increasing complexity; 3) evaluate design choices and prototypes, possibly with users. UCD requires understanding reality: who will use the system, where, how, and to do what. Then, the system is designed iterating a design-implementation-evaluation cycle. In this way it is possible to avoid serious mistakes and to save re-implementation time, since the first design is based on empirical knowledge of user behavior, needs, and expectations. These principles have been captured in the standard ISO 9241-210 (Human-centred design for interactive systems), that is shown in Fig. 3. The design solutions mentioned in the model are implemented through prototypes that are evaluated and, if they do not meet the specified requirements, the process is iterated and goes again through a revision of the requirements and the proposal of a new prototype. The iterative process is stopped when requirements are met. It is evident that evaluation plays a critical role. It is highly recommended to evaluate early prototypes, e.g. paper mock-ups, sketching the screens of the visual interface, because the earliest interface problems are detected, the easiest is to correct them with very limited cost. Chapter [Catarci & Kimani in this book] discusses different evaluation methods.

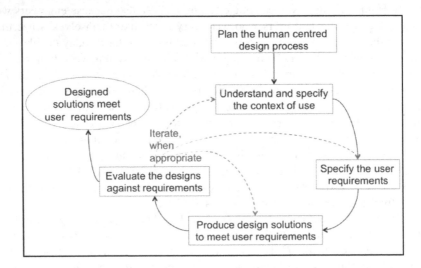

Fig. 3. ISO 9241-210 "Human-centred design process for interactive systems"

4   From Usability to User Experience

Over the last years, the concept of usability has been evolving, along with the emerging IT landscape. HCI has become increasingly concerned with user experience (UX), including subjective attributes like, for instance, aesthetic, emotions, and social involvement in a design space which has previously mainly concerned with ease-of-use. The tenet of UX is well expressed by McCarthy and Wright [8]:

"Today we don't just use technology, we live with it. Much more deeply than ever before we are aware that interacting with technology involves us emotionally, intellectually and sensually. So people who design, use, and evaluate interactive systems need to be able to understand and analyze people's felt experience with technology".

Until recently, a primary goal of product and service design has been to provide useful and usable functionality to allow people to perform their tasks. These goals are still important but, having so many goods and services now available, we have to make sure that they are pleasurable as well. Pleasure and fun are important components of life: learning, education, work can all benefit from pleasure and fun [9]. UX is still a broadly defined term, including satisfaction of non-instrumental needs (e.g. aesthetic, hedonic, creative and social), and acquisition of positive feeling and well-being. Neither a universal definition of UX nor a cohesive theory of experience yet exists that can inform the HCI community on how to practically design for and evaluate UX, although efforts have been undertaken to develop UX conceptual models [10]. For definition of UX, see, for example, [11].

Traditional usability is characterized as task-oriented and performance-based. Some researchers observe that the three canonical usability metrics – effectiveness, efficiency, satisfaction – basically address not only the instrumental aspects of technology use, but also the non-instrumental ones, since satisfaction is a composite term, amalgamating a cluster of "felt experience". What the current UX research emphasizes is the composition of satisfaction into elemental attributes related to people emotions, such as pleasure, fun, surprise, intimacy, joy, and others, and try to understand, define and quantify such attributes.

It is now acknowledged that designing for experience includes but it is much more than designing for efficiency and other traditional attributes of usability. While efficiency is focused on attributes such as fast, easy, functional, error-free, UX involves feelings and thus focuses on beautiful (harmonious, clear), emotional (affectionate, lovable, erotic), stimulating (intellectual, motivational), and also on tactile (smooth, soft), acoustic (rhythmic, melodious) in case of multimodal interfaces. The experience of a user with a product is certainly influenced by functional quality attributes of the product (e.g. utility, robustness), by non-functional quality attributes (e.g. usability, privacy) and by specific user experience attributes (e.g. desirability, pleasure).

Today's emphasis on UX, after many years of focus on usability, is not surprising, since it is typical of many other technological products. Initially, designers concentrated on utility of the new product. As industry sectors mature, the focus goes towards usability and, later, user experience. Fig. 4 and Fig. 5 report two examples. At the beginning of 20th century, a car was a useful, even if uncomfortable, means of transportation, with a user interface (car controls, see Fig. 4a) different from a model to another. During the last century, cars were becoming more and more usable and confortable, with standardized car controls (Fig. 4b). Today, cars are equipped with several devices (GPS navigator, multimedia devices), in order to provide a positive UX for all people traveling in the car (Fig. 4c). The other example is about TVs. The TV first introduced in the market was black and white, with a very limited number of channels (Fig. 5a). Later, color TVs were produced and were provided with a remote control, which made the TV much more usable, since it could be operated while comfortably seating on a sofa. Today, TV provides a much greater experience: TV is interactive, 3D, connected to the Internet. It is interesting to note that the remote controls for these TVs have many buttons and are often not very usable (see Figure 5c), and yet, because of the overall positive experience users get, they accept these complex devices.

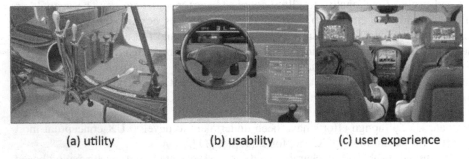

(a) utility   (b) usability   (c) user experience

Fig. 4. (a) Car controls at the beginning of 1900s; (b) car controls at the end of 1900s; (c) devices in a today's car

(a) utility   (b) usability   (c) user experience

Fig. 5. (a) Black-and-white TV; (b) color TV with simple remote control; (c) 3D interactive TV connected to the Internet, with complex and little usable remote control

Summarizing, a product, able to generate a positive UX should be useful, usable, and desirable. In order to create desirable products, UX puts a lot of emphasis on pleasure and thus, on aesthetics and fun. Aesthetics is today much more stressed, even if attractiveness was always considered a characteristic of usability. Aesthetics is very important also in the design of IR interfaces. Some studies show the correlation between aesthetics and the perception of interface quality [12], [13]. It has been shown that interfaces aesthetically appealing are perceived more useful even when they are slightly less useful than an interface with similar functionality but less attractive [14]. Other studies point out the importance of a good layout with proper colors, font styles, blank spaces, showing how small details actually have a great impact on users' perception of the interface. For example, in [15] it is reported that the appropriateness of several graphic design details contributes to a good user experience with Google.

5   Principles for Good Design

As we said in the previous section, a positive user experience makes people more tolerant with respect to some usability problems of a product. Still, usability is very important in order to get a positive UX. Since the '80s, the HCI community has identified various recommendations for designers willing to create usable interfaces. Some of them are expressed in a positive way, such as "choose this solution in order to reach this goal". Others are expressed in a negative way: "don't do this in this situation". Some design recommendations are more general, some are more compulsory. Often, in literature, words such as principles, guidelines, design rules, style guides are used as synonyms. We prefer to be more specific, distinguishing four categories based on different generality and compulsion levels, as shown in Fig. 6.

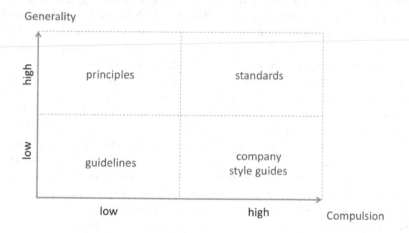

Fig. 6. Classification of design recommendations (adapted from [16])

Principles are more fundamental and widely applicable rules, derived from scientific evidence and general consensus, taking into account psychological and social aspects of human beings, rather than technology. Expressed in general form, they are more enduring. *Guidelines* are more specific recommendations for the design of a certain class of systems, i.e. they are narrowly focused. *Standards* are design rules formulated by an international organization; they must be strictly observed if one has to comply with those standards. *Company style guides* (or company design rules) are very detailed rules to be applied in the design of company systems, so that their user interfaces will have similar look and behavior.

In this chapter, we address design principles, in particular those more relevant for IR interfaces. Many collections of specific guidelines are proposed in the literature, for example the reader may refer to [17]. As an example of standard, the already mentioned ISO 9241 contains guidance on user interfaces design and provides requirements and recommendations, which can be used during the design and evaluation of user interfaces [5]; it reports seven basic and general design rules, called dialogue principles, as well as more specific rules addressing various details of the design of different interface styles, e.g. form-based interfaces, graphical interfaces, etc. Finally, several companies have defined their stile guides, in order to provide indications that their third parties have to strictly follow in developing applications for that company. For example, see the style guides developed by Apple for mobile applications [18].

5.1   Traditional Usability Principles

In the last twenty five years, different authors have proposed sets of design principles which, from one side, offer a way of better understanding usability and, on the other side, provide guidance for a "good design". In his book published in 1993, Nielsen provides ten usability principles, also called usability heuristics, which aim at providing useful indications, not only for the design but also for the evaluation of user interfaces; they are the basis of a well-known inspection technique called heuristic evaluation [3]. Since its formulation in 1993, the ten heuristics have been modified only very slightly; in fact, these are general principles that depend very much on characteristics and behavior of human beings, rather than technology. Thus, while technology changes rapidly, human beings psychological and social aspects do not. Nielsen's heuristics are discussed by many authors and can also be found at [19]; they are reported in Table 1, together with a brief comment that illustrates each heuristic.

Shneiderman proposes eight golden rules, which summarize his view of the key principles of interface design [20]. Other design principles are presented by Dix et al., divided into three main categories, which refer to learnability, flexibility, robustness, for a total of fourteen principles [21]. The ISO 9241 proposes its own set of principles. Of course, one can easily expect that most of those principles are actually the same, even if they are phrased in a slightly different way. A basic principle mentioned by most author is *consistency* (see heuristic 4 in Table 1), which recommends designers to create user interfaces which are consistent, e.g., they show a consistent input/output behavior in similar situations or, in the case of visual interfaces, use consistent colors, layout, fonts. Another well recognized principle is about *feedback* to be provided to users during the interaction. Nielsen refers to it as *visibility of the system status* (see heuristic 1 in Table 1), since the interface has to keep users informed about what is going on in the system, providing appropriate feedback about user actions (e.g., highlight a folder to indicated that the user has selected it) or system operations (e.g.. show a progress bar which indicates the current status of a file download).

Table 1. Nielsen's heuristics for usability [19]

N.	Heuristics	Explanation
1	Visibility of system status	the system should always keep users informed about what is going on, through appropriate feedback within reasonable time
2	Match between system and the real world	the system should speak the users' language (words, phrases and concepts familiar to the user, rather than system-oriented). Follow real-world conventions, information should appear in natural/logical order
3	User control and freedom	users often choose system functions by mistake and will need a clearly marked "emergency exit". Support undo and redo
4	Consistency and standards	users should not have to wonder whether different words, situations, or actions mean the same thing. Follow platform conventions
5	Error prevention	a careful design prevents a problem from occurring in the first place. Eliminate error-prone conditions. Present users with a confirmation option
6	Recognition rather than recall	minimize the user's memory load by making objects, actions, and options visible. The user should not have to remember dialogue Information
7	Flexibility and efficiency of use	accelerators – unseen by the novice user – may often speed up the interaction for the expert user. Allow users to tailor frequent actions
8	Aesthetic and minimalist design	dialogues should not contain information, which is irrelevant or rarely needed. Extra units of information diminishes of relevant units
9	Help users recognize, diagnose, and recover from errors	error messages should be expressed in plain language (no codes), precisely indicate the problem, and constructively suggest a solution
10	Help and documentation	even though it is better if the system can be used without documentation, it may be necessary to provide help and documentation

A very important principle when designing for usability refers to *user control* (see heuristic 3 in Table 1). Even today, many novice users are afraid of approaching interactive systems since they do not feel in control of the system. They want comprehensible and controllable environments. On the other side, the technology tries to support people through systems that are pro-active and anticipate users' operations whenever it is possible. Thus, user interface designers must properly balance the actions automated by the system, which sometimes users might not easily understand, and the users being in control through the actions they perform. Designers should know that users are allowed to make mistakes, so that they have to provide mechanisms for easily recovering from such mistakes. Clearly marked emergency exit, possibility of undo and redo, are powerful mechanisms to keep the user in control of the system. Other principles refer to users' errors and remark the importance of *preventing users' errors* during the interaction, as well as of providing ways to *easily recover from errors* (see heuristics 5 and 9 in Table 1). There are many detailed guidelines that have been derived from these two principles and the reader may refer to them (see, e.g., [17]).

The success of the graphical user interfaces developed since the '80s, which replaced the language-based command interfaces like UNIX® or MS-DOS®, relies on the fact that, for human beings, recognition is better than recall. A corresponding principle (see heuristics 6 in Table 1) is that the interface has to be designed in order to *minimize the user's memory load* by making objects, actions, and options visible, so that the user must not remember dialogue information. For a novice or infrequent user it is certainly more efficient to identify an operation and execute it if it is well represented by an icon or a menu item clearly visible or easily retrieved on the interface screen, rather than to remember the difficult and error prone syntax of an MS-DOS command. However, a good design must also take into account that users are very diverse and that they evolve during time, e.g. a novice user became expert in the use of the system after a continuous use of it. Thus, a further recommendation for designers is to create *flexible interfaces*, which provide mechanisms to accommodate the needs for different types of users, e.g., accelerators that may speed up the interaction for the expert user (see heuristic 7 in table 1).

Heuristic 2 in Table 1 recommends that the system has to speak the user's language, i.e. words, concepts, icons, etc. that are familiar to the users have to be used in the interface. Heuristic 8 recalls that users must not be overloaded with too much information on the screen and suggests to eliminate information rarely needed, which will be available only on users' demand. It also recommends to design interfaces which are simple, paying special attention to graphic details and to the overall aesthetics. Finally, heuristic 10 is about the proper use of help and documentation, especially when the system is rather complex. The documentation should be ready to use, e.g. online help or other types of online documentation. For example, during some tests we observed that users had difficulties in understanding how to use the interface of a portal with many widgets, and they required the help of a more expert person; we next provided the interface with short video-guides (about three minutes long) explaining the main functionalities of the interface, that users can watch on demand. Such video-guides encouraged users to interact without the help of an intermediary person.

5.2   More Specific Design Principles for IR Interfaces

In the book "Search User Interfaces Design", Wilson suggests to take into account primarily the ten heuristics proposed by Nielsen [22]. Principles that have a major impact on the design of IR interfaces have been discussed by Hearst in Chapter 1 of her book [23]. She actually speaks of "design guidelines" but, according to our classification in Figure 6, they are general design principles rather than guidelines. Some of the principles that Hearst reports for IR interfaces are actually applicable to user interfaces of any type of system, and have been described in the previous section, namely *provide feedback, reduce short term memory load, provide shortcuts, reduce errors.* Three other principles mentioned by Hearst are: *balance user control with automated actions, recognize the importance of small details, recognize the importance of aesthetics.* Aesthetics has been discussed at the end of Section 4, highlighting how appropriate graphic details have a very positive impact on the users' perceived quality of the user interface. The reader may refer to Chapter 1 of [23] to see several interesting examples that illustrate the importance of such principles in IR interfaces. In the rest of this section, we discuss three other principles which are very significant for designing IR interfaces capable to provide a positive UX: *simplicity, pleasurability* and *customizability.*

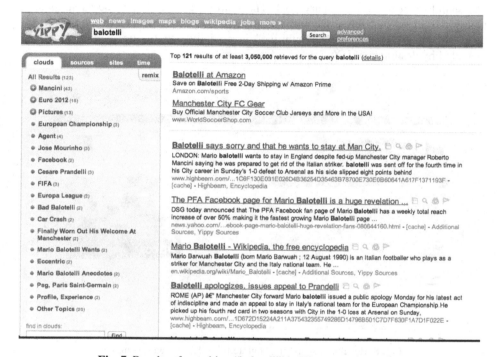

Fig. 7. Results of searching "balotelli" in Yippy search engine

As reported in the introduction, the Web has completely changed the interface of IR systems and its users. Almost any person accessing the Web uses an online search engine. Designers of web search interfaces have to take into account the need of novice and occasional users as well as those of expert and frequent ones. This diversity of end users is one of the main reasons for keeping the interface simple. *Simplicity* is today one of the main principles guiding the design of a search interface: both query formulation and analysis of the search result should be simple. Several studies showed that novice users have difficulties in very basic activities, such as formulating keyword queries and understanding that they do not immediately get the results they seek, but they have to look at the query results and to further navigate in the Web in order to possibly satisfy their information need; examples of such users are children at their first experiences with search interfaces [24], [25]. Designers have to consider that, in most cases, many results are returned to a user query, and such results have to be presented in order to support users to figure out what are the most significant for them and how to proceed to possibly refine such results. For example, the Yippy search engine adds a panel reporting a classification of the top results. Fig. 7 shows the screen obtained when searching for "balotelli". Besides the usual list of the top results, the panel at the left side reports a classification automatically computed by the engine. By clicking on the first item, e.g. 'Mancini' only the 43 results in this cluster are shown. The first three clusters have a plus on their left indicating that a finer classification is available. Another main reason for keeping the interface simple is that nowadays search engines are often used while the user is engaged in a different task, and search is not her/his primary goal. The search interface has to be as simple as possible to avoid distracting the user and to limit the interference with the user main task. "Make things simple and intuitive" is actually one of the main indications provided by designers of UX.

Fig. 8. Results of searching "balotelli" in Lycos search engine

Hess lists 20 guiding principles for Experience Design [26]. Some of them enhance simplicity in the design by recommending principles such as *present few choices*, *limit distraction*, *avoid jargon*, *less is more*. Indeed, providing more alternatives to people makes the choice much more difficult; it is much better to keep the interface simple, providing only the necessary alternative and removing all the less important ones. People have to be concentrated on their current task, and the interface should favor this by avoiding to distract them with less critical tasks. Designers should keep in mind that users are not like them and are very different among themselves, so that the dialogue with the users has to be simple and clear, using a language that users may easily understand. Finally, the design should show only the very necessary and useful information, making sure that any element in the interface has a purpose; it can be a functional purpose or only an aesthetic one. Anything that does not actually contribute to a positive experience should be removed or the user should have the possibility to remove it. Let us consider two examples of showing previews of retrieved web pages. Fig. 8 shows the screenshot of the results obtained by searching "balotelli" with Lycos search engine. A thumbnail of the preview is on the left of each result. Fig. 9

shows the results of the same query, obtained with Google. For each result the user can visualize the preview by moving the cursor to the right of each result. Two arrows will appear and, by clicking on such arrows, the preview is shown, as in Fig. 10. Some very informal test we have performed by asking adult people to compare these two alternatives show that Google solution is preferable since the preview is only on-demand and it is shown at a better resolution.

Fig. 9. Results of searching "balotelli" in Google search engine

Fig. 10. Preview shown in Google when hovering with the mouse pointer on the arrows on the left of an item result

Some of the remaining principles proposed by Hess for UX design are similar to usability principles previously commented, e.g., *make actions reversible, provide feedback, be consistent*. Some others provide suggestions for creating interfaces that are easy to understand and use, and also help people to orient themselves and to be in control of the dialogue, e.g., *group related objects near each other, use appropriate defaults, create a visual hierarchy that matches user's needs* (by appropriately using colors, size position, shape in order to aid in understanding and processing the presented information), *provide signposts and cues, use constraints appropriately* (in order to prevent errors and to guide people to successful interactions).

Nothing really specific is suggested by Hess about designing for *pleasurability*. A well-known slogan when referring to UX is "Make stuff easy and pleasurable to use". This is the consequence of the shift from usability to UX, the latter emphasizing much more subjective emotions, such us fun, engagement, joy, all contributing to create pleasure for the user. A lot of research is going on in order to define models of UX that can serve as a basis for giving designers guidance to cope with the emerging principle of *pleasurability*. UX has a much richer scope that traditional usability, essentially because more attention is devoted to users' emotions, affects, motivations and values that contribute to *pleasurability*. However, currently available UX design principles are much more detailed about those aspects characterizing usability (i.e., easy of learning, ease of use and basic subjective satisfaction), while a little is yet said about *pleasurability*, i.e., about emotions. In the Hess's list, *use emotion* is the only principle addressing the more subjective component of UX. It emphasizes that pleasure is very important and recommends designers to create interfaces that are simple and intuitive for users, without being boring or cold but capable to generate pleasure. Every UX designer pushes for pleasurable interfaces, which can motivate and stimulate persons and make them feel engaged, but specific guidelines are not yet available. In contrast to usability, standard UX metrics are yet to be defined, as well as benchmark that suggest competitive design artifacts and help selecting the right design options. Of course, there are various attempts to measure aspects of the UX. In [27] and [28], it is proposed and evaluated a multidimensional scale to measure user engagement when interacting with technology and in particular with IR systems. Models of UX are also needed to understand, predict and reasoning about processes of UX and their consequences for software design, in order to provide a sound basis for UX measures with desirable properties, such as reliability, sensitivity, validity. Even if some first results are coming, a number of issues about UX modeling remain to be solved [29].

The latter principle discussed here is *customizability*. It was not mentioned in the original 10 heuristics of Nielsen and in the 8 golden rules of Shneiderman, since only more recent technology makes possible to create software that it is easy to adapt, in ways that have to be very intuitive for the users and can make them a lot happier. Dix et al. report *customizability* as one of the principles that affect flexibility [21]. It is also mentioned as a basic principle in the ISO 9241, indicated as *suitability for individualization*. In its wider meaning, *customizability* actually refers to the personalization of the user interface performed by the system or by the user. Personalization accomplished by the system is often called system adaptivity, while the other is called adaptability by the user. Adaptivity is performed if the system, by considering contextual properties, like the current task or situation, or even monitoring users' behavior, is capable to adapt itself for the benefits of users. The following example shows that searches on Google are adapted by the system by taking into account the geographic area in which the user operates. We have asked two persons to perform a search by inputting the word "emiliano" at the same moment but in two different locations: in Bari, our city in South Italy, and in a town of Finland. The screenshots in Fig. 11 show the results of the search performed in Italy (left) and in Finland (right), respectively. The number of results is the same (7.670.000 items), but the order of the results is different. Emiliano is last name of the Bari's major, so for the person in Bari the first result is an item in Wikipedia presenting the major, while for the person in Finland the first result is the Facebook page of Emiliano.

Fig. 11. Results obtained in different order for the same search performed at the same moment by two persons in two different countries

Adaptability occurs when the system allows users to perform modifications; they may go from simple parameter setting, in order to choose among alternative presentations or interaction mechanisms, to more complex activities that imply modifications and/or creations of software artifacts. Such activities are actually examples of End-User Development (EUD) [30], [31] and reflect the new trend toward a more active involvement of end users in tailoring software tools and environments to their own needs [32]. Of course, end users have to be empowered to shape the software they use without being obliged to become programmers [33], [34]. Some EUD-oriented techniques have already been adopted in software for the mass market, such as some Programming by Example techniques in Microsoft Excel™.

So far, search engines have not provided adaptability features, but the situation is quickly changing. For instance, iGoogle™ is an online dashboard in which a user can add widgets of interest. Let us suppose that a user asks every day for weather information. Instead of accessing every time to a weather forecast website, the user may add in his/her iGoogle™ dashboard a weather forecast widget, already set with the geographic area of interest. Every time the dashboard is opened, the weather forecast is available to the user, as shown in Fig. 12. The weather forecast widget is actually a service that the user has added to the dashboard in a very simple way, by clicking on a button available in the iGoogle interface. A page with the more required services is shown to the user, who has also the possibility of searching for other services accessible through the Web. Once the user has selected the service of interest, he/she clicks on the 'Add' button and the widget associated to the service is added to the dashboard, where he/she can position it in the more convenient place.

iGoogle is an example of the new trend to replace fixed, pre-packaged applications with elastic composition environments that allows end users, not necessarily experts of technology, to extract contents and services from various sources and to compose personal information spaces that satisfy their own needs and that can be used on different devices [35], [36].

Fig. 12. iGoogle interface customized by a user

We conclude by summarizing, in Table 2, the main principles that support designers in creating IR interfaces able to provide a positive UX. The first seven principles where already discussed by Hearst in [23]. The last three have been discussed in this paper.

Table 2. Principles for designing IR user interfaces

N.	Principles
1	Offer efficient and informative feedback
2	Balance user control with automated actions
3	Reduce short-term memory load
4	Provide shortcuts
5	Reduce errors
6	Recognize the importance of small details
7	Recognize the importance of aesthetics
8	Keep the interface simple
9	Design for pleasurability
10	Enable users to customize the interface

6   Conclusions

This chapter has presented principles to guide the design of successful user interfaces. The shift from usability to UX has been discussed emphasizing that, in order to generate a positive UX, a software product should be useful, usable and desirable. Design principles that have a major impact on IR interfaces have been analyzed. Very significant are those discussed by Hearst [23]. We have complemented them with three other principles, which focus on simplicity, pleasurability and customizability of the interface, respectively. A lot of emphasis is currently given to such characteristics by both researchers and practitioners, as discussed in the last part of the chapter.

References

1. Pew: A Pew Survey on Internet Adoption, http://www.pewinternet.org/Static-Pages/Trend-Data/Internet-Adoption.aspx. (last access on May, 2012)
2. Pew: A Pew Survey on Search Engine Adoption, http://www.pewinternet.org/Reports/2012/Search-Engine-Use-2012.aspx. (last access on May, 2012)
3. Nielsen, J.: Usability Engineering. Academic Press, San Diego (1993)
4. ISO/IEC: 9126-1: Information Technology – Software Product Quality (1998)
5. International Organization for Standardization: Iso 9241: Ergonomics Requirements for Office Work with Visual Display Terminal (Vdt) - Parts 1-17 (1997)
6. Preece, J., Rogers, Y., Sharp, H., Benyon, D., Holland, S., Carey, T.: Human-Computer Interaction. Addison-Wesley Publishing Company (1994)

7. Dix, A., Finlay, J., Abowd, G., Beale, R.: Human Computer Interaction. Prentice-Hall (1998)
8. McCarthy, J., Wright, P.: Technology as Experience. Interactions 11(5), 42–43 (2004)
9. Norman, D.A.: The Way I See It: The Transmedia Design Challenge: Technology That Is Pleasurable and Satisfying. Interactions 17(1), 12–15 (2010)
10. Roto, V., Law, E.L., Vermeeren, A., Hoonhout, J.: User Experience White Paper. Technical report (2010)
11. Law, E.L.-C., Roto, V., Hassenzahl, M., Vermeeren, A.P.O.S., Kort, J.: Understanding, Scoping and Defining User Experience: A Survey Approach. In: 27th International Conference on Human Factors in Computing Systems, pp. 719–728 (2009)
12. Hassenzahl, M.: The Interplay of Beauty, Goodness, and Usability in Interactive Products. Human-Computer Interaction 19(4), 319–349 (2004)
13. Norman, D.A.: Emotional Design: Why We Love (or Hate) Everyday Things. Basic Books (2004)
14. Ben-Bassat, T., Meyer, J., Tractinsky, N.: Economic and Subjective Measures of the Perceived Value of Aesthetics and Usability. ACM Transactions on Computer-Human Interaction 13(2), 210–234 (2006)
15. Hotchkiss, G.: Q&a with Marissa Mayer, Google Vp, Search Products & User Experience, http://searchengineland.com/070126-124723.php (last access on July 18, 2012)
16. Polillo, R.: Facile Da Usare. Una Moderna Introduzione Alla Ingegneria Dell'usabilità. Apogeo, Milano, pp. xvi+414 (2010)
17. Galitz, W.O.: The Essential Guide to User Interface Design: An Introduction to Gui Design Principles and Techniques. John Whiley & Sons, Inc., New York (2007)
18. Apple Inc.: Ios Human Interface Guidelines, http://developer.apple.com/library/ios/#DOCUMENTATION/UserExperience/Conceptual/MobileHIG/Introduction/Introduction.html (last access on July 18, 2012)
19. Nielsen, J.: Ten Usability Heuristics, http://www.useit.com/papers/heuristic/heuristic_list.html. (last access on July 19, 2012)
20. Shneiderman, B.: Designing the User Interface – Strategies for Effective Human-Computer Interaction, 3rd edn. Addison-Wesley (1998)
21. Dix, A., Finlay, J.E., Abowd, G.D., Beale, R.: Human-Computer Interaction, 3rd edn. Prentice-Hall, Upper Saddle River (2004)
22. Wilson, M.L.: Search User Interface Design. Synthesis Lectures on Information Concepts, Retrieval, and Services. Morgan & Claypool (2011)
23. Hearst, M.: Search User Interfaces. Cambridge University Press (2009)
24. Bilal, D.: Children's Use of the Yahooligans! Web Search Engine: I. Cognitive, Physical, and Affective Behaviors on Fact-Based Search Tasks. Journal of the American Society for Information Science 51(7), 646–665 (2000)
25. Schacter, J., Chung, G.K.W.K., Dorr, A.: Children's Internet Searching on Complex Problems: Performance and Process Analyses. Journal of the American Society for Information Science 49(9), 840–849 (1998)
26. Hess, W.: Guiding Principles for Ux Designers, http://uxmag.com/articles/guiding-principles-for-ux-designers. (last access on July 19, 2012)
27. O'Brien, H.L., Toms, E.G.: What Is User Engagement? A Conceptual Framework for Defining User Engagement with Technology. J. Am. Soc. Inf. Sci. Technol. 59(6), 938–955 (2008)

28. O'Brien, H.L., Toms, E.G.: Is There a Universal Instrument for Measuring Interactive Information Retrieval?: The Case of the User Engagement Scale. In: Proceedings of the Third Symposium on Information Interaction in Context, pp. 335–340. ACM, New Brunswick (2010)
29. Law, E.L.-C., van Schaik, P.: Editorial: Modelling User Experience - an Agenda for Research and Practice. Interact. Comput. 22(5), 313–322 (2010)
30. Lieberman, H., Paternò, F., Wulf, V.: End User Development. Human-Computer Interaction Series, vol. 9 (2006)
31. Costabile, M.F., Dittrich, Y., Fischer, G., Piccinno, A. (eds.): IS-EUD 2011. LNCS, vol. 6654. Springer, Heidelberg (2011)
32. Ardito, C., Buono, P., Costabile, M.F., Lanzilotti, R., Piccinno, A.: End Users as Co-Designers of Their Own Tools and Products. Journal of Visual Languages & Computing 23(2), 78–90 (2012)
33. Costabile, M.F., Fogli, D., Mussio, P., Piccinno, A.: Visual Interactive Systems for End-User Development: A Model-Based Design Methodology. IEEE Transactions on System Man and Cybernetics Part A-Systems and Humans 37(6), 1029–1046 (2007)
34. Costabile, M.F., Mussio, P., Parasiliti Provenza, L., Piccinno, A.: Supporting End Users to Be Co-designers of Their Tools. In: Pipek, V., Rosson, M.B., de Ruyter, B., Wulf, V. (eds.) IS-EUD 2009. LNCS, vol. 5435, pp. 70–85. Springer, Heidelberg (2009)
35. Latzina, M., Beringer, J.: Transformative User Experience: Beyond Packaged Design. Interactions 19(2), 30–33 (2012)
36. Ardito, C., Costabile, M.F., Desolda, G., Matera, M., Piccinno, A., Picozzi, M.: Composition of Situational Interactive Spaces by End Users: A Case for Cultural Heritage. In: 7th Nordic Conference on Human-Computer Interaction (NordiCHI). ACM Press, Copenhagen

Human-Computer Interaction View
on Information Retrieval Evaluation

Tiziana Catarci[1] and Stephen Kimani[2]

[1] Sapienza, University of Rome, Via Ariosto 25, 00185 Rome, Italy
catarci@dis.uniroma1.it
[2] Jomo Kenyatta University (JKUAT), P.O. Box 62000, 00200, Nairobi, Kenya
stephenkimani@gmail.com

Abstract. The field of information retrieval (IR) has experienced tremendous growth over the years. Researchers have however identified Human-Computer Interaction (HCI) aspects as important concerns in IR research. Incorporation of HCI techniques in IR can ensure that IR systems intended for human users are developed and evaluated in a way that is consistent with and reflects the needs of those users. The traditional methods of evaluating IR systems have for a long period been largely concerned with system-oriented measurements such as precision and recall, but not on the usability aspects of the IR system. There also are no well-established evaluation approaches for studying users and their interactions with IR systems. This chapter describes the role and place of HCI toward supporting and appropriating the evaluation of IR systems.

Keywords: Information Retrieval, Human-Computer Interaction, Evaluation.

1   Introduction

1.1   Motivation for HCI in IR

The field of information retrieval (IR) has experienced tremendous growth over the years. Researchers have however identified Human-Computer Interaction aspects as important concerns in IR research [16]. For instance: IR system design, evaluation, and the study of users' information search behaviours and interactions. Allen [2] indicates that there is a need to establish a link between research within IR and the design of user interfaces. According to the ACM Special Interest Group on Human-Computer Interaction (SIGCHI), Human-Computer Interaction (HCI) is a discipline concerned with the design, evaluation, and implementation of interactive computing systems, and the study of major phenomena surrounding them [37]. Marchionini [56] points out three developments that make it important to incorporate HCI in IR:

- Information Retrieval (IR) and Human-Computer Interaction (HCI) are related fields having strong traditions that have been challenged and energized by the World Wide Web.

M. Agosti et al. (Eds.): PROMISE Winter School 2012, LNCS 7757, pp. 48–75, 2013.
© Springer-Verlag Berlin Heidelberg 2013

- The type and nature of content have evolved and changed e.g. type of content has moved beyond text to include statistics, multimedia, computer code, sensor streams and biochemical sequences.
- The type and nature of users have evolved. Data has become increasingly accessible to a large number of users with no or minimal training in information retrieval e.g. on the Internet through mobile devices, TVs, etc.

According to Marchionini [56], the foregoing three developments lead to the concept referred to as Human-Computer Information Retrieval (HCIR), whereby *"we think of information interaction from the perspective of an active human with information needs, information skills, powerful digital library resources (that include other humans) situated in global and local connected communities – all of which evolve over time."* Marchionini [56] goes on to argue that the concept suggests systems that are characterized by:

- Systems should aim to get people closer to the information they need, especially to the meaning; that is, systems can no longer only deliver the relevant documents, but must also provide facilities for making meaning with those documents.
- Systems should increase user responsibility as well as control; that is, information systems require human intellectual effort, and good effort is rewarded.
- Systems should have flexible architectures so they may evolve and adapt to increasingly more demanding and knowledgeable installed bases of users over time.
- Systems should aim to be part of information ecology of personal and shared memories and tools rather than discrete standalone services.
- Systems should support the entire information life cycle (from creation to preservation) rather than only the dissemination or use phase.
- Systems should support tuning by end users and especially by information professionals who add value to information resources.
- Systems should be engaging and fun to use.

Incorporation of HCI techniques in IR can ensure that IR systems intended for human users are developed and evaluated in a way that is consistent with and reflects the needs of those users [57].

1.2   Motivation for HCI in IR Evaluation

The study of IR systems has prescribed and dominant evaluation methods that can be traced back to the work by Cleverdon [17]. The traditional methods of evaluating IR systems have over a long period of time been mainly concerned with system-oriented measurements such as precision and recall, but not on the usability aspects of the user interface such as how well users can accomplish their goals and tasks, interactive, and cognitive issues. There are no well-established evaluation approaches for studying users and their interactions with information retrieval systems [33], [48].

1.3   User Interface Techniques for IR

During the user interface design process, the primary focus is on who the users are and what the tasks are. The main role of the system is to support user in their tasks. A task could be some activity that involves achieving a particular goal or purpose. In general, the user interface of an IR system has the role of guiding, supporting and transforming user's information problems, goals or needs [33]. The user interface can be described as the elements that the user comes into contact with when using a computing system. According to Hix and Hartson [38], the user interface generally comprises two parts: the interaction part and the interface software part. The interaction part or the interaction component is concerned with how the user interface works and its behaviour in response to what the user does while performing a task. The interface software part is concerned with the implementation of the interaction component. In the sequel, is a description of various existing user interface techniques for supporting users to interact with and use information retrieval systems.

Query Formulation and Query Reformulation

Many search engines expect the user to formulate an initial information request in a manner understandable by the underlying search engine. The user interface for such search engines typically accepts the information request (i.e. query) in form of a keyword-based statement. Users often need to reformulate their query after an initial query has been executed. Most search engines support query reformulation features such as: spelling suggestions, spelling corrections, and automatic query term reformulation [36]. Such features support the user by suggesting potential search directions and paths that can yield results that are relevant to the user. The features strive to put control of selection and interpretation of results in the user's hands.

Browsing

Traditional user interfaces of information retrieval systems have been geared toward analytical searching rather than browsing. Analytical search approaches to information retrieval necessitate the systematic formulation of specific, well-structured queries. Browsing involves broad query terms and scanning larger sets of information in a relatively unstructured manner. Browsing is generally considered to virtually involve no planning, preparation or focus. For instance, Marchionini [55] notes that browsing does not involve planning and is often utilized as an alternative to an analytical search strategy. Many studies have been reported that show the benefits of browsing, for instance [11], [40], [53].

Faceted Search and Navigation

Unlike traditional taxonomies in which the hierarchy of categories is fixed and inflexible, faceted search enables users to decide how to navigate information hierarchically. For instance, users can decide how they will move from a category to its sub-categories, and at the same time decide the order in which the categories are presented. Faceted navigation guides users by showing them available categories without requiring them to browse through hierarchies that may not suit their needs or way of thinking [35].

Lookahead

Lookahead [9] supports exploration with no penalty. For instance, some web applications automatically complete query terms and suggest popular searches such as shown in Fig. 1.

Fig. 1. Lookahead

Surrogates

It is important for the user to be able to assess search results. Objects such as images can be displayed in the results as complete objects. It is therefore relatively to assess such results. However, for other objects such as videos and documents, it is often not practical to display them in the results as complete objects. In the latter case, information about those objects is included e.g. key-frames for video objects; titles and abstracts for documents; thumbnails for Web pages; etc. This type of information is sometimes referred to as a surrogate [5].

Relevance Feedback

Relevance feedback enables users to guide an IR system by indicating whether they consider particular results to be more or less relevant [60]. Relevance feedback modifies an existing query based on available user-based relevance judgements for previously retrieved documents. It is worth pointing out that it is also possible to consider automatic relevance feedback, whereby the underlying information retrieval system is fully automated without user interaction, and with many relevance judgments [64].

Summarization, Analytics and Visual Presentation

Summarization and analytics can enable users digest query results. Summarization can be considered to encompass any means of aggregating or compressing the query results into a form that is less likely to lead to information overload on the part of the user. For instance, through clustering, etc. In fact and in general, faceted search, which was described previously, can also be viewed as a form of summarization. The representation of summarization or analytics can be presented using appropriate information visualization techniques.

In Table 1 is a categorization and summary of the user interface techniques for information retrieval.

Table 1. User interface techniques for IR

User interface technique for IR	Examples/References
Query formulation and query reformulation	[36]
Browsing	[11], [40], [53]
Faceted search and navigation	[35]
Lookahead	[9]
Surrogates	[5]
Relevance feedback	[60], [64]
Summarization, analytics and visual presentation	(Mani and Maybury, 1999)

2   HCI in IR Evaluation: Appropriate Evaluation Metrics and Models

2.1   Metrics

Existing literature reports on various metrics or measures regarding information retrieval (e.g., [15], [76], [69], [77]). Over time, four standard categories of measures have emerged: performance measures, interaction measures, usability measures, and contextual measures [48]. For each of the four categories, we in the sequel specifically discuss measures that are appropriate to Human-Computer Interaction in information retrieval evaluation.

Performance Measures
The traditional and classic evaluation measures of information retrieval system performance have been precision and recall. Such and other traditional IR measures can be found in [76]. Other measures include: F-measure, average precision (AP), mean average precision (MAP), and geometric average precision (GMAP). *"Since these measures are document-based, they measure only the performance of the system in retrieving items predetermined to be "relevant" to the information need. They do not consider how the information will be used, or whether, in the judgment of the user, the documents fulfill the information need"* [24].

Interactive Recall and Precision
The traditional IR performance measures are based on an evaluator's relevance judgments. The user's or subject's relevance judgments often do not agree with the evaluator's relevance judgments. It may also be that the evaluator has searched

through hundreds of documents in order to provide relevance judgments. The user or subject may not search long enough to find all of these documents [48].

Toward addressing the mismatch between evaluator's relevance judgments and subjects' relevance judgments, *interactive recall and precision, and interactive TREC precision* [74-75] have been proposed.. For instance: interactive recall is the number of TREC relevant documents saved by the user divided by the number of TREC relevant documents in the corpus; interactive TREC precision is the number of TREC relevant documents viewed by the user divided by the total number of documents viewed.

Multi-level Relevance and Rank Measures

The traditional IR performance measures do not take into account that relevant documents appearing further down on the results list are likely to be less useful because users are less likely to view them. The user needs to put in some effort to get to those documents and by the time the user arrives at the document its content may be less valuable because of what the user has learned on the way to the document. Although MAP was created to address the ordering problem in systems-centered research, it still maintained some of the problematic assumptions of the traditional IR performance measures [48]. The following measures have consequently been proposed:

- J¨arvelin and Kek¨al¨ainen's *cumulated gain* measures [44-45].
- Borlund and Ingwersen's *ranked half-life* measures [14].
- Cooper's expected *search length* [12], [20].
- Dunlop's *expected search duration* [27].
- Losee's *average search length* [54].
- K¨aki and Aula's *immediate accuracy* [47].

Time-Based Measures

Time-based measures are often used as indicators of efficiency. It is worth noting that effectiveness (performance), efficiency and satisfaction are standard usability measures. Although the three measures are interrelated, they can also be looked at separately. Efficiency will be looked at again later when describing usability measures.

- K¨aki and Aula [47] describe two time-based IR measures that are relevant to Human-Computer Interaction, namely *search speed* and *qualified search speed*. Although the measures are based on answers not relevant documents, they can be extended to cover retrieval itself.
- Cleverdon et al. [18] describe the *response time of the system*.

Informativeness

Informativeness is a measure for evaluating search results by focusing on relative evaluations of relevance rather than absolute measures [70-72]. Although informativeness measure has not yet been validated, renewed interest in the measure will perhaps lead to its validation and adoption.

Cost and Utility Measures
A number of authors such as Cooper [21] and Salton [63], [61] have proposed cost
and utility measures.

Contextual Measures
*"Much less attention has been paid to contextual aspects of end-user searching of
electronic information systems, by either librarians or information scientists."* [24].
There exists research evidence, such as seen in Saracevic and Kantor [67] and Dalrymple [23], acknowledging the importance of the user's context in information retrieval.

User Characteristics
Measuring user characteristics (or sometimes referred to as individual differences)
separately from the search process can enable the researcher to use them to predict
performance or to explain differences in performance [15].

- Fenichel [31] highlights common measures of user characteristics including:
  *sex of subject, age, college major, profession, level of computer experience,
  and level of search experience.*
- Ford et al. [32] propose Internet *perceptions* and *cognitive complexity* as additional measures of user characteristics.
- Kelly [48] proposes the following additional measures of user characteristics:
  intelligence, creativity, personality, memory, and cognitive style.

Measures of Information Needs
There are also IR measures that characterize the information need. For instance:

- Task-related measures (e.g. task-typc, task familiarity, task difficulty and
  complexity)
- Topic-related measures (e.g. topic familiarity and domain expertise)
- Persistence of information need
- Immediacy of information need
- Information-seeking stage
- Purpose, goals and expected use of the results

Interaction Measures
Interaction measures are used to describe the activities and processes that subjects
engage in during information retrieval. Interaction measures include:

- Number of queries
- Number of search results viewed
- Number of documents viewed
- Number of documents saved
- Query length

Since most interaction measures are counts, they can be combined to form other measures. For instance, the number of documents saved can be divided by the number of documents viewed [48].

Usability Measures
Usability is the extent to which users can use a system with effectiveness, efficiency and satisfaction to accomplish a task in a specified context of use [43]. Although there exist other definitions of usability, the ISO definition is one of the most commonly used.

Effectiveness
This is the extent to which the user is able to reach goal while using the system. The most common way for measuring effectiveness in HCI studies has been by measuring error rate and binary task completion [39]. In information retrieval, effectiveness can be measured by using appropriate measures from the performance measures that were described earlier (for instance: interactive precision and interactive recall), and also by eliciting self-reported data from subjects about their perceptions of performance.

Efficiency
Efficiency refers to how fast the user takes to finish tasks using the system. One of the most common ways for measuring efficiency is by recording the time it takes a subject to complete a task [39]. Efficiency can therefore include measures such as:

- The overall time the subject takes
- Amount of time the subject spends doing specific things
- Amount of time the subject spends in specific or different modes

In addition to the foregoing efficiency measures, and like with effectiveness, efficiency can also be measured by eliciting self-reported data from subjects about their perceptions of efficiency.

Satisfaction
Satisfaction assesses how much the user is satisfied with the system. Satisfaction can be viewed as the contentment, fulfilment or gratification that users experience when they accomplish particular goals or desires.

Other User-Relevant Measures
Besides the standard usability measures, there are other possible user-oriented measures that are relevant to information retrieval evaluation. They include:

- Preference
- Mental effort and cognitive load
- Flow and engagement: Flow is a *"mental state of operation in which a person is fully immersed in what he she is doing, characterized by a feeling of energized focus, full involvement, and success in the process of the activity."* [22], and engagement is *"a quality of user experiences with technology that*

is characterized by challenge, aesthetic and sensory appeal, feedback, novelty, interactivity, perceived control and time, awareness, motivation, and interest and affect" [58].

- Learning and cognitive transformation: The focus here is on the extent to which the system helps users learn about a particular topic.

In line with the foregoing discussion, the metrics that are appropriate to Human-Computer Interaction in Information Retrieval evaluation can be categorized as seen in Table 2.

Table 2. Categorization of measures appropriate to HCI in IR evaluation

Categorization of measures appropriate to HCI in IR evaluation	
Performance measures	• Traditional IR performance measures [76] ➢ Recall ➢ Precision ➢ F-measure ➢ Average precision (AP) ➢ Mean average precision (MAP) ➢ Geometric average precision (GMAP) ➢ Precision at n ➢ Mean reciprocal rank (MRR) • Performance measures for interactive information retrieval [74-75] ➢ Interactive recall ➢ Interactive user precision ➢ Interactive TREC precision ➢ Relative relevance (RR) • Multi-level relevance and rank measures ➢ Cumulated gain measures [44-45] ➢ Ranked half-life measures [14] ➢ Expected search length [12], [20] ➢ Expected search duration [27]

	➢ Average search length [54]
	
	 ➢ Immediate accuracy [47]
	
	 • Time measures
	   ➢ Search speed [47]
	   ➢ Qualified search speed [47]
	   ➢ Response time of the system [18]
	 • Informativeness [70-72]
	 • Cost and utility measures [21], [63], [61]

Contextual measures	• User characteristics
	   ➢ Sex of subject, age, college major, profession, level of computer experience, and level of search experience [31]
	   ➢ Internet perceptions and cognitive complexity [32]
	   ➢ Intelligence, creativity, personality, memory, and cognitive style [48]
	 • Measures of information needs [48]
	   ➢ Task-related measures (e.g. task-type, task familiarity, task difficulty and complexity)
	   ➢ Topic-related measures (e.g. topic familiarity and domain expertise)
	   ➢ Persistence of information need
	   ➢ Immediacy of information need
	   ➢ Information-seeking stage
	   ➢ Purpose, goals and expected use of the results

Interaction measures	• Number of queries • Number of search results viewed • Number of documents viewed

	• Number of documents saved
	• Query length
	• Combinations of such measures
Usability measures	• Effectiveness [39]
	➢ (Note it can be measured using appropriate performance measures e.g. interactive recall, interactive precision, interactive TREC precision, informativeness, cost, utility, etc)
	• Efficiency [39]
	➢ Overall time the subject takes
	➢ Amount of time the subject spends doing specific things
	➢ Amount of time the subject spends in specific or different modes
	➢ Etc
	• Satisfaction
	• Other relevant measures
	➢ Preference
	➢ Mental effort and cognitive load
	➢ Flow [22]
	➢ Engagement
	➢ Learning and cognitive transformation [58]

2.2   Models and Theories

An information retrieval system can in general be viewed as one that consists of a *"device interposed between a potential user of information and the information collection itself"* [34], containing three major components:

1. Database
2. Communication channel or interface between the user and the database, and which has:

   • A physical component for facilitating interaction.

- A conceptual component that guides the user on how to interact with the information structure and search mechanisms.
3. User

According to Hansen [33], IR research is moving from text representations and related techniques to also include studies of the users and their information needs, behaviour and strategies, and interaction processes.

Information Foraging Theory
Information foraging theory is a theory proposed by Pirolli and Card [59] that describes information retrieval behaviour. The theory is derived from the evolutionary ecological explanations of food-foraging strategies in anthropology and behavioral ecology. It is based on the analogy of an animal deciding what to eat, where it can be found, the best way to obtain it and how much "energy" the meal will provide (how filling the meal will be) as illustrated below:

> *"Imagine a predator, such as a bird of prey, that faces the recurrent problem of deciding what to eat, and we assume that its fitness, in terms of reproductive success, is dependent on energy intake. Energy flows into the environment and comes to be stored in different forms. For the bird of prey, different types of habitat and prey will yield different amounts of net energy (energetic profitability) if included in the diet. Furthermore, the different food-source types will have different distributions over the environment. For the bird of prey, this means that the different habitats or prey will have different access or navigation costs. Different species of birds of prey might be compared on their ability to extract energy from the environment. Birds are better adapted if they have evolved strategies that better solve the problem of maximizing the amount of energy returned per amount of effort. Conceptually, the optimal forager finds the best solution to the problem of maximizing the rate of net energy returned per effort expended, given the constraints of the environment in which it lives."* [59, p. 8]

Humans may be considered to be "informavores" that constantly make decisions on what kind of information to look for, whether to stay at the current site/place to try to find additional information or whether they should move on to another site/place, which path or link to follow to the next information site/place, and when to finally stop the search. Central to the information foraging theory is the concept of "information scent". Just like animals rely on scents to indicate the chances of finding prey in current area and guide them to other promising patches, humans rely on various cues in the information environment to get similar answers. Humans estimate how much useful information they are likely to get on a given path or direction, and after seeking information they compare the actual outcome with their predictions. When the information scent stops getting stronger (i.e., when users no longer expect to find useful additional information), the human users move to a different information source.

Berrypicking Model
The berrypicking model [6] acknowledges that searches are evolving and occur bit by bit. Users constantly change their search terms in response to the results returned from

the IR system. The very act of searching gives feedback which may cause users to modify their cognitive model of the information being searched for. Moreover, information retrieval can be bit by bit. Therefore, the query is satisfied not by a single final retrieved set of results, but by a series of selections of individual references and bits of information at each stage of the ever-modifying search. The model therefore uses the analogy of picking huckleberries or blueberries in the forest. The berries tend to be scattered on the bushes and do not often come in bunches. They need to be picked one at a time.

Ingwersen's Cognitive Model

The traditional model of IR systems represents IR as a two prong set (system and user) of elements and processes converging on comparison or matching. One attempt to improve on the traditional IR model is made by Peter Ingwersen in his cognitive model [41]. IR interaction is viewed as a set of cognitive processes, which involves system characteristics (representational and retrieval techniques), the user's situational characteristics and the functionalities of the user interface/intermediary. The cognitive viewpoint of IR embraces the complexity inherent in IR when users are involved and focuses attention on the cognitive activities that take place during information seeking and retrieval, and user information, user-system interactions [41]. Ingwersen and Jˇarvelin [42] identify five central and interrelated dimensions of the cognitive viewpoint:

1. Information processing takes place in senders and recipients of messages;
2. Processing takes place at different levels;
3. During communication of information any actor is influenced by its past and present experiences (time) and its social, organizational and cultural environment;
4. Individual actors influence the environment or domain; and
5. Information is situational and contextual.

While it is clear in viewing these dimensions that the cognitive viewpoint focuses on the user, Ingwersen and Jˇarvelin [42] are careful to point out that the cognitive viewpoint is not just about users' cognitive structures, but also about the numerous other cognitive structures represented in the IR system. For instance, cognitive structures represented by document authors and IR system developers.

Belkin's Episodes Model

This model concentrates on what happens in interaction as a process. Ingwerson's model focused on elements. Belkin's episodes model [7] views interaction as a series of episodes where a number of different things happen over time. For instance:

- Processes of judgement, use, interpretation, etc depending on user's goals, tasks.
- Processes of navigation, comparison, summarization, etc.
- Involving different aspects of information and information objects.

The user's interaction with the information system is the central process, which should be understood as interaction, especially as human-computer interaction.

Belkin's Evaluation Model for IRR

Belkin et al. [8] suggest an evaluation model and methodology grounded in the nature of information seeking and centred on usefulness. The model assumes that in accomplishing the general work task and achieving the general goal, the user engaged in information seeking goes through a sequence of information interactions, each having its own short term goal that contributes to achieving the general goal. The model is illustrated in Fig. 2.

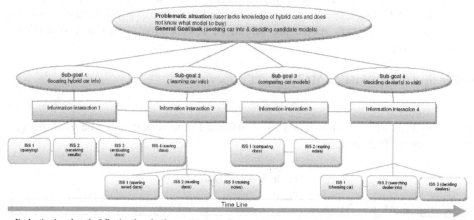

Evaluation based on the following three levels:

1. The usefulness of the entire information seeking episode with respect to accomplishment of the leading task;
2. The usefulness of each interaction with respect to its contribution to the accomplishment of the leading task;
3. The usefulness of system support toward the goal(s) of each interaction, and of each ISS.

Fig. 2. Belkin's evaluation model for IRR

Saracevic's Stratified Model of IR Interaction

The stratified model starts with assumptions that:

- Users interact with IR systems in order to use information
- The use of information is connected with cognition and then situational application.

Saracevic [65-66] proposed and enhanced the stratified interaction model whereby interaction of the interplay among different levels of users and systems is the central component. While users engage in cognitive, affective, and situational levels of interaction, system involvement includes engineering, processing, and content-level. The complexity and dynamic interaction process requires changes and adaptations from both the user and system side.

Ellis' Model of Information-Seeking Behaviours

Ellis' model [28-29] concentrates on the behavior instead of on cognitive activities. The model has six key components which correspond to types of information-seeking characteristics: 1) starting, 2) chaining, 3) browsing, 4) differencing, 5) monitoring, and 6) extracting. In a more recent work, Ellis and Haugan [30] further modeled the information-seeking patterns of engineers and research scientists in relation to their research activities in different phases and types of projects, and identified similar behavior patterns.

Kuhlthau's Model
Kuhlthau [50-51] has proposed a model that describes the tasks involved in the information seeking process from a psychological perspective, containing affective/feelings, cognitive/thoughts, and physical/action activities. The model actually complements Ellis' model by attaching to stages of the 'information search process' the associated feelings, thoughts and actions, and the appropriate information tasks. The stages of Kuhlthau's model are initiation, selection, exploration, formulation, collection and presentation.

Other Specific Evaluation Models and Frameworks

Allen's Model
This model [3] which is shown in Table 3 offers a framework that can be used to support and guide IR evaluation.

Table 3. Allen's model

Component	Method	Task
Resource Analysis	Description of information system functionality	Describe resources used to complete the tasks
User Needs Analysis	• Questionnaire (qualitative and quantitative data) • Log statistics (quantitative data)	• Users goals, purpose, objectives, actions, individual preferences • Measures like time, number of actions, and type of actions
Task analysis	Hierarchical Task Analysis	Users tasks, goals and activities that they accomplish when meeting their needs
User Modeling		Merging needs, user tasks and goals, and system tasks
Designing for usability	Requirement lists (qualitative data)	Requirements for user interface redesign

Ahmed et al.'s User-Centred Approach to the Design and Evaluation of IR Interfaces
Ahmed et al. [1] have proposed a user-centred approach for designing IR interfaces. The approach is based on performing the following:

1. A competitive analysis of an existing IR system to perform usability testing.
2. A user task analysis based on activities during usability test.
3. An initial prototype design drawn from task analysis.
4. A heuristic evaluation of the initial prototype design.
5. An interactive prototype design, incorporating input from heuristic evaluation.

6. A formative evaluation of the interactive prototype using task scenarios.
7. A revised prototype design based on formative evaluations, and finally.
8. A summative evaluation of the final prototype design and a comparison of the results with the results of competitive analysis for performing the same tasks.

IIR (Interactive Information Retrieval) Evaluation Model
Borlund [13] proposes the IIR evaluation model whose key elements are the use of realistic scenarios (referred to as simulated work task situations), and the (call for) alternative performance measures such as the ones that were described earlier.

The information retrieval theories and models can be categorized as summarized in Table 4.

Table 4. Categorization of IR theories and models

General approach	Specific view of IR	Examples of theories/models
Cognitive	Elements	• Ingwersen's cognitive model [41]: IR viewed as a set of cognitive processes (i.e. elements of cognitive processes).
Interaction	User's interaction with system as episodes	• Belkin's episodes model [7]: Focuses on user's interaction with IR system, where interaction is viewed as a series of episodes. • Belkin's evaluation model for IRR [8]: IR interaction viewed as a series information interactions each with a short term goal that contributes to achieving the general goal.
	Complex and dynamic interplay of users and systems	• Saracevic's stratified model of IR interaction [65-66]: IR interaction viewed as the interplay among different levels of users and systems requiring changes and adaptations.

Table 4. (*Continued*)

Behaviour	Standard	• Ellis' model [28-29]: IR viewed as some specific information-seeking behaviour or activities.
	Extended	• Kuhlthau's model [50-51]: complements Ellis' model by including the associated feelings, thoughts and actions.
	Ecological	• Information foraging theory [59]: IR viewed analogically as evolutionary ecological food-foraging behavioral strategies. • Berrypicking model [6]: IR viewed as evolving and occurring bit by bit, analogous to picking huckleberries or blueberries in the forest.

3   Framework for Usability Evaluation in Information Retrieval

A framework for the usability evaluation of an Information Retrieval system would entail aspects or parameters such as described in the sequel.

3.1   Participants

HCI Experts
It is common in HCI to involve HCI experts in evaluating interactive systems. This is normally done during the early phases of the design process. Evaluation methods that involve HCI experts are referred to as expert-based methods. They include: heuristic evaluation and cognitive walkthrough. This approach to evaluation where the participants are HCI experts is relevant also specifically to IR systems.

Users
It is also useful to conduct evaluations whose participants are the intended users of the IR system. According to Siatri [68], it is interesting to note that the first user studies were investigating people's information seeking needs [73], [10]. There are many

different types of evaluations where the participants are the intended users, for instance usability tests, observational methods (e.g., think-aloud and stimulated recall), query techniques (e.g., questionnaires and interviews), physiological monitoring methods (e.g., eye tracking, measuring skin conductance, measuring heart rate), etc. It is worth noting that involving the intended users in the evaluation of the IR system makes the evaluation set up more closely resemble the actual information retrieval processes and settings users would experience in the real world.

Surrogate Users

Sometimes it is extremely difficult to find and recruit actual users to participate in an evaluation. For example: high-powered individuals, national intelligence personnel, etc. In such cases, it is often better to involve surrogate users as a proxy for the actual users than not to conduct a user-based evaluation at all. It is however important to appropriately manage risks associated with surrogate users [52]. For instance: surrogate users should as much as possible resemble the actual users i.e. they should share key and relevant characteristics with the actual users.

There exist many methods for recruiting participants for IR evaluations, including newspaper advertising, posting signs, sending solicitations to mailing list, online advertising, using market research companies, etc. An interesting development in this area is the use of crowdsourcing, for instance through Mechanical Turk [4].

3.2 Tasks

During the evaluation of information retrieval systems, it is important to ensure that the set up is close to the actual information retrieval processes and contextual aspects users would experience in the real world. One way of introducing this realism is by involving the potential users in the evaluation of the IR system, as was mentioned earlier. Another way is by appropriately incorporating user tasks in the evaluation. The tasks can take many forms, for instance: standard tasks in information retrieval, real world work tasks, and simulated work tasks.

Standard Tasks in Information Retrieval

During information retrieval, users primarily engage in the following typical tasks [62],[5]:

- Formulation and submission of a query,
- Examination of the results, with a
- Possible feedback loop to re-formulate the query, and
- Integration of search results and evaluation of the whole search.

Each task or step indicates some statement of user requirement i.e. what the goal-directed user is trying to do with the system [46].

Simulated Work Task Situations

Borlund [13] proposes evaluation model for interactive information retrieval systems, whose key elements are the use of realistic scenarios that simulate real world work task situations. The scenarios are referred to as simulated work task situations. A simulated work task situation is a semantically rather open description of a scenario of a given IR requiring situation. A simulated work task situation is aimed at triggering and developing a simulated information need by allowing for user interpretations of the situation, leading to cognitively individual information need interpretations as in real-life. Research suggests that a simulated work task situation is more time consuming for the participants because it requires them to complete an additional and more complex task beyond finding relevant documents [48]. The additional task is to actually use the information in a manner that matches the user model behind the search task. It is therefore important to ensure that the simulated work task situations that the participants are presented with are not overly involving or tedious.

3.3   Measures

We had previously, in Section 2.1, described in detail the metrics or measures that are appropriate to Human-Computer Interaction in Information Retrieval evaluation. In the sequel we focus on the measures that would be relevant specifically to the usability evaluation of IR systems.

Standard Usability Measures

Effectiveness
In information retrieval evaluation, effectiveness can be measured by eliciting self-reported data from users about their perceptions of performance. Effectiveness in information retrieval can also be measured by using appropriate measures from the performance measures that were described previously. In particular:

- *interactive recall*
- *interactive precision*
- *interactive TREC precision*

Efficiency
In information retrieval evaluation, efficiency can be assessed using such measures as:
- The overall time the user takes
- The time the user takes doing specific things
- The time the user takes in specific or different modes

Efficiency can also be measured in information retrieval by eliciting self-reported data from users about their perceptions of efficiency.

Satisfaction
In information retrieval evaluation, satisfaction can be measured by eliciting self-reported data from users about their level of contentment, fulfilment or gratification as a result of using or interacting with the information retrieval system.

Interaction Measures

Interaction measures are relevant to usability evaluation of information retrieval systems. They include:

- Number of queries
- Number of search results viewed
- Number of documents viewed
- Number of documents saved
- Query length
- Appropriate combinations of the above measures

It is worth pointing out that interaction measures can be resourceful when assessing effectiveness.

User Characteristic Measures

It is important to measure user characteristics when conducting usability evaluation of information retrieval systems. Such information can for instance enable the researcher explain differences (such as in effectiveness) between different users. Measures of user characteristics could include: *sex, age, profession, computer experience, search experience*, Internet *perceptions, cognitive style*, etc.

Information Need Measures

Measures of information need are important when conducting usability evaluation of information retrieval systems. Such measures can for instance enable the researcher to predict or explain efficiency and effectiveness regarding particular topics. Information retrieval measures that characterize the information need include:

- Task-related measures (e.g. task-type, task familiarity, task difficulty and complexity)
- Topic-related measures (e.g. topic familiarity and domain expertise)
- Persistence of information need
- Immediacy of information need
- Information-seeking stage
- Purpose, goals and expected use of the results

Other User-Relevant Measures

There are also other measures that are closely related to the standard usability measures, and are therefore relevant to the usability evaluation of information retrieval systems. They include:

- Preference
- Mental effort and cognitive load
- Flow and engagement
- Learning and cognitive transformation

3.4   Evaluation Method(s)

There exist many methods that can be used for usability evaluation. Although there are several different ways of classifying them, they can generally be categorized as expert-based evaluation methods and user-based evaluation methods. User-based evaluation methods include: usability tests, observational methods (e.g. think aloud, stimulated recall/post-task walkthrough, transaction logging), query techniques (e.g., questionnaires and interviews), and physiological monitoring methods (e.g., eye tracking, measuring skin conductance, measuring heart rate). Expert-based evaluation methods include: heuristic evaluation and cognitive walkthrough.

After collecting the evaluation data, there are some basic things one should do before embarking on the actual data analysis [25], including:

- Looking at the data: A simple glance at the data could be all that is necessary.
- Saving the data: One might need to do more analysis in the future.

According to Dix et al. [25], the choice of the statistical technique for data analysis depends on factors such as:

- The questions we want to answer e.g., "Is there a difference?" (e.g., is one IR system better than another?), "how big is the difference?", "how accurate is the estimate?"
- Type of data/variables e.g. discrete data vs. continuous data; number of independent variables vs. number of dependent variables.

In the following we highlight important considerations when using some specific methods in the usability evaluation of information retrieval systems.

Heuristic Evaluation vs. Usability Testing

Doubleday et al. [26] compared heuristic evaluation with user testing on an IR system. The expert evaluators identified 86 usability problems whereas 38 problems were identified in the user testing. However, not all of the 38 problems found by user testing were identified by the expert evaluators. Some genuine problems would therefore have gone undetected if there had been no user testing. Another example is reported by Cogdill [19], where the expert evaluators identified 27 usability problems compared to 21 problems found in the usability test. Cogdill also noted that using both heuristic evaluation and usability testing resulted in a high degree of comprehensiveness in the study. It is therefore worth pointing out that expert-based and user-based evaluation methods can play a complementary role in evaluating information retrieval systems.

Transaction Logging

Although transaction logging is one of the oldest and most common methods for collecting data when evaluating interactive information retrieval systems, the recent explosion of studies using Web transaction log data has re-popularized the approach. The method relies on computer and Web monitoring tools in order to collect logs characterizing user's interaction with the system. There are various types of logging including: system, proxy, server, and client logging. The researcher however needs to be aware of the following main challenges when using transaction log data: ensuring the validity and reliability of the logger, extracting and preparing data generated by the logger, and interpreting the data [48]. Most transaction logging tools can run in the background while the user interacts with the information retrieval system, without causing any distractions or disruption. Transaction logging is therefore a potentially useful observational method because it can capture users' natural search behaviours without interrupting them. Transaction logs can also be resourceful in providing an objective dimension to the information retrieval evaluation measures that the research is interested in.

Questionnaires

Questionnaires are common in information retrieval evaluations. Questionnaires can be used at various points during an evaluation of an IR system. Consequently there are several types of questionnaire, for instance: screening questionnaire, pre-study questionnaire, and post-study questionnaire. Questionnaires can be administered electronically or manually (pen-and-paper). Kelly et al. [49] found that in the context of interactive information retrieval evaluation, subjects' responses to closed-questions were significantly more positive when elicited electronically, than manually.

Interviews

Research suggests that in information retrieval evaluation, interviews are more appropriate when one is asking complex, abstract questions than when one is asking relatively easy questions [49]. Interviews can also be useful in information retrieval evaluation during simulated recall/post-task walkthrough [48].

Think-Aloud

In think-aloud the user is expected to perform an information retrieval task and at the same time articulate their thoughts as they carry out the task. One of the challenges with the think-aloud is that users may have a difficult time simultaneously articulating their thoughts and carrying out the information retrieval task that they have been given. In many evaluations, the information retrieval system is novel. Users may therefore not be able to handle the additional cognitive demands placed by think-aloud, while they are also learning how to interact with the system. Some researchers have proposed that subjects complete a short training task before they start searching in order to get accustomed to think-aloud [48]. It is worth noting that stimulated recall (i.e. post-task walkthrough) can serve as an alternative to think-aloud. In stimulated recall, the researcher records the screen of the computer as the user performs the searching task. After the searching task is complete, the recording is played back to the user who is then asked to articulate their thoughts and decision-making as the recording is played.

The kinds of parameters that would be typically expected in a framework for the usability evaluation of an Information Retrieval system are summarized in Table 5.

Table 5. Parameters expected in a framework for the usability evaluation of IR systems

Evaluation aspect	Parameters
Participants	• HCI experts • Users • Surrogate users

Tasks	• Standard tasks in information retrieval e.g.
	  ➢ Formulation and submission of a query,
	  ➢ Examination of the results, with a
	  ➢ Possible feedback loop to re-formulate the query, and
	  ➢ Integration of search results and evaluation of the whole search [62], [5]
	• Simulated work task situations [13]

Measures	• Standard usability measures
	  ➢ Effectiveness (interactive recall, interactive precision, interactive TREC precision, informativeness, cost, utility, etc)
	  ➢ Efficiency (overall time user takes, time user takes doing specific things, time user takes in specific or different modes, etc)
	  ➢ Satisfaction
	• Interaction measures e.g.
	  ➢ Number of queries
	  ➢ Number of search results viewed
	  ➢ Number of documents viewed
	  ➢ Number of documents saved
	  ➢ Query length
	  ➢ Appropriate combinations
	• User characteristic measures e.g.
	  ➢ Sex
	  ➢ Age
	  ➢ Profession
	  ➢ Computer experience
	  ➢ Search experience
	  ➢ Internet perceptions
	  ➢ Cognitive style
	• Information need measures e.g.
	  ➢ Task-related measures (task-type, task familiarity, task difficulty, complexity, etc)
	  ➢ Topic-related measures (topic familiarity and domain expertise, etc)
	  ➢ Persistence of information need
	  ➢ Immediacy of information need
	  ➢ Information-seeking stage

	➢ Purpose, goals and expected use of the results
	• Other relevant measures e.g.
	  ➢ Preference
	  ➢ Mental effort and cognitive load
	  ➢ Flow and engagement
	  ➢ Learning and cognitive transformation

Evaluation method(s)	• User-based evaluation methods e.g.
	  ➢ Usability tests
	  ➢ Observational methods (think aloud, stimulated recall/post-task walkthrough, transaction logging, etc)
	  ➢ Query techniques (questionnaires and interviews)
	  ➢ Physiological monitoring methods (eye tracking, measuring skin conductance, measuring heart rate, etc)
	• Expert-based evaluation methods e.g.
	  ➢ Heuristic evaluation
	  ➢ Cognitive walkthrough

4   Conclusions

In this chapter, we have observed that the traditional methods of evaluating IR systems have over a long period of time been primarily concerned with system-oriented measurements such as precision and recall, but not on the usability aspects of the IR system. Moreover, there are no well-established evaluation approaches for studying users and their interactions with IR systems. It is therefore important to consider, appropriately adjust and invent user interface techniques that can support the user in their information retrieval tasks by guiding, supporting and transforming the user's information problems, goals or needs. Human Computer Interaction researchers and designers should also endeavour to appropriately use, revise and propose user-information seeking models and evaluation techniques for information retrieval systems. In line with that, we have in this chapter described: existing user interface techniques for supporting users to interact with and use information retrieval systems, measures that are appropriate to Human-Computer Interaction in information retrieval evaluation, existing IR information seeking theories and models, and IR evaluation frameworks. We have also described the typical elements that would constitute a framework for the usability evaluation of an Information Retrieval system.

It is worth noting that there are some trends that are not only posing unique challenges but also providing tremendous opportunities to the IR community and other communities including the HCI community. For instance: IR of massive user-generated content (e.g. microblogs, social network discussion forums data, user-generated multimedia, etc), user-participation and crowdsourcing in IR, dynamic or continuously evolving and growing data (e.g. sensor data), etc. There is a need to realize user interface techniques that can support users in information retrieval tasks in the context of such trends. It is also worth noting that such trends challenge standard approaches to the usability evaluation of IR systems. For instance, crowdsourcing introduces aspects such as collaboration, trust, etc to the standard IR evaluation measures.

All in all, Human-Computer Interaction aspects are important in information retrieval. Efforts aimed at appropriately incorporating HCI techniques in IR can realize IR systems that meet and possibly exceed the needs of the intended users.

References

1. Ahmed, S.M.Z., McKnight, C., Oppenheim, C.: A user-centred design and evaluation of IR interfaces. Journal of Librarianship and Information Science 38(2), 157–172 (2006)
2. Allen, B.: From research to design: A user-centered approach. In: Ingwersen, P., Pors, N.O. (eds.) CoLIS 2. Second International Conference on Conceptions of Library and Information Science: Integration in Perspective, pp. 45–59. The Royal School of Librarianship, Copehagen (1996)
3. Allen, B.: Information tasks. Towards a user-centered approach to information systems. Academic Press, San Diego (1996)
4. Alonso, O., Rose, D.E., Stewart, B.: Crowdsourcing for relevance evaluation. SIGIR Forum 42, 10–16 (2008)
5. Baeza-Yates, R., Ribeiro-Neto, B.: Modern information retrieval. Addison-Wesley, Reading (1999)
6. Bates, M.J.: The design of browsing and berrypicking techniques for the online search interface. Online Review 13(5), 407–424 (1989)
7. Belkin, N.J., Cool, C., Stein, A., Thiel, U.: Cases, scripts and information seeking strategies: on the design of interactive information retrieval systems. Expert Systems with Applications 9, 379–395 (1995)
8. Belkin, N., J., Cole, M., Liu, J.: A Model for Evaluation of Interactive Information Retrieval. In: SIGIR Workshop on the Future of IR Evaluation (2009)
9. Berger, L.: Look ahead caching process for improved information retrieval response time by caching bodies of information before they are requested by the user. United States Patent (1999)
10. Bernal, J.D.: Preliminary Analysis of Pilot Questionnaires on the Use of Scientific literature. In: The Royal Society Scientific Information Conference, pp. 589–637 (1948)
11. Borgman, C.L., Hirsh, S.G., Walter, V.A., Gallagher, A.L.: Children's searching behaviour on browsing and keyword online catalog: the Science Library Catalog Project. Journal of the American Society for Information Science 46(9), 663–684 (1995)
12. Borlund, P.: The concept of relevance in IR. Journal of the American Society for Information Science 54, 913–925 (2003)
13. Borlund, P.: The IIR evaluation model: a framework for evaluation of interactive information retrieval systems. Information Research 8(3) (2003)
14. Borlund, P., Ingwersen, P.: Measure of relative relevance and ranked halflife: Performance indicators for interactive information retrieval. In: Proceedings of the 21st ACM SIGIR Conference on Research and Development of Information Retrieval (SIGIR 1998), Melbourne, Australia, pp. 324–331 (1998)

15. Boyce, B.R., Meadow, C.T., Kraft, D.H.: Measurement in Information Science. Academic Press, Inc., London (1994)
16. Callan, J., Allan, J., Clarke, J.L.A., Dumais, S., Evans, D.A., Sanderson, M., Zhai, C.: Meeting of the MINDS: An information retrieval research agenda. SIGIR Forum 41, 25–34 (2007)
17. Cleverdon, C.W.: The Cranfield tests on index language devices. In: Spark-Jones, K., Willett, P. (eds.) Readings in Information Retrieval. Reprinted from Aslib Proceedings, pp. 173–192. Morgan Kaufman Publishers, San Francisco (1967)
18. Cleverdon, C. W., Mills, L., Keen, M.: Factors Determining the Performance of Indexing Systems. Design, vol. 1. Aslib Cranfield Research Project, Cranfield (1996)
19. Cogdill, K.: MEDLINEplus Interface Evaluation: Final Report, University of Maryland, Human-Computer Interaction Lab (HCIL), College Park, MD (1999)
20. Cooper, W.S.: Expected search length: A single measure of retrieval effectiveness based on the weak ordering action of retrieval systems. American Documentation 19, 30–41 (1968)
21. Cooper, W.S.: On selecting a measure of retrieval effectiveness, part 1: The "subjective" philosophy of evaluation. Journal of the American Society for Information Science 24, 87–100 (1973)
22. Csikszentmihalyi, M.: Finding Flow: The Psychology of Engagement with Everyday Life. Basic Books, New York (1997)
23. Dalrymple, P.W.: Retrieval by reformulation in two university library catalogs: Toward a cognitive model of searching behavior. Journal of the American Society (1990)
24. Dalrymple, P.W.: User-Centered Evaluation of Information Retrieval. In: Allen, B. (ed.) Evaluation of Public Services and Public Services Personnel, pp. 85–102. University of Illinois, Urbana (1991)
25. Dix, A., Finlay, J., Abowd, G., Beale, R.: Human-Computer Interaction. Prentice Hall (2003)
26. Doubleday, A.R., Ryan, M., Springett, M., Sutcliffe, A.: A comparison of usability techniques for evaluating design. In: Proceedings of the Conference on Designing Interactive Systems: Processes, Practices, Methods, and Techniques, August 18-20, pp. 101–110. ACM, Amsterdam (1997)
27. Dunlop, M.: Time, relevance and interaction modeling for information retrieval. In: Proceedings of the 20th ACM Conference on Research and Development in Information Retrieval (SIGIR 1997), Philadelphia, PA, pp. 206–213 (1997)
28. Ellis, D.: The derivation of a behavioral model for information system design. Unpublished doctoral dissertation. University of Sheffield, England (1987)
29. Ellis, D.: A behavioural approach to information retrieval system design. Journal of Documentation 45(3), 171–212 (1989)
30. Ellis, D., Haugan, M.: Modeling the information seeking patterns of engineers and research scientists in an industrial environment. Journal of Documentation 53(4), 384–403 (1997)
31. Fenichel, C.H.: Online searching: Measures that discriminate among users with different types of experience. Journal of the American Society for Information Science 32, 23–32 (1981)
32. Ford, N., Miller, D., Moss, N.: The role of individual differences in Internet searching: An empirical study. Journal of the American Society for Information Science and Technology 52, 1049–1066 (2001)
33. Hansen, P.: Evaluation of IR User Interface. Implications for user interface design. Human IT (2), 28–41 (1998)

34. Harter, S.: Online information retrieval. Concepts, principles, and techniques. Academic Press, Orlando (1986)
35. Hearst, M.: User Interfaces and Visualization. In: Baeza-Yates, R., Ribeiro-Neto, B. (eds.) Modern Information Retrieval, ch.10 (1999)
36. Hearst, M.: Query Reformulation. In: Search User Interfaces, ch. 6. Cambridge University Press (2009)
37. Hewett, T., Baecker, R., Card, S., Carey, T., Gasen, J., Mantei, M., Perlman, G., Strong, G., Verplank, W.: ACM SIGCHI Curricula for Human-Computer Interaction (1992)
38. Hix, D., Hartson, H.R.: Developing user interfaces. Ensuring usability through product and process. Wiley, New York (1993)
39. Hornbaek, K.: Current practice in measuring usability: Challenges to usability studies and research. International Journal of Human–Computer Studies 64, 79–102 (2005)
40. Hutchinson, H.B., Drunin, A., Bederson, B.B.: Supporting elementary-age children's searching and browsing: design and evaluation using the International Children's Digital Library. Journal of the American Society for Information Science 58(11), 1618–1630 (2007)
41. Ingwersen, P.: Cognitive perspectives of information retrieval interaction: Elements of a cognitive IR theory. Journal of Documentation 52, 3–50 (1996)
42. Ingwersen, P., Järvelin, K.: The Turn: Integration of Information Seeking and Retrieval in Context. Springer, Dordrecht (2005)
43. ISO: Ergonomic Requirements for Office Work with Visual Display Terminals (VDTs): Part II, Guidance on Usability, ISO 9241- 11:1998 (1998)
44. Järvelin, K., Kekäläinen, J.: IR evaluation methods for retrieving highly relevant documents. In: Proceedings of the 23rd ACM SIGIR Conference on Research and Development of Information Retrieval (SIGIR 2000), Athens, Greece, pp. 41–48 (2000)
45. Järvelin, K., Kekäläinen, J.: Cumulated gain-based evaluation of IR techniques. ACM Transactions on Information Systems (TOIS) 20, 422–446 (2002)
46. Johnson, F.C., Griffiths, J.R., Hartley, R.J.: Task dimensions of user evaluations of information retrieval systems. Information Research 8(4) (2003)
47. Käki, M., Aula, A.: Controlling the complexity in comparing search user interfaces via user studies. Information Processing and Management 44, 82–91 (2008)
48. Kelly, D.: Methods for evaluating interactive information retrieval systems with users. Foundations and Trends in Information Retrieval 3(1-2), 1–224 (2009)
49. Kelly, D., Harper, J., Landau, B.: Questionnaire mode effects in interactive information retrieval experiments. Information Processing and Management (2008)
50. Kuhlthau, C.C.: Inside the search process: information seeking from the user's perspective. Journal of the American Society for Information Science 42, 361–371 (1991)
51. Kuhlthau, C.C.: Seeking meaning: a process approach to library and information services. Ablex Publishing, Norwood (1994)
52. Lievesley, M.A., Yee, J.S.R.: Surrogate Users – A Pragmatic Approach to Defining User Needs. In: Conference Proceedings and Extended Abstracts, CHI 2007, San Jose. ACM Press (2007)
53. Lin, X.: Map displays for information retrieval. Journal of the American Society for Information Science 48(1), 40–54 (1997)
54. Losee, R.M.: Evaluating retrieval performance given database and query characteristics: Analytical determination of performance surfaces. Journal of the American Society for Information Science 47, 95–105 (1996)
55. Marchionini, G.: An invitation to browse: designing full text systems for novice users. Canadian Journal of Information Science 12(3), 69–79 (1987)

56. Marchionini, G.: Toward Human-Computer Information Retrieval Bulletin. Bulletin of the American Society for Information Science (June/July 2006), http://www.asis.org/Bulletin/Jun-06/marchionini.html
57. Mira working group: Evaluation Frameworks for Interactive Multimedia Information Retrieval Applications (1996), http://www.dcs.gla.ac.uk/mira
58. O'Brien, H., Toms, E.: What is user engagement? A conceptual framework for defining user engagement with technology. Journal of the American Society for Information Science and Technology 59, 938–955 (2008)
59. Pirolli, P., Card, S.K.: Information foraging. Psychological Review 106(4), 643–675 (1999)
60. Rocchio, J.: Relevance feedback in information retrieval. In: Salton, G. (ed.) The SMART Retrieval System (1971)
61. Salton, G.: Evaluation problems in interactive information retrieval. Information Storage and Retrieval 6, 29–44 (1970)
62. Salton, G.: Automatic text processing: the transformation, analysis and retrieval of information by computer. Addison-Wesley, Reading (1989)
63. Salton, G.: The state of retrieval system evaluation. Information Processing and Management 28, 441–449 (1992)
64. Salton, G., Buckley, C.: Improving retrieval performance by relevance feedback. Journal of the American Society for Information Science 41(4), 288–297 (1990)
65. Saracevic, T.: Modeling interaction in information retrieval (IR): A review and proposal. In: Proceedings of the 59th ASIS Annual Meeting 1996, vol. 33, pp. 3–9 (1996)
66. Saracevic, T.: The stratified model of information retrieval interaction: Extension and applications. In: Proceedings of the 60th ASIS Annual Meeting 1997, vol. 34, pp. 313–327 (1997)
67. Saracevic, T., Kantor, P.: A study of information seeking and retrieving. Journal of the American Society for Information Science 39(3), 177–216 (1988)
68. Siatri, R.: The Evolution of User Studies. Libri 49, 132–141 (1999)
69. Su, L.T.: Evaluation measures for interactive information retrieval. Information Processing and Management 28, 503–516 (1992)
70. Tague, J.: Informativeness as an ordinal utility function for information retrieval. SIGIR Forum 21, 10–17 (1987)
71. Tague-Sutcliffe, J.M.: The pragmatics of information retrieval experimentation, revisited. Information Processing and Management 28, 467–490 (1992)
72. Tague-Sutcliffe, J.M.: Measuring Information: An Information Services Perspective. Academic Press, San Diego (1995)
73. Urquhart, D.J.: The Distribution and Use of Scientific and Technical Information. In: The Royal Society Scientific Information Conference, pp. 408–419 (1948)
74. Veerasamy, A., Belkin, N.J.: Evaluation of a tool for visualization of information retrieval results. In: Proceedings of the 19th Annual International ACM SIGIR Conference on Research and Development in Information Retrieval, Zurich, Switzerland, pp. 85–92 (1996)
75. Veerasamy, A., Heikes, R.: Effectiveness of a graphical display of retrieval results. SIGIR Forum 31, 236–245 (1997)
76. Voorhees, E.M., Harman, D.K.: TREC: Experiment and Evaluation in Information Retrieval. MIT Press, Cambridge (2005)
77. Yuan, W., Meadow, C.T.: A study of the use of variables in information retrieval user studies. Journal of the American Society for Information Science 50, 140–150 (1999)

User-Oriented Information Retrieval

Elaine G. Toms

Information School, The University of Sheffield, Sheffield, United Kingdom
e.toms@sheffield.ac.uk

Abstract. User models of information seeking and retrieval reflect a rich culture of exploring the relationshipns among users, task, and their context. This lecture examines briefly the complex information use environment in which information retrieval systems are situated.

Keywords: Information models, Information seeking and retrieval, searching, browsing.

1   Introduction

What do we mean by "user-oriented" information retrieval (IR)? In general, information retrieval has been about how to extract precise nuggets from a vast collection of initially, unstructured documents, and now, information and data in all of its various formats, from text to video and architectural drawings. User oriented IR moves the orientation from a "closed system" in which the IR "engine" is tuned to handle a given set of documents and queries, to one that integrates the IR system within a broader information use environment that includes people, and the context in which they are immersed. This latter situation may include human lab experimentation, that is, the IR system is used in an artificial setting in which participants perform simulated tasks that fit within a particular work or pleasure environment; or, the IR system is implemented in a real world setting in which the system is actively in use to assist with the daily work. Regardless of which scenario, the intent of the research is to examine how well the system fits a particular user or group context, or to research how users interact with the system and its content. As a consequence, the IR system is not just a lab artifact, but also has value in a socio-cultural-organisational context, which could be construed as the raison d'être for its existence. Ruthven and Kelly's [25] edited volume have brought together succinct summaries of the broad aspects of the topic and serves as a useful starting point.

In this short overview, we will examine: a) the elements of the context in which an IR system is used; b) some of fundamental models of information seeking and retrieval that have emerged over the past decades in information science to explain the environment or aspects of the environment in which the system is used, and c) the multiple layers involved in the interactive process.

M. Agosti et al. (Eds.): PROMISE Winter School 2012, LNCS 7757, pp. 76–85, 2013.
© Springer-Verlag Berlin Heidelberg 2013

2   Context and Information Use Environments

That broader context – the information use environment – in which an IR system is deployed, has a significant influence on the IR system's success. Indeed, without a context in which to operate, an IR system is nothing more than a bunch of algorithms that accepts queries and outputs results. Unfortunately, "[t]here is no term that is more often used, less often defined, and when defined, defined so variously as Context. Context is something you swim in like a fish. You are in it. It is you" [9]. It is Dervin's understanding of context that defines how context is applied on the user-centric side of the IR problem.

The broader context has three important elements:

1) The user who comes to the system with a bag of potentially influential characteristics such as age (child or adult), level of education, knowledge (novice or expert), and experience (none to a lot). The user may bring a host of "individual differences" that make that person somewhat unique among the global user community. These include reading level, cognitive style, need for cognition, personality type, intellectual ability, and spatial ability. At the point of interacting with a system, the user may vary in any of these characteristics as well as those that pertain directly to the reason for using an IR system at that time, such as motivation, and the user's mental model of the system. Additionally, any of these physical settings may be occupied by *groups*, which may also affect the style of "work" activity; that is, the user may act alone, but also may work collaboratively.

The challenge to date has been in identifying which among this very large set of characteristics may influence a person's use of IR systems. Arguably the work to date is primarily descriptive rather than causal. We can only rarely say because a person has characteristic X, that the person will behave in a particular way or use a search system in a particular way. Personalisation emerged as a way to examine and manage that individual process, but the evidence has yet to be demonstrated despite the research interest and plethora of publications.

2) The *social/organisational environment* – the information use environment in which the user is immersed, such as law, health, or education, or even everyday life. What domain or type of work is involved? This is not limited to formal work settings but also pertains to leisure activities and home life.

3) The *task* that drove a person to an IR system in the first place which interacts with a user's motivation for doing said task. Task has been interpreted in a multitude of ways, likely because the word task is so generic, and can be specified at multiple levels of activity. A *work* task is an "activity to be performed to accomplish a goal" [13] where work may be interpreted as any human activity that occurs in the home, or at a place of employment, or indeed as an aspect of any leisure activity. A task may be simple – a single activity or action is required; it may be a composite requiring multiple actions in multiple activities, each with its own objective, and may require multiple pieces of information or data that have to be humanly aggregated and digested to make a *human* decision.

The task at the point of interaction with an IR system is a type of *information* task that is being deployed to find information to support achieving the work task's outcome. This may range from a simple Q&A or the typical known-item search tasks, to a multi-facetted process that requires a series of inter-related queries that extract a set of information objects for other forms of analyses, e.g., comparison, synthesis, etc.

These three elements are encapsulated in this example:

> The user may be a student writing a term paper, a lawyer preparing an argument, a member of a social group choosing a movie to watch, or a mom (or dad) looking for age-specific health information. The user in each of these scenarios may be the same person; the scenarios represent the roles that the user may play in a day. Each role will influence how the user approaches the IR system, what the user inserts as a query or queries, the sources of information that may be used, and what the user might expect to find or be satisfied with to achieve a useful outcome.

Thus the user as human being may not vary, but the roles and their associated tasks suggest that task environment may take supremacy over user variability, or interact with that variability in considering the "fit" of an IR system. Once an IR system moves outside the traditional IR lab setting and into a human use environment, the challenge is in tuning the system to satisfy a host of potential options based on the information use environment, i.e., its context.

3   Models of Information Seeking and Retrieval

Over the years a plethora of models and frameworks have emerged to explain the various facets and elements of information use environments (see a sample of 20 in Table 1). Noted decades ago and still true today, we have no central theory or even a common model [18]. Ideally, a model simplifies reality and enables understanding of the essence of complex phenomena, which in this case is the information seeking, searching and retrieval of information for some purpose. These models tend to be descriptive (rather than predictive). The challenge for any student, particularly those new to the field, is in navigating the list. Which ones represent a documented and validated model or theory? Which ones are still unsubstantiated hypotheses? Some emerged from a single data set, and some have never been validated, or the data collection replicated to confirm the initial findings. This remains a conundrum in this rich, complex research area. Case [6], and Ingwersen and Jarvelin [16] have done substantial "meta" analyses of some of these and both can serve as useful guides for the novice.

The information use environment and its elements have been succinctly and elegantly represented in Ingwersen and Jarvelin's [16] conceptual model of *Interactive Information Seeking, Retrieval and Behavioral* processes and is a useful starting point in grappling with the area. As illustrated in Figure 1, the IR system represented by "IT" acts on Information Objects that may be text, video, audio or any information bearing object, which are then viewed and interacted with through an interface by a set of users (called cognitive actors by Ingwersen and Jarvelin) who are influenced by the social, cultural and organisational milieu in which they are immersed. This bird's view illustrates the role of the IR system as one aspect in a large, multi-faceted system (that was described simply in Section 2, and more comprehensively in [16]. What is missing from this illustration is the notion of task, which is hidden within context in this model. Others, such as Saracevic [26] and Wilson [35, 36] have presented variations on this theme.

Table 1. Model Mania – Models of Information Seeking, Search and Retrieval

Source	Type
Bates [3]	Information search/browse process
Bates [1,2]	Information search Tactics
Belkin [4]	Information search process
Bystrom & Jarvelin [5]	Information need/seeking process
Ellis [10,11]	Information Task Activities
Guthrie [12]	Information Search process/procedure
Henry et al [15]	Information search process
Ingwersen & Jarvelin [16]	Context-oriented
Johnson [17]	Information seeking process
Krikelas [18]	Information seeking process
Kuhlthau [19]	Information seeking process
Leckie et al. [20]	Information seeking process
Marchionini [22]	Information search process
Saracevic [26]	Context-oriented
Savolainen [27]	Context-oriented
Sonnewald [28]	Context-oriented
Taylor [29]	Information needs
Vakkari [31, 32]	Information search process
Wang & Soergel [33]	Information seeking
Wilson [35, 36]	Context-oriented

Some like Kuhlthau [19] and Vakkari [31], [32] have substantive research to support their assertions and have nicely integrated each other's work to illustrate similarities and where perspectives diverge. Others such as Bates' tactics [1,2] and Ellis' activities [10], [11] provide insights into the development of tools to support how information is sought and found. Regardless of which model one uses to explain a particular research problem, the conclusion is irrefutable: an IR system does not operate in a vacuum; many other aspects influence its design and implementation.

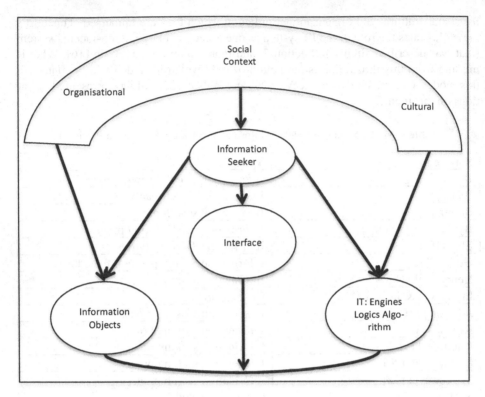

Fig. 1. Ingwersen and Jarvelin's Interactive Information Seeking, Retrieval and Behavioral processes (modified from [16])

4   Models that Represent the Information Interaction Process

The process of information seeking and retrieval operates in a mixed human and technological environment. From the emergence of information needs and the subsequent seeking perspective, we can view the process at a high conceptual level (such as the work of Ingwersen and Jarvelin [16] previously discussed). But once one engages with an interactive process for information searching, retrieval and use, then many other processes are invoked. Figure 2 illustrates those nested layers, from a conceptual view of the entire process to computer input; Sandwiched between the two, multiple processes are invoked that may be explained by existing models, theories or frameworks.

At the top are the models of context that represent in whole or in part the information use environment as described by Ingwersen and Jarvelin [16], Wilson [35], [36] and Saracevic [26]. Although they represent the space in differing ways, they conceptually bring the various threads together for a broad perspective. These abstract representations present rich pictures, but are difficult to apply in a specific user-system interaction, the typical interactive IR scenario, when the IR system is in use.

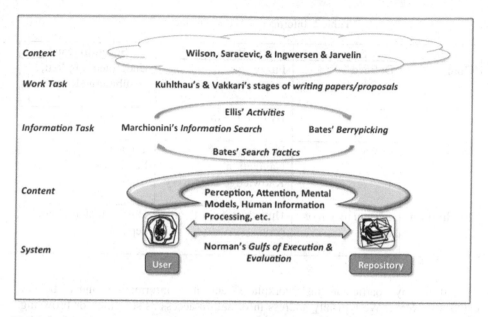

Fig. 2. Layers in the Human Information Seeking, Searching and Retrieval Process from broad conceptual level to the keystroke level (adapted from [30])

Information use environments have purpose, and those purposes are rendered as work tasks, or leisure activities, and provide the intent to use an IR system. Unfortunately, the concept of task has been badly maligned in IR research in the past. Initially, the concept of task was modeled after first, the Cranfield studies [7], and more recently TREC (Text Retrieval Conference – http://trec.nist.gov), INEX (Initiative for the Evaluation of XML Retieval) and CLEF (Conference and Labs of the Evaluation Forum – http://www.clef-initiative.eu//); task for the most part has been equated with topics used to tune search algorithms, and sometimes even considered equivalent to query. In systems design and in particular, user-centred design, the task is elemental to defining functional requirements.

As noted earlier, a work task can be equated with writing a term paper or a research proposal, or deciding among potential cancer treatments. The example that best illustrates this concept and is perhaps the most robust (although still relatively unspecified from a procedural perspective) is Kuhlthau's [19] process for writing term papers, and Vakkari's [31], [32] stages of writing a research proposal. We have yet to consider an IR system tuned to a particular information use environment designed to support particular tasks. Examples from e-commerce could be the shopping task, the travel task and even the online dating task. Provision of good design prescriptions at this level are limited to date, and as a result we have few models or frameworks.

Table 2. Information Access Distinctions

	Search	**Browse**	**Serendipitous**
Goal	Defined	Fuzzy	Undefined, implicit, or submerged
Mode	By specifying	By recognising	By recognising
Method	Query	Scanning Navigation Knowledge Discovery	Trigger Landmark Cue
Evaluation	System match of terms	Human match of concepts	Human match of concepts

Within any particular task/workplace activity, information must be located/discovered. We typically address information access as searching or browsing. But, information access can be explained as three core processes (see Table 2) that may be distinguished primarily by goal and the method by which the IR system facilitates the process. The search process has been well defined since the early days of online searching but is often ascribed to the succinctly and clearly explained dynamic process presented by Marchionini [22]. Historically, browsing has been about finding information without a specific goal in mind, and is often confused with the manner in which it is achieved which is to physically scan a display until a cue disrupts the scanning process. Bates' [3] berrypicking explanation (which later informed conceptually the foundation for Pirolli and Card's [24] information foraging theory) has yet to be fully deployed in any systems development, but is often used to explain user-browsing behavior. The third, type, serendipitous access, is very rarely considered and is often confused with pure chance, although recent work suggests that serendipity is much more complex than that, an interaction of past knowledge and experience juxtaposed new or old information that may now be interpreted in new ways.

At present, there is only a limited set of deployed techniques to accomplish these information tasks. The bulk of the effort has been placed on the development of algorithms rather than on tools to aid the user in search interaction. With respect to search, it is the quintessential query box. Despite the series of information tactics developed by Bates [1], [2] decades ago, few tools have been developed and deployed to realize their objectives. Along similar lines, Ellis [10], [11] identified a set of core activities to facilitate information access that included chaining, differentiating, monitoring, extracting, and verifying. The principles of each could form the design prescription for "soft" tools that facilitate human access to an IR system. Wilson's [37] taxonomy for a search interface (influenced by Hearst's in-depth coverage of the search interface issue [14]) and White's [34] set of interactive techniques provides a useful starting point for defining how information tasks can be operationalised.

At the level of the interface, the user is engaged in a generic user-system base-level operation that plays out in all user-system interactions regardless of application and input/output device. In some respects it is comparable to reader-text interaction and how humans process information. It includes models that explain everything from how people comprehend text, and decode cues on the display, to how they read an article, activities not typically addressed in IR, although very important in how people interpret what appears on a display – from the mechanisms that support scanning actions to how query input is implemented and results presented. At the very base level and now nearly three decades old, Norman's Gulfs of Execution and Evaluation [23] still describe the seven-stage process that a person invokes from intent to interpretation and evaluation of response from the system. At this level some aspects have been explained in a predictive way [21].

In general, the information access problem for which IR systems are a solution can be addressed at any of these "user" levels. The broad perspective at the top informs research at the information needs and seeking perspective. Those in the middle address the problem from a human computer interaction combined with an interactive IR perspective (that is now being described as "human computer information retrieval" or HCIR). At the bottom, the research focuses on information presentation, and how people process information. The value in isolating these various layers is in understanding which aspects of user interaction directly or indirectly influence and thus should inform IR systems design.

5   Final Words

User-oriented IR places an "ordinary" IR system into a complex information use environment that includes not just a document collection and a system, but an integrated "system" of people, their work and activities and the context in which they are immersed. In such an environment an IR system plays a supporting and supportive role that facilitates user access to and use of information. Over the past several decades we have seen tremendous improvement in what an IR system delivers, but some of the remaining challenges is in how to map those outcomes to user requirements and task.

References

1. Bates, M.: Information search tactics. Journal of the American Society for Information Science 30(4), 205–214 (1979)
2. Bates, M.: Idea tactics. Journal of the American Society for Information Science 30(4), 280–289 (1979)
3. Bates, M.: The design of browsing and berrypicking techniques for the online search interface. Online Review 13(5), 407–431 (1989)
4. Belkin, N.: Anomalous state of knowledge as a basis for information retrieval. Canadian Journal of Information Science 5, 133–143 (1980)

5. Bystrom, K., Jarvelin, K.: Task complexity affects information seeking and use. Information Processing & Management 31, 191–213 (1995)
6. Case, D.O.: Looking For Information: A Survey of Research on Information Seeking, Needs, and Behaviour, 2nd edn. JAI Press (2007)
7. Cleverdon, C.W.: Report on the Testing and Analysis of an Investigation into the Comparative Efficiency of Indexing Systems. Aslib Cranfield Project (1962)
8. Dillon, A.: Designing Usable Electronic Text, 2nd edn. CRC Press (2004)
9. Dervin, B.: Given a context by any other name: methodological tools for taming the unruly beast. In: Vakkari, P., Savolainen, R., Dervin, B. (eds.) Information seeking in context: Proceedings of an International Conference on Research in Information Needs, Seeking and use in Different Contexts, pp. 13–38. Taylor Graham, London (1997)
10. Ellis, D.: A behavioural approach to information retrieval design. Journal of Documentation 45(3), 171–212 (1989)
11. Ellis, D., Cox, D., Hall, K.: A comparison of the information seeking patterns of researchers in the physical and social scientists. Journal of Documentation 49, 356–369
12. Guthrie, J.T.: Locating information in documents: examination of a cognitive model. Reading Research Quarterly 23, 178–199 (1988)
13. Hackos, J., Reddish, J.: User and Task Analysis for Interface Design. Wiley (1998)
14. Hearst, M.: Search User Interfaces. Cambridge University Press (2009)
15. Henry, W.M., et al.: Online Searching: An Introduction. Butterworth (1980)
16. Ingwersen, P., Jarvelin, K.: The Turn: Integration of Information Seeking and Retrieval in Context. Springer (2005)
17. Johnson, J.D.: Cancer-related information seeking. Hampton Press, Cresskill (1997)
18. Krikelas, J.: Information seeking behavior: patterns and concepts. Drexel Library Quarterly 19, 5–20 (1983)
19. Kuhlthau, C.C.: Inside the search process: information seeking from the user's perspective. Journal of the American Society for Information Science 42(5), 361–371 (1991)
20. Leckie, G.J., Pettigrew, K., Sylvain, C.: Modeling the information seeking of professionals: a general model derived from research on engineers, health care professionals and lawyers. Library Quarterly 66, 161–193 (1996)
21. MacKenzie, I.S.: Motor behaviour models for human-computer interaction. In: Carroll, J.M. (ed.) HCI Models, Theories, and Frameworks: Toward a Multidisciplinary Science, pp. 27–54. Morgan Kaufmann, San Francisco (2003)
22. Marchionini, G.: Information seeking in electronic environments. Cambridge University Press, Cambridge (1995)
23. Norman, D.A.: Cognitive engineering. In: Norman, D.A., Draper, S.W. (eds.) User Centered System Design: New Perspectives on Human-Computer Interaction, pp. 31–61. Lawrence Erlbaum Associates, Hillsdale (1986)
24. Pirolli, P., Card, S.: Information foraging. Psychological Review 106(4), 643–675 (1999)
25. Ruthven, I., Kelly, D. (eds.): Interactive Information Seeking, Behaviour and Retrieval. Facet Publishing (2011)
26. Saracevic, T.: Modeling interaction in information retrieval (IR): a review and proposal. In: Hardin, S. (ed.) 59th Annual Meeting of the American Society for Information Science, pp. 3–9. American Society for Information Science, Silver Spring (1996)
27. Savolainen, R.: Everyday life information seeking: approaching information seeking in the context of 'way of life'. Library and Information Science Research 17, 259–294 (1995)

28. Sonnewald, D.: Evolving perspectives of human information behavior: contexts, situations, social network and information horizons. In: Wilson, T.D., Allen, D.K. (eds.) Exploring the Contexts of Information Behavior: Proceedings of the Second International Conference on Research in Information Need, Seeking and Use in Different Contexts, pp. 176–190. Taylor Graham (1999)

29. Taylor, R.S.: Information Use Environments. In: Dervin, B., Voigt, M.J. (eds.) Progress in Communication Sciences, pp. 217–255. Ablex Publishing (1991)

30. Toms, E.G.: Models that inform digital library design. In: Dobreva, M., et al. (eds.) User Studies of Digital Library Development, pp. 21–32. Facet Publishing (2011)

31. Vakkari, P.: A theory of the task-based information retrieval process: a summary and generalization of a longitudinal study. Journal of Documentation 57(1), 44–60 (2001)

32. Vakkari, P., Pennanen, M., Serola, S.: Changes of search terms and tactics while writing a research proposal. Information Processing & Management 39(3), 445–463 (2003)

33. Wang, P., Soergel, D.: A cognitive model of document use during a research project: Study 1. Documents selection. Journal of the American Society for Information Science 49(2), 115–133 (1998)

34. White, R.W.: Interactive Techniques. In: Ruthven, I., Kelly, D. (eds.) Interactive Information Seeking, Behaviour & Retrieval, pp. 171–188. Facet Publishing (2011)

35. Wilson, T.D.: Models in information behaviour research. Journal of Documentation 55(3), 249–270 (1999)

36. Wilson, T.D.: Evolution in information behavior modeling: Wilson's model. Journal of Documentation 55(3), 249–270 (2005)

37. Wilson, M.: Search User Interface Design. Morgan & Claypool (2011)

6   Recommended Reading

Case, D. O.: *Looking for Information: A Survey of Research on Information Seeking, Needs, and Behavior.* 2nd ed. Academic Press. (2007).

Choo, C. W.: *The Knowing Organization: How Organizations use Information to Construct Meaning, Create Knowledge and Make Decisions* (2nd ed.) Oxford University Press (2006).

Dillon, A.: *Designing Usable Electronic Text* (2nd ed.). CRC Press (2004)

Hearst, M.: *Search User Interfaces.* Cambridge University Press (2009)

Ingwersen, P. & Järvelin, K.: *The Turn: Integration of Information Seeking and Retrieval in Context.* Springer (2005)

Ruthven, I. & Kelly, D. (Eds.): *Interactive Information Behaviour, Seeking and Retrieval.* Facet. (2010)

User-Oriented Evaluation in IR

Kalervo Järvelin

University of Tampere, Finland
Kalervo.Jarvelin@uta.fi
www.uta.fi/~likaja

Abstract. The paper discusses briefly user-oriented evaluation in test collections with simulated users and real users, as well as operational systems evaluation. It concludes by a glimpse of issues beyond evaluation. The paper provides pointers to literature where much more thorough discussion of each topic may be found.

1 Introduction

"My search engine is better than yours." Statements like this are often sought after in IR research. If such statements are not mere opinions, they are based on IR evaluation, which is sometimes referred to as a hallmark and distinctive feature of IR research. No claim in IR is granted any merit unless it is shown, through rigorous evaluation, that the claim is well founded. Technological innovation alone is not sufficient. In fact, much research in IR deals with IR evaluation methodology.

The present paper discusses briefly user-oriented evaluation in test collections with simulated users and real users as well as operational systems evaluation. The paper concludes by a glimpse of issues beyond evaluation. It is a short paper largely based on other publications by the author, see [2], [3], [7], [8], [10], in particular. These papers provide a much more thorough discussion of each topic.

2 What Is Evaluation?

Evaluation, in general, is the systematic determination of merit and significance of something using criteria against a set of standards [7].[1] Evaluation therefore requires some object that is evaluated and some goal that should be achieved or served. In IR, both can be set in many ways. The object usually is an IR system or a system component – but what is an IR system? The goal is typically the quality of the retrieved result – but what is the retrieved result and how does one measure quality? These questions can be answered in alternative ways, which lead to different kinds of IR evaluation.

---

[1] See also Wikipedia, http://en.wikipedia.org/wiki/Evaluation

M. Agosti et al. (Eds.): PROMISE Winter School 2012, LNCS 7757, pp. 86–91, 2013.

3   IR Evaluation Landscape

Figure 1 presents IR evaluation as nested frameworks of IR context, seeking context, work-task context, and socio-organizational and cultural contexts. Some types of evaluation criteria in each context are given at A – D. First, IR may be designed and evaluated in its own specific context – the test-collection approach (A). Here the evaluation measures relate to the quality of the retrieval result, the system's efficiency, and the quality of the search process like searcher's effort (time) and satisfaction. [5]

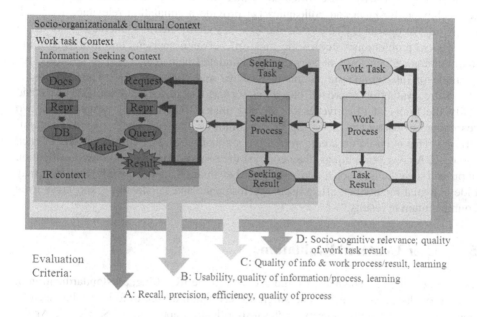

Fig. 1. Evaluation frameworks for (I)IR [5, p. 322]

However, information retrieval is just one means for information access in the searcher's information seeking context (B). This context provides a variety of information sources and systems for coordinated access. One may evaluate what is the contribution of an IR system at the end of a seeking process. Next, the real impact of information retrieval is its contribution to the work task (e.g., effort, time) and the quality of its result. Therefore, IR should be evaluated for its contribution to the work task context (C). Finally, work tasks are performed in a socio-organizational and cultural context (D) and may be evaluated for their contribution therein. [5]

4   User-Oriented Evaluation in Test Collections without Users

Test-collection based IR evaluation is performed in laboratory IR environments. The methodology of such evaluations is discussed in Harman [4], Järvelin [7], and Sanderson [12]. The methodology tries to abstract away much of users' individual variability and traditionally focuses on evaluating search engine performance based on individual queries and without user interaction. The system being evaluated consists of a test collection (documents, topics, and relevance assessments), its goal is a high-quality ranking of documents for topics, and the evaluation criteria are the traditional, such as mean average precision (MAP). This fosters controllability and comparability of experiments. Despite of its simplicity and neglect of interaction (users), this methodology has served the IR community well.

However, it is possible to go beyond the limitations of the traditional test collection methodology and toward user-oriented evaluation through *explicit simulation* of user's behavior. Baskaya and colleagues [2] provide a simulation relevance feedback behavior. Azzopardi [1] addressed the cost aspect by treating interactive IR as an *economical* problem and studied the trade-off between querying and browsing while maintaining a given level of normalized cumulated gain (NCG) [5] in sessions. An example of full session simulation is Baskaya and colleagues [3]. They propose a pragmatic evaluation approach based on scenarios with explicit subtask costs and study the limits of effectiveness of diverse interactive searching strategies in two searching environments – desk-top PCs and mobile phones – under overall cost constraints. This is based on a comprehensive simulation of 20 million sessions in each use case. Among other things, they contrast the proposed time (cost) based evaluation approach with the traditional one, rank based evaluation, and show how the latter may hide essential factors that affect users' performance and satisfaction - and gives even counter-intuitive results.

5   User-Centered Evaluation

When one brings a human actor ("the user") into the IR setting, all standardization of evaluation disappears. There is no single experimental design to follow. This must be one key factor in the popularity of the test-collection approach of Section 4. Again, one needs to define the system being evaluated, its goals, and the evaluation criteria. A range of possibilities becomes available – some close to test-collection based evaluation with hired test users and others task-based studies where humans are given controlled tasks to perform, aided by an IR system and a document collection. And there is a whole range between these cases – as discussed in Jarvelin [7]. For a discussion of the methodologies, see Kelly [9].

There are both challenges and limitations in user-oriented interactive IR evaluation experiments. This evaluation domain is challenging because it is open and multifaceted enough so that very different kinds of studies can be performed. Practical limitations in the studies emanate from the need to control several factors as soon as test persons are part of the evaluation design. In addition, the number of test persons and the complexity of test protocols make the evaluations expensive and time-consuming. Due to the variety of designs, building a coherent theoretical knowledge base becomes difficult.

It may be claimed that it becomes in a broader system framework increasingly difficult to analyze system's contributions because subjects compensate for poor systems. To see the systems contributions, one needs to focus on the narrow engine-and-its-user subsystem. However, seen in another direction, this is an indication that the search engine is not a dominating factor in the larger system evaluated – also other factors should be looked at in rational attempts to improve information access.

6   User-Oriented Evaluation in Operational Systems

When one moves further out from the laboratory into real-life IR settings, not only standardization of evaluation disappears but also the control of evaluation designs becomes increasingly difficult. There is no single experimental design to follow, and one may have to give up *experimentation* in evaluation entirely. Again, one needs to define the system being evaluated, its goals, and the evaluation criteria.

At the *system* end, evaluation of operational systems may roughly follow the test-collection based approach in the collection and formulation of test requests, defining the document collection, and obtaining relevance assessments. However, such evaluation is often broader in that the system evaluated consists of a search engine deployed in some environment, document collections indexed for the engine, and users generating queries and perhaps providing relevance assessments. The goal of the system may be to find relevant documents – a high quality ranked list. Additional goals may involve efficiency – fast response times and high throughput. Due to the sheer size of the operational environments, and lack of competing evaluation teams, obtaining relevance assessments requires new solutions like crowdsourcing or relying on click data. As there are no standard search topics, there may be no automatic ways of deriving queries – users are needed.

At the extreme *user study* end, one encounters real tasks, real users, and real needs in their natural contexts. The goal of the studies may be to understand human behavior related to information problems. In as much *evaluation* is concerned, the system being evaluated includes the databases, search engine(s), and humans using them due to their tasks and in their socio-organizational and system context. The goal of the system is, again, to get work (or leisure activity) done (well). Additional goals may be user satisfaction, efficiency (time), and the quality of the search result. Increasing openness allows a great number of evaluation designs but also puts many challenges on the generalizability of the findings.

Jarvelin [7] discusses operational systems evaluation – designs, metrics, data collection and limitations – in more detail. Operational systems evaluation for real life decision-making requires greater effort and much more varied data than user or system oriented evaluations in the laboratory. The latter benefit from available test collections and simplified standard evaluation designs where the goal may be as simple and purified as the quality of the ranked list. The strengths of operational systems evaluation include realistic and rich data that can put the 'more scientific' evaluation findings from the lab studies into perspective. The findings are however usually limited to the particular evaluation case, affected by several hard-to-control variables and difficult to repeat.

7   Beyond Evaluation?

The goals of a research area may be classified as (a) theoretical understanding, (b) empirical description, prediction and explanation, and (c) technology development. While much of research in IR is driven by the technological interest of developing retrieval tools, the technological interest becomes blind if not nurtured by the other goals.

One may reasonably ask, without an immediate requirement of technological application, what, for example, explains human retrieval behavior? Which behaviors are popular or effective? The major types of IR evaluation study cover (a) *empirical* studies (evaluation experiments), (b) *methodological* studies (creating and analyzing methods), and (c) *constructive* studies (designing and testing better systems) [6]. Evaluation can serve all of these study types.

It would be simplistic to stop with evaluation in IR research. True science is about theory development, i.e., understanding and explaining, making hypotheses and testing them. Evaluation helps to confirm / refute theories. Figure 2 illustrates building user-and-interaction based theories for IR.

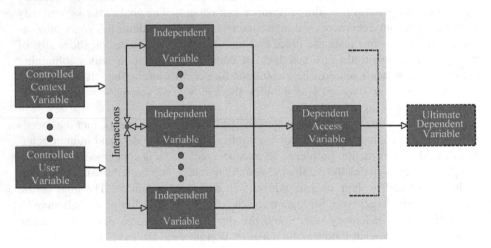

Fig. 2. Building user and interaction based theories for IR

In traditional test-collection based IR evaluation (e.g. [12]) we may focus on the topic and document representation methods, and their matching methods are studied experimentally with the aim of explaining the quality of ranking. Experimental evaluation seeks to improve the quality of ranking. It is tacitly assumed that the quality of ranking is related to effectiveness in IR interaction. That is, more of MAP would bring more of interaction effectiveness.

However, this may no more hold when considered from the user point-of-view. This is why user studies / user-oriented evaluation are necessary in IR. Technology alone is blind. In order to develop it sensibly we need to understand how (or how well) technology together with users-in-context produces the desired outcomes in information access and the ultimate benefits. This again requires that users and context are taken into account as independent variables in study designs, see Figure 2. The dashed lines in Figure 2 suggest that the ultimate benefits may also depend on other factors than just the access variables.

Such evaluation may be based on test-collections and simulation, real-user experiments in test collections, or operational systems evaluations. All approaches can be beneficial. Narrowly defined component-based evaluation is useful when accompanied with reality checks at reasonable intervals.

References

1. Azzopardi, L.: The economics of interactive information retrieval. In: 34th ACM SIGIR Conference (ACM SIGIR 2011), pp. 15–24. ACM Press, New York (2011)
2. Baskaya, F., Keskustalo, H., Järvelin, K.: Simulating Simple and Fallible Relevance Feedback. In: Clough, P., Foley, C., Gurrin, C., Jones, G.J.F., Kraaij, W., Lee, H., Mudoch, V. (eds.) ECIR 2011. LNCS, vol. 6611, pp. 593–604. Springer, Heidelberg (2011)
3. Baskaya, F., Keskustalo, H., Järvelin, K.: Time Drives Interaction: Simulating Sessions in Diverse Searching Environments. In: 35th ACM SIGIR Conference (ACM SIGIR 2012), pp. 97–106. ACM Press, New York (2012)
4. Harman, D.: Information retrieval evaluation. Morgan & Claypool (2011)
5. Ingwersen, P., Järvelin, K.: The Turn: Integration of Information Seeking and Retrieval in Context. Springer, Heidelberg (2005)
6. Järvelin, K.: An Analysis of Two Approaches in Information Retrieval: From Frameworks to Study Designs. Journal of the American Society for Information Science and Technology (JASIST) 58, 971–986 (2007)
7. Järvelin, K.: Evaluation. In: Ruthven, I., Kelly, D. (eds.) Interactive Information Seeking, Behaviour and Retrieval, pp. 113–138. Facet Publishing, London (2011)
8. Järvelin, K.: IR Research: Systems, Interaction, Evaluation and Theories. ACM SIGIR Forum 45, 17–31 (2011), http://www.sigir.org/forum/2011D/conferences/2011d_sigirforum_jarvelin.pdf
9. Kelly, D.: Methods for evaluating interactive information retrieval systems with users. Foundations and Trends in Information Retrieval (FnTIR) 3, 1–224 (2009)
10. Kumpulainen, S., Järvelin, K.: Information Interaction in Molecular Medicine: Integrated Use of Multiple Channels. In: 3rd Information Interaction in Context Conference (IIiX 2010), pp. 95–104. ACM Press, New York (2010)
11. Kumpulainen, S., Järvelin, K.: Barriers to Task-based Information Access in Molecular Medicine. Journal of the American Society for Information Science and Technology (JASIST) 63, 86–97 (2012)
12. Sanderson, M.: Test Collection Based Evaluation of Information Retrieval Systems. Foundations and Trends in Information Retrieval (FnTIR) 4, 247–375 (2010)

Multimedia Information Retrieval in a Social Context

Stéphane Marchand-Maillet

Viper Group
Deparment of Computer Science
University of Geneva
http://viper.unige.ch

Abstract. This note presents an overview of the literature related to multimedia information retrieval, as a tool in the context of inter-connected media. The goal is to propose and motivate a structure to present key focus and successful achievements in the domain. We go through the base foundations of multimedia information retrieval and investigate new challenges.

Here, we particularly focus on providing large-scale accurate access to the data from both the user and the computation perspectives. We identify and discuss information representation and fusion as key building blocks of an efficient and accurate information access strategy.

1 Introduction

The multiplication of large-scale document collections has created the need for robust and adaptive access strategies in many applicative areas such as education or culture [1–3], business [4] or public domain [5]. Multimedia search and retrieval strategies have installed themselves as a base paradigm for accessing documents from within a collection.

In this note, we review the state of advancement of multimedia information retrieval systems and the challenges they face in a context where social networks develop over the World Wide Web. We walk through challenges induced by the new *social media* content and focus on the opportunities these challenges create on the way to facilitate multimedia content understanding and access.

2 Challenges in Multimedia Information Retrieval

While Information Retrieval [6, 7] has essentially developed over textual data, the advent of new media has created associated new challenges. Perception models and similarity measures adapted to audio, visual and temporal media [8, 9] have been the base to cater for the *semantic gap*, which has been extensively discussed in the scientific literature [10].

The overwhelming volume of such media, generated either professionally (eg news agencies) but also personally [11, 12] has forced efficient solutions to be

M. Agosti et al. (Eds.): PROMISE Winter School 2012, LNCS 7757, pp. 92–96, 2013.

found. Many further dimensions to the issue of new media content access have thus been adding up.

The first issue is how to face the large volume of data for processing and retrieval. Not only distributed computing [13] should come as a solution but appropriate distributed indexing strategies should be defined. A deep understanding of indexing strategies is required both to adapt computational models to distributed architectures [14] but also to propose efficient scalable approximations [15].

One further important factor is the fact that users and media are now mixed together [16]. Starting from recommendation systems [3, 17] this has extended to social networks over which media is viewed as a support for interconnections between users (and vice verse). The redundancy of the media (eg repetition via approximate copies) is a challenge for today's systems. However, the new type of inter-connectivity of this media-user-knowledge network may be an opportunity to extract the best out of the available data and take an overall different approach to the content understanding problem [1, 16, 18, 19].

The next challenge is in the change in consumption mode for media. The classical desktop setup is surpassed by mobile and tactile accesses [11]. Again, far from limiting the efficiency of current techniques, this may open the door to the design of novel, more natural access modes [5, 20–23], as one major topic of this volume.

In all cases, what is required to gain proper and suitable access to the content is to be able to propose accurate content models that can accommodate adaptation based on some form of user interaction (eg feedback, or judgements). From there, as discussed above, scalable models may be derived by approximating nearest-neighbour computation, content may be attached to high-level interpretations via (collaborative or social) interaction operated on a selection of devices with proper interfaces.

3 Multimodal Information Representation for Multimedia Information Retrieval

Classical perception models for multimedia generally emulate the human cognitive process, and a number of content features have been derived in that respect [24, 25]. Such features have been used to reach high-level content interpretation with more or less success, also depending on the implication of a human operator in the process [10, 26].

It has however recently been noticed that, as much as text does not require complete understanding to be searched for, multimedia may also be looked at from its recurring properties. This result has led to the new trend of indexing solutions based on automatically derived codebooks (eg [27, 28]). Used primarily for recognition or tagging [29, 30], such features have also proved useful in retrieval setups based on learning [31–35].

One issue however is the high-dimensionality of representations they induce, leading to sparsity and the so-called *curse of dimensionality* [36]. Such sparse representations should therefore be made compact using information fusion [37] or dimension reduction strategies [38]. The objective is to define new, compact representations that preserve initial properties with possibly filtering out unreliable or redundant information.

Such mappings may be derived in an unsupervised (or semi-supervised) way [39] or adaptively based on user supervision [35].

4   Outlook

We have walked through the multimedia information retrieval literature, immersed in the context of social media. This context is both challenging due to the complexity in data, volume and access mode but also favourable for human (collaborative) supervision to be exploited, in order to get a finer understanding of the content. Information should be taken and looked at from its various facets that may be fused or compacted using appropriate strategies. The aim is to gain scaling properties to adapt to actual collections sizes.

The evaluation of such methods should adapt to encompass the assessment of related properties such as scale and interactivity [40]. Existing benchmarks such as ImageCLEF [41] are perfect platforms to accommodate evolution, as discussed along this volume.

Acknowledgments. The support of the Swiss National Science Foundation (SNSF) via the Swiss National Center of Competence in Research (NCCR) on Interactive Multimodal Information Management (IM2) and the European COST Action on Multilingual and Multifaceted Interactive Information Access (MUMIA) via the Swiss State Secretariat for Education and Research (SER No. C11.0043) is gratefully acknowledged.

References

1. Brusilovsky, P., Cassel, L.N., Delcambre, L.M., Fox, E.A., Furuta, R., Garcia, D.D., Shipman III, F.M., Yudelson, M.: Social navigation for educational digital libraries. In: Procedia Computer Science (Proceedings of the 1st Workshop on Recommender Systems for Technology Enhanced Learning, RecSysTEL 2010), vol. 1(2), pp. 2889–2897 (2010)
2. Carbonaro, A.: Collaborative and semantic information retrieval for technology-enhanced learning. In: Proceedings of the 3rd International Workshop on Social Information Retrieval for Technology-Enhanced Learning (SIRTEL 2009), Aachen, Germany (2009)
3. Manouselis, N., Drachsler, H., Vuorikari, R., Hummel, H.G.K., Koper, R.: Recommender Systems in Technology Enhanced Learning. In: Kantor, P.B., Ricci, F., Rokach, L., Shapira, B. (eds.) Recommender Systems Handbook, pp. 387–415. Springer, Berlin (2011)
4. Seidel, S., Muller-Wienbergen, F.M., Rosemann, M., Becker, J.: A conceptual framework for information retrieval to support creativity in business processes. In: Proceedings 16th European Conference on Information Systems, Galway, Ireland (2008)
5. van Zwol, R., Sigurbjörnsson, B.: Faceted exploration of image search results. In: Proceedings of the 19th International Conference on World Wide Web, WWW 2010 (2010)

6. Dominich, S.: Mathematical foundations of information retrieval. In: Mathematical Modelling: Theory and Applications. Kluwer Academic Publishers (2001)
7. Baeza-Yates, R., Ribeiro-Neto, B.: Modern Information Retrieval: the concepts and technology behind search, 2nd edn. Addison Wesley (2011)
8. Datta, R., Joshi, D., Wang, J.: Image retrieval: Ideas, influences and trends of the new age. ACM Computing Surveys (CSUR) 40(2), 1–60 (2008)
9. Orio, N.: Music retrieval: a tutorial and review. Now Publishers (2006)
10. Smeulders, A.W.M., Worring, M., Santini, S., Gupta, A., Jain, R.: Content-based image retrieval at the end of the early years. IEEE Transactions on Pattern Analysis and Machine Intelligence 22(12), 1349–1380 (2000)
11. Baeza-Yates, R.: Web data mining. Tutorial at the 4th Russian Summer School in Information Retrieval, Voronezh, Russia (2010)
12. Good, J.: How many photos have ever been taken? 1000 memories blog (September 15, 2011), http://blog.1000memories.com/94-number-of-photos-ever-taken-digitaland-analog-in-shoebox (last visited May 2012)
13. Dean, J., Ghemawat, S.: Mapreduce: Simplified data processing on large clusters. In: OSDI 2004: Sixth Symposium on Operating System Design and Implementation, San Francisco, CA (2004)
14. Mohamed, H., Marchand-Maillet, S.: Distributed media indexing based on MPI and MapReduce. In: 10th Workshop on Content-Based Multimedia Indexing, Annecy, France (2012)
15. Amato, G., Savino, P.: Approximate similarity search in metric spaces using inverted files. In: InfoScale 2008: Proc. of the 3rd Inernational Conference on Scalable Information Systems (2008)
16. Marchand-Maillet, S., Morrison, D., Szekely, E., Kludas, J., Von Wyl, M., Bruno, E.: Mining Networked Media Collections. In: Detyniecki, M., García-Serrano, A., Nürnberger, A. (eds.) AMR 2009. LNCS, vol. 6535, pp. 1–11. Springer, Heidelberg (2011)
17. Park, D.H., Kim, H.K., Choi, I.Y., Kim, J.K.: A literature review and classification of recommender systems research. Expert Systems with Applications (in press, 2012)
18. Baldi, P., Frasconi, P., Smyth, P.: Modeling the Internet and the Web: Probabilistic Methods and Algorithms. Wiley (2003)
19. Morrison, D., Tsikrika, T., Hollink, V., de Vries, A.P., Bruno, E., Marchand-Maillet, S.: Topic modelling of clickthrough data in image search. Multimedia Tools and Applications (to appear, 2012)
20. Chen, C., Börner, K.: Top Ten Problems in Visual Interfaces to Digital Libraries. In: Börner, K., Chen, C. (eds.) Visual Interfaces to Digital Libraries. LNCS, vol. 2539, pp. 226–231. Springer, Heidelberg (2002)
21. Hearst, M.A.: UIs for faceted navigation: Recent advances and remaining open problems. In: Workshop on Computer Interaction and Information Retrieval, HCIR, Redmond, WA (2008)
22. Heesch, D.: A survey of browsing models for content based image retrieval. Multimedia Tools and Applications 40, 261–284 (2008)
23. Zhang, J.: Visualization for information retrieval. The information retrieval series. Springer (2008)
24. Rorissa, A., Clough, P., Deselaers, T.: Exploring the relationship between feature and perceptual visual spaces. Journal of American Society for Information Science and Technology (JASIST) 58(10), 1401–1418 (2007)
25. Zhang, D., Lu, G.: Review of shape representation and description techniques. Pattern Recognition 37, 1–19 (2004)

26. Zhou, X.S., Huang, T.S.: Relevance feedback for image retrieval: A comprehensive review. Multimedia Systems 8(6), 536–544 (2003)
27. Lowe, D.G.: Distinctive image features from scale-invariant keypoints. International Journal of Computer Vision 60(2) (2004)
28. Csurka, G., Dance, C., Fan, L., Williamowski, J., Bray, C.: Visual categorization with bags of keypoints. In: ECCV 2004 Workshop on Statistical Learning in Computer Vision (2004)
29. Quack, T., Leibe, B., Van Gool, L.: World-scale mining of objects and events from community photo collections. In: CIVR 2008: Proceedings of the 2008 International Conference on Content-based Image and Video Retrieval, pp. 47–56. ACM, New York (2008)
30. Lee, Y., Grauman, K.: Shape discovery from unlabeled image collections. In: Proc. Computer Vision and Pattern Recognition (CVPR) Conference, Miami (2009)
31. He, X., King, O., Ma, W.Y., Li, M., Zhang, H.J.: Learning a semantic space from user's relevance feedback for image retrieval. IEEE Transactions on Circuits and Systems for Video Technology 13(1), 39–48 (2003)
32. Bruno, E., Moënne-Loccoz, N., Marchand-Maillet, S.: Design of multimodal dissimilarity spaces for retrieval of multimedia documents. IEEE Transactions on Pattern Analysis and Machine Intelligence 30(9), 1520–1533 (2008)
33. von Wyl, M., Mohamed, H., Bruno, E., Marchand-Maillet, S.: A parallel cross-modal search engine over large-scale multimedia collections with interactive relevance feedback. In: Proceedings of the 1st ACM International Conference on Multimedia Retrieval, ICMR 2011, pp. 73:1–73:2. ACM, New York (2011)
34. Ferecatu, M., Geman, D.: A statistical framework for image category search from a mental picture. IEEE Transactions on Pattern Analysis and Machine Intelligence 31(6), 1087–1101 (2009)
35. Yan, F., Mikolajczyk, K., Kittler, J.: Multiple Kernel Learning via Distance Metric Learning for Interactive Image Retrieval. In: Sansone, C., Kittler, J., Roli, F. (eds.) MCS 2011. LNCS, vol. 6713, pp. 147–156. Springer, Heidelberg (2011)
36. Aggarwal, C.C., Hinneburg, A., Keim, D.A.: On the Surprising Behavior of Distance Metrics in High Dimensional Space. In: Van den Bussche, J., Vianu, V. (eds.) ICDT 2001. LNCS, vol. 1973, pp. 420–434. Springer, Heidelberg (2000)
37. Kludas, J., Marchand-Maillet, S.: Effective multimodal information fusion by structure learning. In: 14th International Conference on Information Fusion (FUSION 2011), Chicago, IL (July 2011)
38. Szekely, E., Bruno, E., Marchand-Maillet, S.: High-dimensional multimodal distribution embedding. In: IEEE ICDM 2010 Workshop on Visual Analytics and Knowledge Discovery (VAKD 2010), Sydney, Australia (December 2010)
39. van der Maaten, L.: Learning a parametric embedding by preserving local structure. In: Proceedings of the Twelfth International Conference on Artificial Intelligence and Statistics, AI-STATS (2009)
40. Müller, H., Müller, W., Squire, D.M., Marchand-Maillet, S., Pun, T.: Performance evaluation in content-based image retrieval: Overview and proposals. Pattern Recognition Letters (Special Issue on Image and Video Indexing) 22(5), 593–601 (2001); Bunke, H., Jiang, X. (eds.)
41. Müller, H., Clough, P., Deselaers, T., Caputo, B.: ImageCLEF – Experimental evaluation of visual information retrieval. Springer (2010)

TREC-Style Evaluations

Donna Harman

National Institute of Standards and Technology, Gaithersburg, USA
donna.harman@nist.gov

Abstract. TREC-style evaluation is generally considered to be the use of test collections, an evaluation methodology referred to as the Cranfield paradigm. This paper starts with a short description of the original Cranfield experiment, with the emphasis on the how and why of the Cranfield framework. This framework is then updated to cover the more recent "batch" evaluations, examining the methodologies used in the various open evaluation campaigns such as TREC. Here again the focus is on the how and why, and in particular on the evolving of the older evaluation methodologies to handle new information access techniques. The final section contains advice on using these existing test collections and building new ones.[1]

Keywords: information retrieval evaluation, Cranfield paradigm, TREC, batch evaluation.

1 Introduction

Information retrieval has been very fortunate in that we early on had an emphasis on strong evaluation, and also general agreement on the evaluation methodologies. One of today's important evaluation methodologies, the so called "TREC-style" evaluation, follows a basic framework started over 50 years ago. This first section discusses these early beginnings and examines the important concepts in the framework.

If we step back in time to the late 1950s, we see very different types of information access methods–text was not available electronically, and information could only be found by "word-of-mouth" or specialist librarians, who mainly used manually produced, massive indexes to publications. Examples of these systems still exist today, such as the Medical Subject Index, or the Engineering Index. These indexes were very expensive to create and there was lots of contention as to which type of indexing system to use.

Cyril Cleverdon, Librarian of the College of Aeronautics, Cranfield, England was concerned about finding better indexing methods and ran two experiments in the early 1960's to investigate indexing practices [7,9]. The second of these experiments led to the well-known Cranfield paradigm of testing in information retrieval.

---

[1] Parts of this paper have been taken from the Morgan/Claypool lecture notes *Information Retrieval Evaluation* [15].

M. Agosti et al. (Eds.): PROMISE Winter School 2012, LNCS 7757, pp. 97–115, 2013.
© Springer-Verlag Berlin Heidelberg 2013

This paradigm was (and is) essentially a user/task simulation; that is, instead of using different indexing methods for user studies with librarians, he modeled the user search task by building a *test collection* and then repeatedly using this test collection in laboratory experiments. This allowed him to run many experiments, enough to allow significance testing, and also to have an existing resource that could reliably be used for additional experiments. This would not have been possible if he had done user studies.

He took great care in modeling both the tasks and his users to build this test collection. The documents needed to be ones they would naturally search, the questions needed to reflect ones they might ask, and the relevance judgments needed to mirror the type of judgments researchers would make for documents they examined in the search process.

He used a "source document" method to gather questions, The titles of 271 papers published in 1962 on the subject of high speed aerodynamics and the theory of aircraft structures were sent to their authors, along with a listing of up to 10 papers that were cited by these papers. The following instructions were also sent to these authors.

1. State the basic problem, in the form of a search question, which was the reason for the research being undertaken leading to the paper, and also give not more than three supplemental questions that arose in the course of the work, and which were, or might have been, put to an information service.
2. Assess the relevance of each of the submitted list of papers which had been cited as references, in relation to each of the questions given. The assessment is to be based on the following scale of five definitions:
   (a) References which are a complete answer to the question.
   (b) References of a high degree of relevance, the lack of which either would have made the research impractical or would have resulted in a considerable amount of extra work.
   (c) References which were useful, either as general background to the work or as suggesting methods of tackling certain aspects of the work.
   (d) References of minimal interest, for example, those that have been included from a historical viewpoint
   (e) References of no interest

There were 173 useful forms returned, with an average of 3.5 questions per form. The document collection was built by merging the 173 source documents with their cited documents (those that had been previously sent to the authors for judgments), and 209 similar documents, for a total of 1400 documents.

The next stage involved getting relevance assessments for the questions. Five graduate students spent the summer of 1963 making preliminary (and liberal) judgments for the questions against all 1400 documents. These judgments were then conveyed to the question authors for a final decision, based on the five graded levels of judging shown above. Judgments were returned for 279 of the questions, although for various reasons usually only 221 of them were used in testing (compound questions were removed for example).

This gave him the test collection, and his experiments then involved trying two types of indexing: manual indexing of the full documents at 3 levels of exhaustivity (averaging 31, 25, and 13 descriptors per document), and "automatic" indexing using the natural language abstracts and titles. For the manual indexing, there were four types of indexing languages used: single terms, simple concepts, controlled terms, and use of only the abstracts and titles. On top of this there were recall devices, such as the use of synonyms and/or hierarchies from a thesaurus and the use of the (stemmed) word forms. There were also precision devices such as weighting and the use of co-ordination (the Boolean "anding" of terms or concepts during the search process).

The documents were indexed at the simple concept level, i.e., "terms which in isolation are weak and virtually useless as retrieval handles were given the necessary context; such terms as 'high', 'number', 'coefficient', etc.". These simple concepts could then be broken into the single terms, with weights assigned to these terms. The controlled terms were created by translating the simple concepts into the vocabulary of the Thesaurus of Engineering Terms of the Engineers Joint Council.

The experiments were done by creating a series of rules that governed each of the many possible combinations of variables. The searchers then manually followed these rules using coded cards stored in what was known as the "Beehive". So for example, one specific type of index was selected, such as the use of the simple concepts and then a series of precision device experiments were done by using different levels of co-ordination on a per question basis. First all simple concepts in the question were "anded"; then one less concept was used, and so on until only one concept was used for searching.

Cleverdon also wanted to use metrics that would be intuitive to his users. There had been a lot of discussion previously about metrics, centering around the well-known categories shown in Table 1. Cleverdon decided to use the "Recall Ratio" defined as $a/(a+c)$, and the "Precision Ratio" $a/(a+b)$.

Table 1. Possible categories of documents in searching

	Relevant	Non-relevant	
Retrieved	a	b	a + b
Not Retrieved	c	d	c + d
	a + c	b + d	a + b + c + d = N

It should be noted that for each of the 221 questions the recall and precision ratios measured a *single* point for each experiment. Using the example experiment described earlier, each of the co-ordinate levels would generate a single recall and a precision point, e.g., co-ordinating 5 terms yields 28% recall at 29% precision, 4 terms gives 40% recall at 12% precision, and using only one term gives 95% recall at 1% precision. These could be plotted on a recall/precision curve looking much like today's curves, but with each point representing a single experiment as opposed to one curve for each experiment.

There were also issues about how to average these points across the full set of questions. The Cranfield experiments usually worked with the grand total figures of the relevant and retrieved across all of the questions, i.e., sum up the total number of relevant retrieved and the total number of documents retrieved for all questions and then divide by the number of questions. This today is called the micro-averaging method and was the simplest to calculate (remember they were not using computers). Cleverdon was aware of the problems with this method, in that questions with many relevant documents skewed the results, and therefore he did some experimentation with per question ratios (known as macro-averaging).

So what were the results of this huge set of experiments? Figure 8.1T in [8], lists the order of effectiveness of 33 different "index languages" encompassing the types of descriptor terms used and the recall and precision devices applied. The top 7 of these are using the single terms, with the very best results found using the word forms (stems) of these single terms.

Of course there was a great furor from the community and arguments over the Cranfield methodology were fierce [24]. These mostly centered on the use of source documents to generate questions (as opposed to real questions) and on the definitions of relevancy. Whereas some of these came from community rejection of the experimental conclusions, many were reasonable objections for the Cranfield paradigm (although the general consensus was that the experimental results are valid).

Today the Cranfield paradigm is generally taken to mean the use of a static test collection of documents, questions, and relevance judgments, often with standard recall and precision metrics. But there are two other subtle components that Cleverdon was insistent on. The first was the careful modeling of the task being tested by the test collection. So his collection of scientific documents, his selection of "users" (via the source document method) that would heavily use this collection, and his careful definition of relevance based on how these *particular* users might judge documents were critical pieces of the Cranfield paradigm. The second component was his strict separation of the building of the test collection from the experimentation itself.

There were other small test collections built in the late 1960s, mostly by Gerard Salton of the SMART project at Cornell [21], all following the Cranfield paradigm. However unfortunately there was little funding to build a larger collection that would mirror the increasing online data that was becoming available in the 1980s.

2   The TREC Evaluations

The National Institutes of Standards (NIST) was asked in 1991 to build a test collection to evaluate the results of the DARPA (Defense Advanced Research Projects Agency) TIPSTER project [20] . The goal of this project was to significantly improve retrieval from large, real-world data collections, and whereas only four DARPA contractors were involved, the TREC initiative opened the evaluation to the wider information retrieval research community, with 25 additional groups taking part in 1992.

TREC has now been running for over 20 years. Full coverage of the research is clearly beyond the scope of this paper and readers are referred to [26] as a general reference and to the full series of online proceedings at `http://trec.nist.gov/` for details relating to each year.

Other evaluation campaigns, often starting in a similar vein as TREC, and then branching out into new areas especially appropriate for their participants have been started. An Asian version of TREC (NTCIR) started in 1999, with the conferences occurring every 18 months since then. NTCIR pioneered retrieval evaluations with patents, developing appropriate evaluation techniques for searching, classification, and translation efforts in this field. Online proceedings and more information about NTCIR can be found at `http://research.nii.ac.jp/ntcir`. The CLEF conference in Europe took over the TREC cross-language work for European languages in 2000, expanding it to more languages and new tasks such as image retrieval. Information including working notes from all of the CLEF workshops can be found at `http://www.clef-initiative.eu/`, with formal proceedings produced in the Springer Lecture Notes in Computer Science each year. The INEX conference, now combined with CLEF, has worked with structured data, and the FIRE evaluation (`http://www.isical.ac.in/~fire/`) has concentrated on work with various Indian languages.

3   The TREC Ad Hoc Tests (1992-1999)

The term "ad hoc" here refers to the classic information retrieval user model in the Cranfield method where "new" requests are searched against a fixed document collection. This section discusses the TREC ad hoc test methodology (test collection and metrics) in detail both because this methodology was extended for later TREC tasks (and other evaluation efforts) and because the ad hoc test collections are still heavily used in research today and it is important to understand how and why they were built.

3.1   Building the Ad Hoc Collections

The TIPSTER/TREC test design was based squarely on the Cranfield paradigm, with a test collection of documents, user requests (called topics in TREC), and relevance judgments. Like Cranfield, it was important to create all parts of the collection based on a realistic user model, in this case the TIPSTER application. The TIPSTER users were presumed to be intelligence analysts, but could also be other types of users that work with information intensively, such as journalists, medical researchers, or legal staff.

The document collection needed to have a very large number of full-text documents (2 gigabytes of text was generally used each year), of varied length, writing style, level of editing and vocabulary. Table 2 lists the document sources used during the initial eight years of the ad hoc evaluations; these were selected based on availability and suitability to the TIPSTER task. Articles from newspapers and newswires covered all domains and contrasted in their format, style, and level of editing. Documents from *Computer Selects* were from different initial sources, but dealt with the single domain of computer technology. Finally there were documents selected less for their content than for the length of articles: the *Federal Register* ones were especially long, and of non-uniform length, and the DOE abstracts were very short. All documents were converted to an SGML-like format with enough uniformity to allow easy processing by the systems. Note that at 2 gigabtyes these collections were beyond the ability of most research systems in 1992 to handle, mainly because the storage to index them (say a total of 4 gigabytes) cost around $10,000 at that time.

Earlier test collections had typically provided only sentence-length requests; however the TIPSTER/TREC topics contained multiple fields, including a user

Table 2. TREC ad hoc document collection statistics

	Size: MB	# Docs	Median # Words	Mean # Words
Disk 1				
Wall Street Journal				
1987–1989	267	98,732	245	434.0
Associated Press 1989	254	84,678	446	473.9
Computer Selects	242	75,180	200	473.0
Federal Register 1989	260	25,960	391	1315.9
abstracts from DOE	184	226,087	111	120.4
Disk 2				
Wall Street Journal				
1990–1992	242	74,520	301	508.4
Associated Press 1988	237	79,919	438	468.7
Computer Selects	175	56,920	182	451.9
Federal Register 1988	209	19,860	396	1378.1
Disk 3				
San Jose Mercury News 1991	287	90,257	379	453.0
Associated Press 1990	237	78,321	451	478.4
Computer Selects	345	161,021	122	295.4
U.S. patents, 1993	243	6,711	4445	5391.0
Disk 4				
Financial Times				
1991–1994	564	210,158	316	412.7
Federal Register 1994	395	55,630	588	644.7
Congressional Record 1993	235	27,922	288	1373.5
Disk 5				
Foreign Broadcast Information				
Service	470	130,471	322	543.6
Los Angeles Times				
1989-1990	475	131,896	351	526.5

need statement that is a clear statement of what criteria make a document relevant. Having these multiple fields allowed for a wide range of query construction methods, and having clear statements about relevancy improved the consistency of relevance judgments. All topics were designed to mimic a real user's need, although the actual topic writers, the topic format and the method of construction evolved over time. The first two TRECs (topics 1-150) involved actual users of a TIPSTER-like search system and had very elaborate topics. By TREC-3 the topics were reduced to three fields and were written by the same group of "stand-in" users who did the relevance assessments. Figure 1 shows a sample topic from TREC-3. Each topic contains a number and title, followed by a one-sentence description of the information need. The final section is the narrative section, meant to be a full description of the information need in terms of what separates a relevant document from a nonrelevant document.

The definition of relevance has always been problematic in building information retrieval test collections [3,6,10,17]. The TIPSTER task was defined to be a high-recall task where it was important not to miss information. Therefore the assessors were instructed to judge a document relevant if information from that document would be used in some manner for the writing of a report on the subject of the topic, even if it was just one relevant sentence or if that information had already been seen in another document. This also implies the use of binary relevance judgments; that is, a document either contains useful information and is therefore relevant, or it does not. Documents retrieved for each topic were judged by a single assessor so that all documents screened would reflect the same user's interpretation of topic.

```
<num> Number: 168
<title> Topic: Financing AMTRAK

<desc> Description:
A document will address the role of the Federal Government in financing the
operation of the National Railroad Transportation Corporation (AMTRAK).

<narr> Narrative:
A relevant document must provide information on the government's
responsibility to make AMTRAK an economically viable entity. It could
also discuss the privatization of AMTRAK as an alternative to continuing
government subsidies. Documents comparing government subsidies given to air
and bus transportation with those provided to AMTRAK would also be relevant.
```

Fig. 1. Sample topic statement from TREC-3

There was the additional requirement that the relevance assessments be as complete as possible. This became a critical piece of both the implementation of TREC and the later analysis of the collections. Three possible methods for finding the relevant documents could have been used. In the first method, full relevance judgments could have been made on over a million documents for each topic, resulting in over 100 million judgments (clearly impossible). The second approach, a true non-biased random sample of the documents, would have been prohibitively expensive for acceptable completeness levels. Therefore a biased sampling method called "pooling" was adopted from the 1977 proposal to the British Library for building an "ideal" test collection [23]. To construct the pools for TREC, the following was done. Given a ranked list of results from a single system, for each topic select the top X ranked documents for input to the pool. Then merge this set with sets from all systems, sort the final list based on the document identifiers, and remove duplicates (identical documents found by multiple systems in the pool). This created the pooled list for each topic that was then judged by the assessors.

3.2   Analysis of the Ad Hoc Collections

Since the ad hoc evaluations were run for 8 years (see Table 3 for details of the eight collections), it was possible to analyze how well the various evaluation decisions were working and to modify them as necessary. This analysis is presented in detail here because these large collections are still in heavy use and it is critical to know their strengths and weaknesses in order to avoid experimental bias. It also provides guidance for some of the types of issues that need to be investigated in building future test collections.

Table 3. Document and topics sets for the first 8 TRECs

TREC ad hoc	Document sets	Topic Numbers
TREC-1	disks 1 & 2	51-100
TREC-2	disks 1 & 2	101-150
TREC-3	disks 1 & 2	151-200
TREC-4	disks 2 & 3	201-250
TREC-5	disks 2 & 4	251-300
TREC-6	disks 4 & 5	301-350
TREC-7	disks 4 & 5 (minus Congressional Record)	351-400
TREC-8	disks 4 & 5 (minus Congressional Record)	401-450

The ad hoc topics built for TREC underwent major evolution across the first five TRECs. Part of this evolution came as a result of changes in the personnel constructing the topics, but most was the result of deliberate changing of the topic specifications. The elaborate topics in the first two TRECs contained a field with manually-selected keywords (the concepts field) and this was removed in TREC-3 because it was felt that real user questions would not contain this field, and because inclusion of the field discouraged research into techniques for expansion of "too short" user need expressions. The TREC-4 topics were made even shorter, with removal of the title and the narrative field, however this turned out to be too short, especially for groups building manual queries, so the TREC-3 format became standard.

There was also a change in how the topics were constructed. In TREC-3 the assessors brought in "seeds" of topics, i.e. ideas of issues on which to build a topic. These seeds were then expanded by the assessor, based on looking at the items that were retrieved. To avoid this tuning to the data, starting in TREC-4 the assessors were asked to bring in a one-sentence description that was used for the initial searching to estimate the number of relevant documents that are likely to be found. Topics with "reasonable" numbers of relevant documents were then kept for further development into the final TREC ad hoc topics.

Another issue about the topics relates to measuring the difficulty of a given topic. There has been no attempt in TREC to build topics to match any particular characteristics, partly because the emphasis was on real user topics, but also because it is not clear what particular characteristics would be appropriate. A measure called topic "hardness" was defined for each topic as the average over a given set of runs of the precision at R (where R is the number of relevant documents for that topic) OR the precision at 100 if there were more than 100 relevant documents. This measure is therefore oriented towards high recall performance and how well systems do at finding all the relevant documents. In TREC-5 an attempt was made to correlate topic characteristics with this hardness measure, but neither topic length nor the number of relevant documents were found to be correlated [30], and it is still unclear what topic characteristics make a topic harder. Further work on topic characteristics has been carried out in an extended workshop, the Reliable Information Access (RIA) workshop in 2004 [16].

A related issue concerns the "required" number of topics for a test collection, i.e., how many topics are needed in order for the performance averages to be stable, much less show significant differences between systems or techniques. There has always been a huge variability in the performance across topics, and TREC was no exception here, with a huge variability in the "hardness" of the topics, in the system performance on each topic, and in the performance of different techniques, such as relevance feedback on each topic. However it is critical that the average performance measure truly reflect differences rather than just random performance points. Although TREC's 50-topic sets have been shown to produce stable averages [5,29], the measurement of significant differences is still a problem in information retrieval, with some TREC-specific work starting in TREC-3 [25], and much more work since then (see Chapter 5 in [22]).

The TREC relevance judgments were specifically designed to model users interested in high recall tasks and therefore the more complete the relevance judgments are, the better the test collection models the high-recall needs of these users. Additionally, the more complete the test collection, the more likely that future systems using the collection for evaluation can trust that all/most of the relevant documents in the collection have been identified. Note that the pooling methodology *assumes* that all documents that have not been judged can be considered non-relevant.

A test of the relevance judgment completeness assumption was made using TREC-2 results, and again during the TREC-3 evaluation. In both cases, a second set of 100 documents was examined from each system, using only a sample of topics and systems in TREC-2, and using all topics and systems in TREC-3 [13]. The more complete TREC-3 testing found well less than one new relevant document per run. These levels of completeness are quite acceptable; furthermore the number of new relevant documents found was shown to be more strongly correlated with the original number of relevant documents, i.e., topics with many relevant documents are more likely to have additional ones, than with the number of documents judged.

These findings were independently verified by Justin Zobel at the Royal Melbourne Institute of Technology (RMIT) [33]. Additionally Zobel found that lack of completeness did not bias the results of particular systems and that systems that did not contribute documents to the pool can still be evaluated fairly using the pooled judgments. Since the goal of the TREC collections is to allow comparisons of multiple runs, either across systems or within systems, having the exact number of relevant documents, or having an exact recall number is not as important as knowing that the judgments are complete enough to insure that comparisons of two methods using the test collections will be accurate.

A second issue important to any set of relevance judgments is their consistency, i.e. how stable are the judgments and how does their stability or lack thereof affect comparison of performance of systems using that test collection. For TREC each topic was judged by a single assessor to ensure the best consistency of judgment and testing of this consistency was done after TREC-2, and more completely for TREC-4 [14]. All the ad hoc topics had samples rejudged by two additional assessors, with the results being about 72% agreement (using the overlap measure of the intersection over the union) among all three judges, and 88% agreement between the initial judge and either one of the two additional judges. This remarkably high level of agreement is probably due to the similar background and training of the judges, and a general lack of ambiguity in the topics as represented by the narrative section.

Unfortunately, most of this agreement was for the large numbers of documents that were clearly nonrelevant. Whereas less than 3% of the initial nonrelevant documents were marked as relevant by secondary judges, 30% of the documents judged relevant by the initial judge were marked as nonrelevant by both the additional judges. This average hides a high variability across topics; for 12 of the 50 topics the disagreement on relevant documents was higher than 50%.

While some of these disagreements were likely caused by mistakes, most of them were caused by human variation in judgment, often magnified by a mismatch between the topic statement, the task, and the document collection. For example, topic 234 is "What progress has been made in fuel cell technology?". A lenient interpretation might declare relevant most documents that discuss fuel cells. A strict judge could require that relevant documents literally present a progress report on fuel cell technology. Additionally some of the more problematic topics were either very open to different interpretations (topic 245: "What are the trends and developments in retirement communities?") or so badly mismatched to the document collection that the initial assessor made extremely lenient relevance judgments (topic 249: "How has the depletion or destruction of the rain forest effected the worlds weather?").

Note that this type of topic and user variation is very realistic and must be accepted as part of any testing. Users come to retrieval systems with different expectations, and most of these expectations are unstated. If test collections do not reflect this noisy situation, then the systems that are built using these collections to test their algorithms will not work well in operational settings.

A critical question is how variation affects system comparisons. Voorhees [27] investigated this by using different subsets of the relevance judgments from TREC-4. As her most stringent test, she used the intersection of the relevant document sets (where all judges had agreed), and the union of these judgements (where any judge had marked a document relevant). She found that although the mean average precision of a given set of system results did change, the changes were highly correlated across systems and the relative ranking of different system runs did not significantly change. Even when the two runs were from the same organization (and therefore are more likely to be similar), the two systems were ranked in the same order by all subsets of relevance judgments. This clearly demonstrates the stability of the TREC ad hoc relevance judgments in the sense that groups can test two different algorithms and be reasonably assured that results reflect a true difference between those algorithms.

These results were independently verified as a result of the University of Waterloo's work in TREC-6 [11]. Waterloo personnel judged over 13,000 documents for relevance, and these judgments were used by Voorhees in a similar manner as the TREC-4 multiple judgments. Even though there was even less agreement between the NIST assessors and the Waterloo assessors (very different backgrounds and training), the changes in system rankings were still not significant. The one exception to this was the comparison between two same-system runs in which one run had used manual relevance feedback. For this reason, comparison between automatic runs and runs with manual intervention, particularly manual relevance feedback which basically adds a third relevance judge, should be more carefully analyzed as they are the comparisons most likely to be affected by variations in relevance judgments.

4 The TREC Metrics

TREC followed the Cranfield metrics, with Chris Buckley making available the evaluation program used by SMART called trec_eval. Figure 2 shows the set of metrics provided for a run in the TREC-8 ad hoc track. The recall level and document level precision averages across the 50 topics are shown, in addition to a new non-interpolated average precision, defined as "the precision at each relevant document, averaged over all relevant documents for a topic" [4]. The non-interpolated average precision is then averaged over all the topics to produce the "mean average precision" or MAP, which has been used as the main measure

Ad hoc results — SabIR Research/Cornell University

Summary Statistics	
Run Number	Sab8A4
Run Description	Automatic, title + desc
Number of Topics	50
Total number of documents over all topics	
Retrieved:	50000
Relevant:	4728
Rel-ret:	2986

Recall Level Precision Averages	
Recall	Precision
0.00	0.7860
0.10	0.5229
0.20	0.4324
0.30	0.3644
0.40	0.3084
0.50	0.2498
0.60	0.1912
0.70	0.1360
0.80	0.0776
0.90	0.0362
1.00	0.0133
Average precision over all relevant docs	
non-interpolated	0.2608

Document Level Averages	
	Precision
At 5 docs	0.5200
At 10 docs	0.4800
At 15 docs	0.4413
At 20 docs	0.4090
At 30 docs	0.3733
At 100 docs	0.2384
At 200 docs	0.1702
At 500 docs	0.0985
At 1000 docs	0.0597
R-Precision (precision after R docs retrieved (where R is the number of relevant documents))	
Exact	0.3021

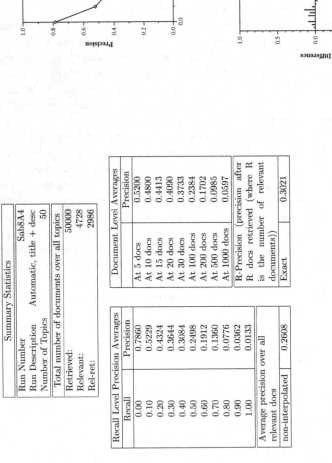

Recall-Precision Curve

Difference from Median in Average Precision per Topic

Fig. 2. Sample evaluation report from TREC-8

in TREC. Other new metrics include the R-Precision which was proposed by Buckley to better measure the high-recall task being modeled in TREC. For more details on these metrics, including a discussion of their relative strengths and weaknesses, see [4,22]. Note that this result page also includes a histogram showing the results for all of the 50 topics so that groups could easily spot how their systems had performed with respect to the median system performance per topic.

There has been considerable interest and work on new metrics since 1992, coming from perceived needs of TREC and other evaluations, but also from the explosion of information access available today. For a much more detailed discussion, see [22] and recent papers at the SIGIR conference.

5   Other TREC Retrieval Tasks

New tasks called tracks were added in TREC-4, and led to the design and building of many specialized test collections. None of these test collections were as extensive as nor as heavily used as the ad hoc collections described earlier, but the necessary changes in the design criteria provide useful case studies in building test collections. Note that these changes were required either because of the specific data characteristics, or because the track research goals dictated modifications to the standard Cranfield implementation.

A brief summary of the changes necessary for some of the TREC tracks follows–for a more complete description see [15,26] or the appropriate online TREC proceedings.

- Streamed Text (Routing/Filtering): Filtering required set-based metrics and new pooling mechanisms
- Human-in-the-Loop: Tasks designed specifically for user studies
- Beyond Just English: Cross-language retrieval required that topic building and relevance judgments be distributed across native speakers of the included languages
- Beyond Text: OCR using known item searching with a new mean reciprocal rank metric, also speech and video retrieval necessitating appropriate definitions of document boundaries
- Large Corpora and Web: New pooling techniques, additional task models for the web such as home page finding
- Searching corporate documents: Enterprise track and legal track needing careful modeling of the actual user task
- Answers, not documents: Question answering specifying new metrics, new ways of creating topics
- Retrieval in a domain: Genomics, chemical, medical all needing domain experts for building the test collection
- Personal documents: Blog, tweets, and spam involving new ways of collecting documents, new task models

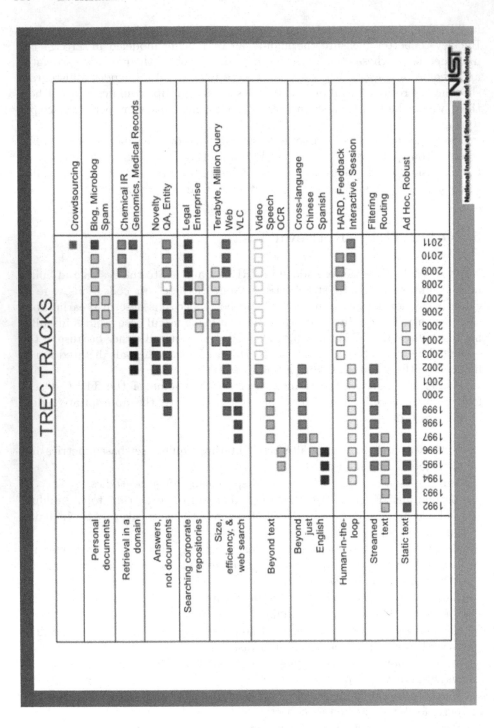

Fig. 3. TREC tracks

6   Some Advice on Using, Building and Evaluating Test Collections

This final section departs from the more formal coverage of the batch evaluations by offering some advice on selecting appropriate test collections, building new test collections, and evaluating those collections. This advice is not meant to be a complete manual on this topic but rather comes from personal observations during many years of working with test collections.

6.1   Using Existing Collections

The easiest evaluation method for batch experiments is to use an existing collection. This method not only cuts the major costs of building a collection, but also provides training material. An equally important issue is the universal acceptance of these test collections, including the ability to compare results to other work. However this decision should not be taken automatically; the user task and the assumptions about the users should be appropriately matched to the selected test collection and test collection characteristics need to be considered in any analysis of the results.

The most heavily used test collections for monolingual English retrieval are the TREC ad hoc ones. These collections are based mainly on newspapers and newswires, along with government documents. The topics are general-purpose and domain-independent, and there is a reasonable assumption that the relevance judgments are complete. But there are 9 sets of topics (1-450), searched against different document sets, so which to pick? The best choice for most experiments are the 3 sets used in TRECs 6-8, consisting of 150 topics (numbers 301-450) searched against (mostly) the same data (disks 4 and 5). This set provides 150 topics, enough for good statistical analysis, plus this group is the most consistent in terms of topic format and relevance judgments.

Some of the earlier TREC ad hoc collections need to be used with caution. Topics 1-50, used for minimal training in TREC-1, are poor topics with only minimal relevance judgments. Topics 51-150, used in TRECs 1 and 2 have an expanded format; this may be useful for particular kinds of experiments, such as structured query experiments, however the topics themselves were created in a possibly unnatural manner, with the relevance judgments being done by another person. Topics 150-200 (TREC-3), were constructed with reference to the documents, and because they often use terms from the documents, are the "easiest" of the TREC topic sets. Topics 201-250 for TREC-4 have no narrative field, which may or may not be necessary depending on the experiment.

Other TREC track test collections are also available (http://trec.nist.gov/data.html), including test collections for OCR and speech, non-English ad hoc collections, and collections for web, blog, genomics, legal, etc. Whereas the Chinese and European language collections are available (the Chinese one for TREC-6 is not recommended because of issues with the topic building process), it is better to get the NTCIR and CLEF collections for these languages. The Arabic collections (TRECs 2001 and 2002) are available at NIST, although the second one (2002) is the recommended one since the improved systems meant better pooling. Other collections are also available, usually with the topics and other auxiliary data on the TREC web site and a pointer to the documents which are available elsewhere. Note however that these collections are all specialized, based on possibly narrower tasks and/or user models and these issues should be throughly understood (by reading track overviews about the collection characteristics) before using these collections.

What about using the much older small collections? These collections are much too small for testing and validating new technology; furthermore most of them use abstracts rather than full documents and results may well be misleading because of this. However one exception to this would be to use them (particularly the TIME collection) as teaching tools; but here again the benefits of a much smaller collection for failure analysis need to be weighed against the different insights one gains when working on the larger collections.

6.2   Modifying Existing Collections

Modifying a collection is more difficult and (possibly) loses some of the advantages of using an existing collection. One obvious modification would be to change the relevance judgments, either by changing the unit of judgment (doing passage retrieval for example) or by changing the definition of relevance. The TREC relevance judgments for the ad hoc task are the broadest type of judgments, i.e., the fact that a document contained ANY information about a topic/question was enough to make it relevant. This was important because the perceived definition of the TREC task/user was that of a high-recall task. But it also was important in terms of creating the most complete set of relevance judgments possible. The current judgments could be used as the starting point for other types of relevance judgments, such as removal of "duplicate" documents [2], or the use of graded relevance judgments [19] or even the measurement of some type of learning effect. This type of modification is very tricky; in essence a second relevance judgment is being made, with all of the consistency difficulties discussed earlier, which may affect the experiment. For some discussion of the problems, see [32].

6.3   Building and Evaluating New Ad Hoc Collections

Building a new collection is a major step to take; it is costly in terms of time and money and full of pitfalls for those new to this task. However if it is to be done, then the critical thing is that the experiments and the new collection they use be modeled on some real user task and that the characteristics of likely users be considered as part of this task. Are the users searching the web for a nearby restaurant with good reviews, are they searching their company's intranet for patents, or are they browsing the web for information about some specific type of tree they want to plant? Each of these applications requires a different set of documents, different types of "topics", different definitions of relevance, and different types of metrics to use in evaluation. These decisions need to be made long before the collection is built.

Once this piece of the design is done, then the next step is to find some documents. Again the easiest place to start would be some existing set of documents that can either be used as is or be sub-setted in some manner. Possibly the news collections from TREC/NTCIR/CLEF are useful, but more likely the new web collection (http://boston.lti.cs.cmu.edu/Data/clueweb09), is a candidate. Note that any sub-setting of these collections needs to be done carefully; the web collections were carefully sampled during their construction process and any subsets need to reflect the new user task design being envisioned. The small web collection [18] design gives some clues on how to do this, the construction of the WT10g [1] also discusses web collection design or see the discussion of the recent "Category B" of the ClueWeb09 collection. Note that subsets of these collections cannot be re-distributed, however one could make subsets using the "docids" for reuse by others. If completely new document sets need to be collected (a major job), then hopefully this can be done in some manner so that the work can be used by others. This means that any intellectual property rights need to be resolved and that the data has to be formatted for ease of use.

Given that the documents are collected, the next step is the topics. Again the user task/characteristics need to be modeled; ideally some real topics from a log can be gathered, or some topics can be built by "surrogate" users such as those used in the TREC/NTCIR/CLEF ad hoc tasks. Enough topics need to be built to overcome topic variation in performance [29,28]; 25 can be taken to be the absolute minimum, with 50 a more reasonable number. The format of the topics needs to mirror the task; for example browsing the web looking for a specific item may need a series of related topics to mimic the interactive search process. Topics for a specific domain need to be appropriate for that domain, either by getting domain experts to build the topics (such as the legal track), or by using a survey such as that done before topic construction by the genomics track to gather representative needs of the genomics community. It is equally critical to closely examine the issues with searching a given genre, such as the patent tracks in NTCIR, TREC and CLEF. The NTCIR efforts in multiple years have tackled different pieces of the patent retrieval problem, but all based on realistic analysis of the needs of that community [12]. If multiple languages are involved, then the topics need to be constructed so that there is no bias towards one language [31].

The methodology for making the relevance judgments for the topics is again reliant on the user task and characteristics. Does the user want only document level judgments or are passage (or even sentence) level judgments needed? What types of judgments are required (binary, graded or other), how many judgments per topic (a major cost factor), and of course setting up the mechanics of getting the documents to judge (pooling, manual search, or some other method such as sampling). Many different approaches to pooling have been tried over the years (see section 6.3 in [22]), each with some advantages and weaknesses that need to be considered in light of the goals of the test collection. Finally, of course, the judging needs to be done.

Once the collection is built, some types of validation need to be made. If this collection is used only for a single experiment, the validation is needed only to understand any likely biases that affect the analysis of the results. However if the test collection can be used by others, then some measures must be made of the consistency and completeness of the relevance judgments.

References

1. Bailey, P., Craswell, N., Hawking, D.: Engineering a Multi-Purpose Test Collection for Web Retrieval Experiments. Information Processing and Management 39(6), 853–871 (2003)
2. Bernstein, Y., Zobel, J.: Redundant Documents and Search Effectiveness. In: Proceedings of the 2005 ACM CIKM International Conference on Information and Knowledge Management, pp. 736–743 (2005)
3. Bookstein, A.: Relevance. Journal of the American Society for Information Science, 269–273 (September 1979)
4. Buckley, C., Voorhees, E.: Retrieval System Evaluation. In: TREC: Experiment and Evaluation in Information Retrieval, ch. 3. The MIT Press (2005)
5. Buckley, C., Voorhees, E.M.: Evaluating Evaluation Measure Stability. In: Proceedings of the 23rd Annual International ACM SIGIR Conference on Research and Development in Information Retrieval, pp. 33–40 (2000)
6. Burgin, R.: Variations in Relevance Judgments and the Evaluation of Retrieval Performance. Information Processing and Management 28(5), 619–627 (1992)
7. Cleverdon, C.: Report on the Testing and Analysis of an Investigation into the Comparative Efficiency of Indexing Systems. Aslib Cranfield Research Project, Cranfield, England (1962)
8. Cleverdon, C., Keen, E.: Factors Determining the Performance of Indexing Systems, vol. 2: Test Results. Aslib Cranfield Research Project, Cranfield, England (1966)
9. Cleverdon, C., Mills, J., Keen, E.: Factors Determining the Performance of Indexing Systems, vol. 1: Design. Aslib Cranfield Research Project, Cranfield, England (1966)
10. Cooper, W.: A Definition of Relevance for Information Retrieval. Information Storage and Retrieval 7, 19–37 (1971)
11. Cormack, G.V., Clarke, C.L.A., Palmer, C.R., To, S.S.L.: Passage-based Refinement(MultiText Experiments for TREC-6). In: Proceedings of the Sixth Text REtrieval Conference (TREC-6), pp. 303–320 (1998)
12. Fujii, A., Iwayama, M., Kando, N.: Introduction to the special issue on patent processing. Information Processing and Management 43, 1149–1153 (2007)
13. Harman, D.: Overview of the Third Text REtrieval Conference (TREC-3). In: Overview of the Third Text REtrieval Conference (TREC-3), Proceedings of TREC-3. (1995) 1–20
14. Harman, D.: Overview of the Fourth Text REtrieval Conference (TREC-4). In: Proceedings of the Fourth Text REtrieval Conference (TREC-4). (1996) 1–23
15. Harman, D.: Information Retrieval Evaluation. Morgan/Claypool (2011)
16. Harman, D., Buckley, C.: Overview of the Reliable Information Access Workshop. Information Retrieval 12, 615–641 (2009)
17. Harter, S.P.: Variations in Relevance Assessments and the Measurement of Retrieval Effectiveness. Journal of the American Society for Information Science 47(1), 37–49 (1996)

18. Hawking, D., Voorhees, E., Craswell, N.: Overview of TREC-8 Web Track. In: Proceedings of the Eighth Text REtrieval Conference (TREC-8), pp. 131–151 (2000)
19. Järvelin, K., Kekäläinen, J.: IR Evaluation Methods for Retrieving Highly Relevant Documents. In: Proceedings of the 23rd Annual International ACM SIGIR Conference on Research and Development in Information Retrieval, pp. 41–48 (2000)
20. Merchant, R. (ed.): The Proceedings of the TIPSTER Text Program—Phase I. Morgan Kaufmann Publishing Co., San Mateo (1994)
21. Salton, G. (ed.): The SMART Retrieval System. Prentice-Hall, Englewood Cliffs (1971)
22. Sanderson, M.: Test Collection Based Evaluation of Information Retrieval Systems. Foundations and Trends in Information Retrieval 4, 247–375 (2010)
23. Sparck Jones, K., Bates, R.: Report on a Design Study for the "Ideal" Information Retrieval Test Collection. British Library Research and Development Report 5488, Computer Laboratory. University of Cambridge (1977)
24. Swanson, D.: Some Unexplained Aspects of the Cranfield Tests of Indexing Language Performance. Library Quarterly 41, 223–228 (1971)
25. Tague-Sutcliffe, J., Blustein, J.: A Statistical Analysis of the TREC-3 Data. In: Overview of the Third Text REtrieval Conference (TREC-3), Proceedings of TREC-3, pp. 385–398 (1995)
26. Voorhees, E., Harman, D. (eds.): TREC: Experiment and Evaluation in Information Retrieval. The MIT Press (2005)
27. Voorhees, E.M.: Variations in Relevance Judgments and the Measurement of Retrieval Effectiveness. Information Processing and Management 36(5), 697–716 (2000)
28. Voorhees, E.M.: Topic Set Size Redux. In: SIGIR 2009, pp. 806–807 (2009)
29. Voorhees, E.M., Buckley, C.: The Effect of Topic Set Size on Retrieval Experiment Error. In: Proceedings of the 25th Annual International ACM SIGIR Conference on Research and Development in Information Retrieval, pp. 316–323 (2002)
30. Voorhees, E.M., Harman, D.: Overview of the Fifth Text REtrieval Conference (TREC-5). In: Proceedings of the Fifth Text REtrieval Conference (TREC-5), pp. 1–28 (1997)
31. Womser-Hacker, C.: Multilingual Topic Generation within the CLEF 2001 Experiments. In: Peters, C., Braschler, M., Gonzalo, J., Kluck, M. (eds.) CLEF 2001. LNCS, vol. 2406, pp. 389–393. Springer, Heidelberg (2002)
32. Zhang, Y., Callan, J., Minka, T.: Novelty and Redundancy Detection in Adaptive Filtering. In: Proceedings of the 25th Annual International ACM SIGIR Conference on Research and Development in Information Retrieval, pp. 81–88 (2002)
33. Zobel, J.: How Reliable are the Results of Large-Scale Information Retrieval Experiments. In: Proceedings of the 21st Annual International ACM SIGIR Conference on Research and Development in Information Retrieval, pp. 307–314 (1998)

Visual Analytics and Information Retrieval

Giuseppe Santucci

"La Sapienza" University of Rome, Italy
santucci@dis.uniroma1.it

Abstract. *Visual Analytics (VA)* [1] is an emerging multi-disciplinary area that takes into account both ad-hoc and classical *Data Mining (DM)* algorithms and *Information Visualization IV (IV)* techniques, combining the strengths of human and electronic data processing. Visualisation becomes the medium of a semi-automated analytical process, where human beings and machines cooperate using their respective distinct capabilities for the most effective results. Decisions on which direction analysis should take in order to accomplish a certain task are left to the user. Although IV techniques have been extensively explored [2], combining them with automated data analysis for specific application domains is still a challenging activity [3]. This chapter provides an introduction of the main concepts behind VA and presents some practical examples on how apply it to *Information Retrieval (IR)*.

1 What Is Visual Analytics

Around the year 2000, for the purpose of supporting human beings in analyzing large and complex datasets, synergies between Information Visualization and Data Mining started to be considered, defining *Visual Data Mining* (VDM) as a new area focused on the explorative analysis of visually represented data. In 2001, the first VDM workshop was held in Freiburg. In 2004, first in the United States, and almost at the same time in Europe, researchers started talking about Visual Analytics [4]. Compared to VDM, there is the clear intention to focus on the analysis process that leads to explanation, interpretation, and presentation of hidden information in the data, taking advantage of dynamic visualizations. From that moment on, the term VDM is superseded by the term Visual Analytics (VA). Daniel Keim, one of the major European experts in the field, provides the following definition: "Visual analytics is more than just visualization and can rather be seen as an integrated approach combining visualization, human factors and data analysis. ..." On a grand scale, Visual Analytics provides technology that combines the strengths of human and electronic data processing. Visualization becomes the medium of a semi-automated analytical process, where humans and machines cooperate using their respective distinct capabilities for the most effective results. The user has to be the ultimate authority in giving the direction of the analysis along his or her specific task. At the same time, the system has to provide effective means of interaction to concentrate on this specific task since in many applications different people work along the path from data to decision.

M. Agosti et al. (Eds.): PROMISE Winter School 2012, LNCS 7757, pp. 116–131, 2013.

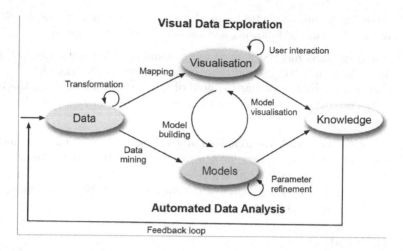

Fig. 1. The Visual Analytics process

Figure 1 (from [5]) schematizes the VA process that combines automatic and visual analysis methods with a tight coupling through human interaction in order to gain knowledge from data. The figure shows an abstract overview of the different stages (represented through ovals) and their transitions (arrows) in the visual analytics process. The first step is often to preprocess and transform the data to derive different representations for further exploration (as indicated by the Transformation arrow). Other typical preprocessing tasks include data cleaning, normalization, grouping, or integration of heterogeneous data sources. After the transformation, the analyst may choose between applying visual or automatic analysis methods. Alternating between visual and automatic methods is characteristic for the VA process and leads to a continuous refinement and verification of preliminary results. User interaction with the visualization is needed to reveal insightful information, for instance by zooming in on different data areas or by considering different visual views on the data. In summary, in the VA process, knowledge can be gained from visualization, automatic analysis, as well as the preceding interactions between visualizations, models, and the human analysts. With respect to the field of visualization, VA integrates methodology from Information Visualization [6,7,8,9], Visual Data Mining [10], geospatial analytics [11], and scientific analytics. Especially human factors (e.g., interaction, cognition, perception, collaboration, presentation, and dissemination) play a key role in the communication between human and computer, as well as in the decision-making process (see, e.g., [12]).

1.1 Visual Analytics and Information Retrieval

If we want to apply Visual Analytics to *Information Retrieval* (IR) evaluation, in order to find solutions that improve the visualizations, analysis, and interpretation of experimental data, a preliminary study is needed to understand both the data structures that are actually used within IR community and its usage. According to this aim, the following sections will cover two aspects:

1. data analysis, that has the goal of understanding what data are useful for the IR evaluation activities and their organization, see Section 2;
2. visualization analysis, that has the goal of understanding what are the most common visualization patterns and the underlying data feeding them, see Section 3.

It is worth noting that, while the following analysis has been carried on within the *Participative Research labOratory for Multimedia and Multilingual Information Systems Evaluation (PROMISE)* NoE project [13,14], using experiences and data collected within the *Cross-Language Evaluation Forum (CLEF)* conference series [15], its validity is quite general.

2   Data Analysis

In order to understand how data are organized and displayed it is important to define a typical scenario in which these data are used. In particular, we focus on IR evaluation campaigns. An evaluation campaign is an activity aiming at supporting IR researchers by providing large test collection and uniform scoring procedures. Within an evaluation campaign there are many tracks, like multi-media, multilingual, text, images, and so on. A track includes, in turn, several tasks. A task is used to define the experiments' structure, specifying a set of documents, a set of topics, and a relevance assessment. Some ad-hoc metadata allows for partitioning the set of documents. For example, in the same set we can have European or American documents and a mechanism that allows for choosing only one of these subsets. Moreover, it is important to remark that very often, in an evaluation campaign, the so called closed world assumption holds, which means that the set of documents is finite and known a-priori. A topic represents an information need and its structure can change according to the task at hand. Documents can be assessed as being relevant or not (or more or less relevant) for a given information need (topic). The relevance of a document with respect to a specific topic is independent of the other documents in the collection. In some case we can have different sets of relevance assessment for a set of documents. The relevance assessment can be done manually, automatically, or using online approach like Amazon mechanical Turk.

Basically, an evaluation campaign involves two kinds of actors: organizers and participants. Organizers prepare the campaign establishing, among other things, tracks and tasks. Participants run their searching algorithm(s) according to the actual tasks. Each run produces a (ranked) result set on which different metrics are computed and stored. In the following we use the terms run and experiment to indicate the systematic application of an algorithm within a task. The computed metrics can be used by organizers or participant. In general, organizers are interested in evaluating the whole campaign, while participants are interested in evaluating their own algorithms, comparing them with other participants' algorithms.

These data can be represented by the TME (Topics-Metrics-Experiment) cube shown on Figure 2.

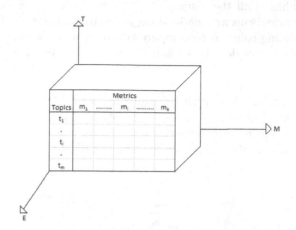

Fig. 2. The TME Data cube

Starting from this cube, we can aggregate or manipulate data in different ways, according to our needs. In particular we are interested in computing four kinds of tables.

The first kind of table describes a single experiment e in terms of topics and metrics and it is a projection of the TME cube on the Topics-Metrics axes. In particular, this table is represented by a matrix T x M where T is the set of topics and M is the set of metrics. In the following we will refer to this kind of tables as TM(e) tables (topics x metrics table of experiment e).

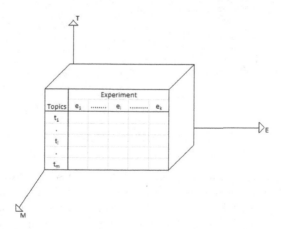

Fig. 3. Projecting the TME data cube on the Topics-Experiments axes

Still considering the TME cube we can derive a second kind of tables (see Figure 3), useful to analyze a single metric m in terms of different topics and experiments. In particular, this table is represented by a matrix T x E where T is the set of topics and E is the set of experiments. In the following we will refer to this kind of tables with the name TE(m) tables (topics x experiments table of metric m). Comparisons are made along rows, to evaluate the behavior of a single topic, or among columns to compare two or more experiments.

The third kind of table describes a single experiment e in terms of descriptive statistics and metrics. In particular, this table is represented by a matrix S x M where S is the set of statistics and M is the set of metrics. In the following we will refer to this kind of table with the name SM(e) table (statistics x metrics table of experiment e). This table is strictly related on the corresponding TM(e) table since values are computed from the TM(e) table's columns. Figure 2 shows an example of how a TM(e) table can be used to calculate values of the SM(e) table.

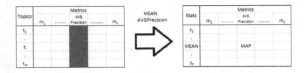

Fig. 4. Relationship between TM and SM tables

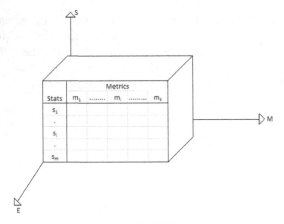

Fig. 5. The SME Data cube

As shown on Figure 4, in an SM table there is the same number of metrics as the related TM table. If we extend this table with respect to experiments we obtain a new cube, the SME (Statistics-Metrics-Experiment) data cube, shown on Figure 5. With respect to the SME cube an SM table is a projection on the Statistics-Metrics axes.

The last kind of table we consider, allows to inspect a single metric m in terms of descriptive statistics and experiments, i.e., it allows for comparing different experiments against a some descriptive statistics computed on a given metric. In

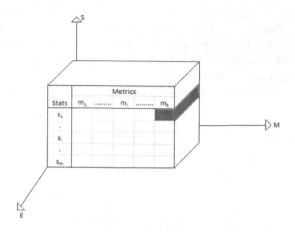

Fig. 6. The SME Data cube projected on the Statistics-Experiments axes

particular, this table is represented by a matrix S x E where S is the set of statistics and E is the set of experiments. In the following we will refer to this table as $SE(m)$ table (statistics x experiment table computed on metric m), and it is a projection of the SME cube on the Statistics-Experiments axes (see Figure 6).

To complete our analysis we recall the concept of meta-attribute. A meta-attribute is a categorical attribute that is associated with a cube component (e.g., the experiments) and it is used to define a further classification of data, with respect to a category. Examples of meta-attributes are: reference track, year, and type of search. Meta-attributes are mainly associated with experiments and documents, but also topics can have their own meta-attributes (for example the data provenance).

3   Visual Analysis

Before discussing the IR evaluation requirements, the overall architecture of the Visual Analytics component is presented, with the main goal of making the following considerations more clear. Such an architecture is depicted on Figure 7 and its structure is totally parametric, without any assumption about the data structure (in the most general case it is contained in non-normalized table). Moreover, there are no assumptions about available visualizations (it is possible to include any kind of visualization), about the mapping between data and visualizations, and about analytical components. The most general situation is the one in which the system presents the user with multiple visualizations, each of them working on a different dataset. Visualizations are synchronized using two main interaction mechanisms: *selection* (it is just a way to focus the attention on a subset of data) and *highlight* (it allows for highlighting a part of the displayed data). In order to produce a visualization, three main steps are, in principle, needed:

1. data extraction from a database (e.g., the historical CLEF data);
2. data manipulation, i.e., deriving new attributes, applying some aggregation operators or analytical algorithms, etc. During such a process the system adds some hidden attributes to the data, in order to support the selection and the highlighting mechanisms;
3. mapping the data obtained from step two on one or more visualizations.

These steps are optional: in some cases the system will automatically perform them, allowing the user to focus only on the mapping and analysis activities.

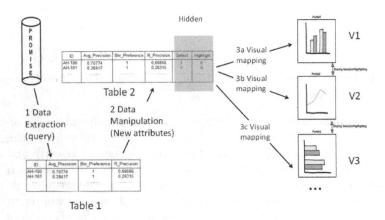

Fig. 7. The PROMISE Visual Analytics architecture

3.1 IR Evaluation Requirements

This section describes the requirements needed to realize a mapping between the data and a suitable visualization. These and the following requirements are derived from the analysis performed on [16,17], collecting both collaborative and VA issues. As an example, annotations are crucial to the extent of reconstructing the operations leading to a visualization. Through annotations one can explain executed operations and can explain, spread, and save particular choices.

According to the performed analysis, we foresee two different user interfaces: General purpose and ad-hoc interfaces.

General Purpose User Interface. In order to obtain an effective visualization there are four main basic activities the system must implement:

1. (quantitative/categorical) attribute classification;
2. data manipulation;
3. visual data mapping;
4. data filtering.

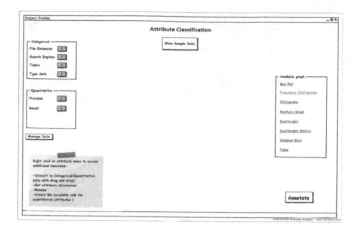

Fig. 8. The attribute classification page

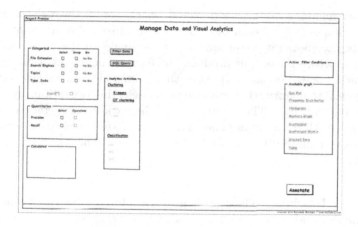

Fig. 9. The data manipulation page

The first activity (see Figure 8) takes a list of attributes as input, and provides the same list as output, but with a (possibly) different attribute classification (into quantitative and categorical). It may allow also for exploring data samples, in order to investigate the data structure and meaning.

The data manipulation activity (see Figure 9) takes as input a table (organized in an arbitrary way) and provides a different table as output that may contain new columns, derived from the "original" table, through some mathematical or ordering/grouping operation. The system checks whether the manipulated table is suitable for the user visualization purposes (otherwise, there are some warning messages leading the user to a more compliant data organization). The Interface should allows also to activate basic statistic and data mining algorithms (e.g., T-test, clustering, etc.).

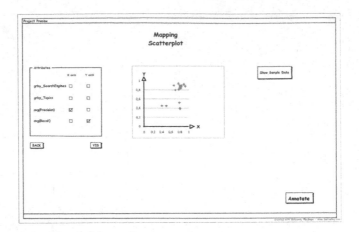

Fig. 10. The mapping page

The visual mapping activity is depicted on Figure 10 through an example, showing the mapping between a table and a bidimensional scatterplot.

Obviously, the above interfaces are part of a sequence of operations, so there is a sort of chain where the output produced by each of them constitutes the input of the following one. The user expresses the commands by dragging attributes from categorical to quantitative and vice versa, selecting operations by means of checkboxes and slide bars. The greater part of them will be implemented through suitable queries. All the activities allow for an "Annotate" operation, providing a means to store an annotation, useful to document and share the analysis choices an patterns.

Ad-Hoc User Interface. The general purpose interface described so far allows for very complex and personalized analysis. However, most of the IR evaluation activities are quite repetitive and follow several basic analysis patterns. To this aim, it is useful to foresee some ad-hoc, highly automated pattern analysis, in which most of the previously described steps are automatically performed according to the analysis pattern at hand. In this scenario the set of available visualizations and their mappings with the data are wired in the interface, according to the most used analysis patterns: *Per topica nalysis* and *Per Experiment* analysis. This is the actual strategy implemented in the PROMISE project, and the following pictures come from the VA prototype under implementation within this project.

Per Topic Analysis. Per topic analysis allows for comparing a set of experiments on each topic with respect to a chosen metric. Therefore the first step for a user is to choose a metric m. Looking at the TME data cube described in the previous section we can note that choosing a metric is equivalent to fix an axis and reduce the set of data to the $TE(m)$ table shown on Figure 3. Per topic analysis implies a comparison on each topic, so we foresee to represent topics on x-axis in each available visualization. We foresee four kinds of visualizations for a per topic analysis: a table, a boxplot chart, a bi-dimensional scatter plots, and a stacked bar chart.

- The table represents the $TE(m)$ table, allowing for looking up details (see Figure 11, upper left);
- The box plot chart (see Figure 11, upper right) is used to evaluate the trend of a topic among experiments with respect to the chosen metric m. It contains a box plot for each topic (x-axis) and the chosen metric (y-axis). Looking at table shown on Figure 3, we can say that each box is built calculating statistical indicators on the set of data represented by a single TE(m) row;
- The bi-dimensional scatter plot (see Figure 11, lower left) allows for comparing topic behavior wrt two experiments. Each topic is represented by a point, according to the values it shows on the two experiments.
- The stacked bar chart (see Figure 11, lower right) has the same purpose as the box plot chart: to evaluate the trend of a topic among experiments with respect to a chosen metric. In such a visualization each topic is associated with all the values the explored metrics m exhibits in all experiments and the height of the bar represents the sum of all these values.

The user can change the metric under analysis and restrict his or her focus on data subsets through select and highlight operations. As an example, Figure 12 shows three topics highlighted in all the four visualizations.

Per experiment analysis In the ad-hoc interface, per experiment analysis allows for analyzing an experiment as a whole and/or comparing the performances of a set of experiments with respect to a chosen descriptive statistics. As an example, on Figure 13, left side, the table chart represents an experiment in each row, showing the descriptive statistics of the metric average_precision (min, max, median, etc.). The box plot chart on Figure 13, right side, shows the percentile values of the observed metric for each experiment represented through boxplots.

4   Combining Automated and Visual Analysis

In this section we show, through an example, how the VA system allows for combining automated and visual analysis, as described on the Introduction (see Figure 1). Let us consider the initial view presented on Figure 11 and assume that the user is interested in focusing on difficult topics. She can run and analytical module (see Figure 14) that partitions the topics in two subsets, namely simple and difficult topics.

The result of the automated analysis is presented to the user visually, using adjacency and color (see Figure 15). After that, the user can sort the two sets, selecting the best topic of the difficult set to inspect its numerical values on the table, and to use it as the input of another automated analysis, e.g., clustering or similarity search, (not discussed in this chapter) to better understand its characteristics (see Figure 16).

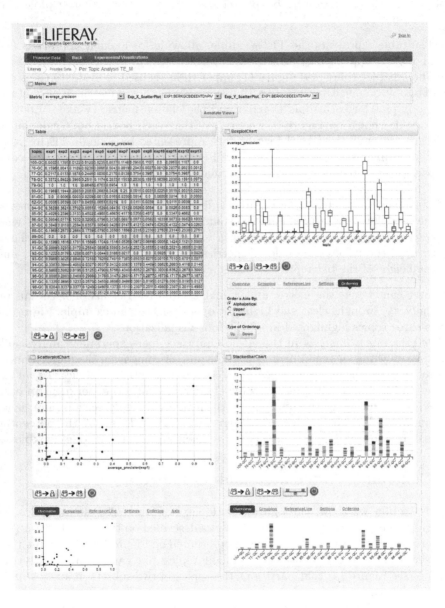

Fig. 11. Per topic analysis

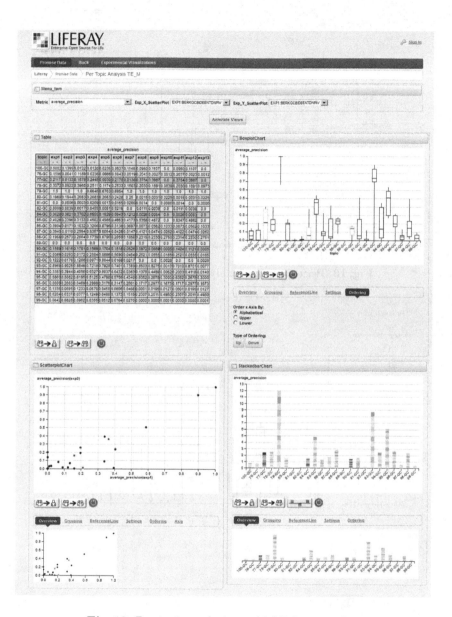

Fig. 12. Per topic analysis: an highlight operation

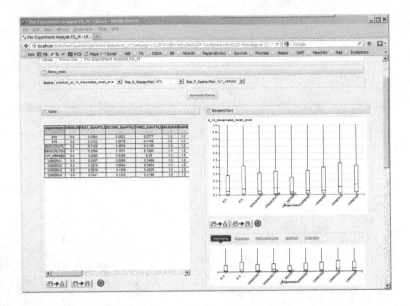

Fig. 13. Per experiment analysis: table and box plot

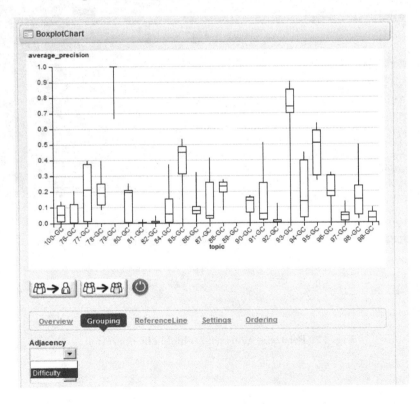

Fig. 14. Per topic analysis: running an automated analysis

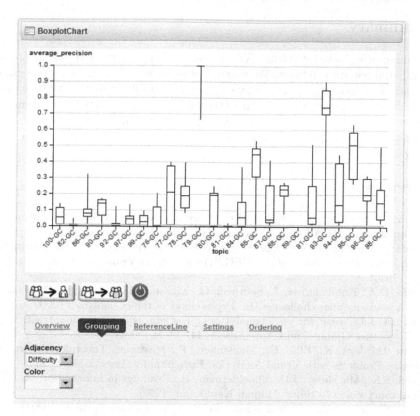

Fig. 15. Per topic analysis: visual feedback of the automated analysis

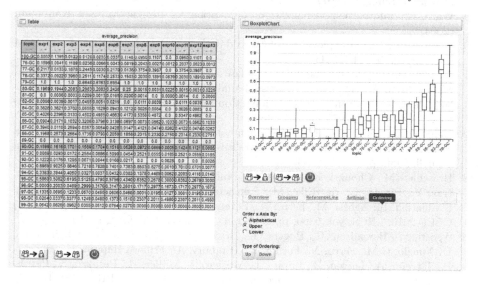

Fig. 16. Per topic analysis: visually selecting a topic as the input of a new automated task

5   Summary

In this chapter we have introduced VA, a new, challenging metodology for analyzing large and complex dataset. We started presenting the main issues associated with such a metodology and we have shown how apply it in the context of IR system evaluation, dealing with data structure and visualization requirements. We have used the European NoE PROMISE and the CLEF conference series as bed tests, but the ideas and the results presented in this chapter have a quite broader scope.

References

1. Keim, D., Andrienko, G., Fekete, J.D., Görg, C., Kohlhammer, J., Melançon, G.: Information visualization, pp. 154–175. Springer, Heidelberg (2008)
2. Shneiderman, B.: The eyes have it: a task by data type taxonomy for information visualizations. In: Proceedings. IEEE Symposium on Visual Languages, pp. 336–343 (1996)
3. Keim, D.A., Kohlhammer, J., Santucci, G., Mansmann, F., Wanner, F., Schaefer, M.: Visual analytics challenges. In: Proceedings of the eChallenges (2009)
4. Thomas, J.J., Wong, P.: Visual analytics - guest editors' introduction. IEEE Trans. on Computer Graphics and Applications 24, 20–21 (2004)
5. Keim, D., Jörn, K., Ellis, G., Mansmann, F.: Mastering The Information Age-Solving Problems with Visual Analytics. Eurographics Association, Goslar (2010)
6. Card, S.K., Mackinlay, J.D., Shneiderman, B.: Readings in information visualization: using vision to think. Morgan Kaufmann (1999)
7. Chen, C.: Information Visualization - Beyond the Horizon. Springer (2004)
8. Spence, R.: Information Visualization - Design for Interaction, 2nd edn. Pearson Education Limited (2007)
9. Ware, C.: Information visualization: perception for design. Morgan Kaufmann (2004)
10. Keim, D.A.: Visual exploration of large data sets. Communications of the ACM (CACM) 44, 38–44 (2001)
11. Andrienko, G., Andrienko, N., Jankowski, P., Keim, D.A., Kraak, M.J., MacEachren, A., Wrobel, S.: Geovisual analytics for spatial decision support: Setting the research agenda. International Journal of Geographical Information Science 21, 839–858 (2007)
12. Keim, D.A., Mansmann, F., Schneidewind, J., Ziegler, H.: Challenges in visual data analysis. In: Proceedings of the Tenth International Conference on Information Visualization, pp. 9–16 (2006)
13. Braschler, M., Choukri, K., Ferro, N., Hanbury, A., Karlgren, J., Müller, H., Petras, V., Pianta, E., de Rijke, M., Santucci, G.: A PROMISE for Experimental Evaluation. In: Agosti, M., Ferro, N., Peters, C., de Rijke, M., Smeaton, A. (eds.) CLEF 2010. LNCS, vol. 6360, pp. 140–144. Springer, Heidelberg (2010)
14. Agosti, M., Berendsen, R., Bogers, T., Braschler, M., Buitelaar, P., Choukri, K., Di Nunzio, G.M., Ferro, N., Forner, P., Hanbury, A., Friberg Heppin, K., Hansen, P., Järvelin, A., Larsen, B., Lupu, M., Masiero, I., Müller, H., Peruzzo, S., Petras, V., Piroi, F., de Rijke, M., Santucci, G., Silvello, G., Toms, E.: PROMISE Retreat Report – Prospects and Opportunities for Information Access Evaluation. SIGIR Forum 46 (2012)

15. Ferro, N.: CLEF, CLEF 2010, and PROMISEs: Perspectives for the Cross-Language Evaluation Forum. In: Kando, N., Kishida, K. (eds.) Technologies: Information Retrieval, Question Answering and Cross-Lingual Information Access, pp. 2–12. National Institute of Informatics, Tokyo (2010)
16. Croce, M., Di Reto, E., Granato, G.L., Hansen, P., Sabetta, A., Santucci, G., Veltri, F.: Deliverable D5.1 – Collaborative user interface requirements. PROMISE Network of Excellence, EU 7FP, Contract N. 258191 (2011), http://www.promise-noe.eu/documents/10156/50834686-2118-48f8-a57b-8553ec3d7981
17. Granato, G.L., Santucci, G., Tino, G.: Deliverable D5.2 – User interface and Visual analytics environment requirements. PROMISE Network of Excellence, EU 7FP, Contract N. 258191 (2011), http://www.promise-noe.eu/documents/10156/21f1512a-5b47-48ae-834a-89d6441d079e

An Introduction to Crowdsourcing for Language and Multimedia Technology Research

Gareth J.F. Jones

Centre for Next Generation Localisation
School of Computing, Dublin City University, Dublin 9, Ireland
gjones@computing.dcu.ie
http://www.computing.dcu.ie/~gjones

Abstract. Language and multimedia technology research often relies on large manually constructed datasets for training or evaluation of algorithms and systems. Constructing these datasets is often expensive with significant challenges in terms of recruitment of personnel to carry out the work. Crowdsourcing methods using scalable pools of workers available on-demand offers a flexible means of rapid low-cost construction of many of these datasets to support existing research requirements and potentially promote new research initiatives that would otherwise not be possible.

Keywords: crowdsourcing, human computation, human language technologies, multimedia technologies.

1 Introduction

Research in multimedia and language technologies often relies heavily on the use of datasets for training and evaluation of the various methods and algorithms proposed to achieve the objectives of the technology currently under consideration. For example, data for the training of machine translation or visual concept recognition algorithms or the evaluation of search effectiveness in information retrieval. The requirement for extensive manual involvement means that the development of these datasets is generally very expensive, and that the cost and logistics of the construction of such resources can represent a considerable obstacle to the exploration of new research directions which are not supported by existing training or test data resources.

Manual contributions to the construction of these datasets include for example the transcription of audio files as a first stage to them being used in the training of a speech recognition system, the labeling of visual concepts in images or frames of video for training of visual classifiers, and the writing of test queries for the evaluation of information retrieval algorithms for a specific document collection and judgement of relevance of the documents to each query. It is notable that these activities can generally be broken into small tasks which are often quite repetitive, and also that many of these tasks do not require any specific skills or rely only on an individual's existing skills. For example natural

M. Agosti et al. (Eds.): PROMISE Winter School 2012, LNCS 7757, pp. 132–154, 2013.

manual translation of text by a bilingual speaker to build a training set for a machine translation system.

The nature of these tasks makes them highly suitable for online *crowdsourcing* methods where individual online workers are allocated and carry out small assignments in return for micro payments. Crowdsourcing is currently being used and explored in a number of areas of language and multimedia technology research. This work makes use of crowdsourcing for simple activities, e.g. speech transcription [20], but is also being explored for more challenging tasks, involving some level of personal creativity, e.g. writing search queries suitable for a particular document collection [6].

This paper provides an introduction to the general topic of crowdsourcing, highlights practical details of designing and using crowdsourcing activities, a short overview of some key existing work in crowdsourcing for language and multimedia research, and illustrates this with an example of the use of crowdsourcing in the MediaEval 2011 Rich Speech Retrieval task [15].

2   What Is Crowdsourcing?

Crowdsourcing is form of *human computation*, where human computation is a method of having people do things that we might otherwise consider assigning to a computing device to calculate automatically, e.g. a language translation task. A *crowdsourcing system* facilitates a crowdsourcing process to complete a specified task. To carry out a task, a crowdsourcing system, enlists a "crowd" of human workers to help solve a defined problem [27]. Currently the best known crowdsourcing system is *Amazon Mechanical Turk (AMT)*[1]. For this reason, the crowdsourcing terminology of AMT is generally adopted in this paper.

In operation someone wishing to undertake a task defines the operations needed to complete it, and then divides them into multiple micro-tasks which when combined solve the problem at hand. The activity is then made available as a set of micro-tasks on a crowdsourcing system. Human workers are then recruited to undertake the micro-tasks for which they typically receive a payment for each completed task.

To operate successfully, a crowdsourcing system must address the following four issues [5]:

- How to recruit and retain workers?
- What contributions can the workers make?
- How to combine worker contributions to solve the target problems?
- How to evaluate workers and their contributions?

There are various forms of collaborative activities not all of which qualify as crowdsourcing. Collaborations between workers in crowdsourcing environments can be explicit or implicit. For example, in the development of Wikipedia or Linux, the crowdsourcing system enlists a crowd of workers to explicitly collaborate to build a long lasting artefact of use to a larger community [5]. By contrast,

---

[1] https://www.mturk.com/

workers in the ESP game implicitly collaborate to label images as a side effect
while playing a game [37][36]. Similarly, workers using AMT collaborate implicitly, e.g. workers enlisted to find a missing boat in thousands of satellite images,
where each worker inspects an individual image [5]. However, not all human-
centric systems address these challenges, and such systems do not fall within the
scope of crowdsourcing. For example, crowd management at a sports event does
not look to recruit more members of the crowd, if anything in this case it would
be preferable for members of the crowd to leave [5].

The availability of online crowdsourcing services such as AMT, is now making
human computation resources available to various research communities. Among
these communities there is currently significant interest in exploring the use of
these services to support research activities in information and data processing
technologies, and investigating how they might be used to open up new research
directions, which might be technically innovative or may previously have been
impractical using other means.

2.1   Creating and Managing a Crowdsourcing Activity

The basic process of creating a crowdsourcing activity is as follows. First, identify an activity which is amenable to being broken into small elemental tasks,
e.g. the need to label the presence or absence of a visual concept in many thousands of images. Rather than give this elemental task to a specific individual,
e.g. an employee, a crowdsource requester outsources it to someone else via the
crowdsourcing system. The crowdsourcing system makes the tasks available to
an ad hoc group of workers (who might be considered "employees" since they
usually receive payment for their work) recruited via a call for participation. The
workers bid for the offered work, the requester has the choice of which workers
to accept to undertake the offered task. The decision of whether to accept an
offer of work can be complex taking account of a number of factors; this issue
is examined in more detail in Section 3. Once a worker has been accepted, they
carry out the agreed work, the requester can then check the quality of the work;
depending on the nature of the task, this checking process may itself be complex
or non-exhaustive. Once the quality of the work has been checked, the requester
then has the option to accept the work and make payment to the worker, or
to reject it, in which case payment is not made. The decision as to whether to
accept the work may not be straightforward, and is also discussed further below.

2.2   Why Use Crowdsourcing?

Many areas of work involve a need to complete a large number of repetitive small
tasks with high short term peak loads. In many cases these tasks do not involve
specialist skills, with the key requirement being that the person undertaking
them should be conscientious and seek to do the job to the best of their ability.
Crowdsourcing is often ideal for this type of situation since it provides rapid
access to a very flexible and cheap workforce enabling fast completion of tasks

at short notice without the need for the development of a long term employment infrastructure.

Established crowdsourcing platforms such as MTurk provide a framework which enables new tasks to be developed very rapidly using a standard set of interface components, and to be made available to workers straightaway with a well defined mechanism for making payments. This enables early stage experimentation to develop a crowdsource task for completion. For example, to develop a task for assessment of document relevance to some user information need. The initial version of the task can then be deployed on the crowdsource platform in a pilot study. The outputs of the workers attempts to complete this pilot task can then be examined, any problems or unexpected responses noted, the structure or content of the task iterated, and the task run again until the workers complete the task as required, at which point the full set of tasks can be offered for completion.

2.3   Who Are the Workers?

A question that arises in respect of offering crowdsource tasks on an online platform such as MTurk where anyone can register as a potential worker and bid for work is, who are these workers? Surveys have found that initially they were frequently based in the USA, often based in the home for family reasons, and who probably undertook the work for the sake of interest, rather than for the financial reward. However, workers are increasingly diverse and international, where some of them are much more motivated by the available financial rewards. For example students based in countries with emerging economies [25][30].

3   High Level Issues in Crowdsourcing

Effective use of crowdsourcing requires a number of high level issues to be addressed. Assuming that an activity amenable to crowdsourcing has been selected, and broken down into elemental tasks, then the requester of the work needs to consider the following points: the level of payment or other incentives for the work, the design of the interface and interaction design of the task, and the choice of crowdsourcing platform.

In addition to these very practical issues, the requester also needs to give careful consideration to management of human factors relating to workers, including: recruitment of workers, retention of good workers, quality control of the work, trust in and reliability of workers, and detection of poor quality work [35]. The remainder of this section examines each of these issues in more detail.

3.1   Recruitment

As outlined earlier, once they are happy with the design of their task, the requester makes their task available to the registered workers on their selected crowdsourcing platform. Workers are able to search a list of currently available tasks, and request to be assigned to a task that they want to do. The list of available tasks typically makes the registered identify of the requester available to the worker, as well as summary details of their history as a requester in terms of completed tasks, payment record to workers, etc. The requester is similarly shown summary details of a worker requesting their task, in terms of amount of successfully completed previous tasks, etc. Workers are thus able to determine whether a potential "employer" treats their workers fairly, and employers can see whether their potential employees are reliable high quality workers. Thus, requesters and workers with established strong reputations are likely to be successful in the recruitment process: the requester gets the worker they want, and the worker gets chosen for the task they want A reputable requester can often have their pick from among reputable workers applying for their tasks.

Further to their general history of successful completion of tasks, other practical issues relating to the workers suitability for a specific task may need to be addressed in the recruitment process, e.g. for a language translation task, the worker must have the requisite level ability as a translator between the required languages. In order to ensure the workers skill level, the requester can set a qualifying test before agreeing to let the worker take the task, e.g. to translate and check some sample text. On other occasions, the quality of previous tasks completed can be taken as sufficient proof of the worker's skills.

3.2   Reputation

As indicated in the previous section, workers and requesters can make selections based on each others reputations. Reputations within a crowdsourcing system are based on previous task activities which are made available at the selection stage. A worker's reputation can act as an incentive for a requestor to accept their offer to undertake a task, and to trust the likely quality of their work. A requester can also select a worker based on their own previous experience of the worker.

In terms of the requestor's reputation, as indicated above, the requester has the option of approving completed work or not, if they don't approve the work, they don't pay the worker. They may also have the option of paying a bonus to individual workers for completing work of exceptional quality or above some agreed standard as part of the task specification. The requester can approve the work, pay for it, and then not use, e.g. if it is clear that the worker expended reasonable effort in attempting to complete the task, but that the output is just not useable for some reason. The requester's fairness in recognising the genuine effort of workers can have a long term effect on their success in recruiting for subsequent tasks. By contrast if they are perceived to reject large amounts of work, with or without good reason, then they can damage their reputation with workers, and workers may not request to take their tasks. This can create a dilemma for requesters, if they accept poor quality work then they can waste money, but if they set their standards too high, they may fail to attract enough workers to complete the full set of tasks required for their overall objective. One consequence of this situation is that it creates an incentive for requesters to develop their task so that it is easy enough for reliable completion by suitably qualified workers, but still enables them to fulfill their overall objectives.

Overall, the reputation of both requesters and workers can be important for the success of a crowdsourcing ecosystem. A requester with a reputation for posting well structured and clearly described tasks, with fair and prompt payments is likely to prove popular with regular workers. A worker who undertakes tasks in a professional manner is likely to prove popular with requesters.

3.3   Payment and Incentives

As already stated workers generally undertake tasks for micro-payments - very small payments for completion of individual tasks. Workers may volunteer for an available task because it looks interesting, but often they will do so because it looks a good way to earn some money [30]. For the requester, offering a suitable level of payment is a trade-off between:

- Underpayment, for either or both of worker's time or expertise.
- Overpayment, which may attract workers keen to earn money without undertaking the task properly.
- Sufficient payment to motivate the worker to complete the task conscientiously, with the possibility of offering bonus payments for excellent work.

Thus the requester needs to offer sufficient payment to attract enough suitably qualified workers, to motivate them to complete the task well, but not to make the task too attractive to undesirable workers who just want to make money without completing the work properly [35]. The relationship between incentives and quantity and quality of work is often complex. For example, if has been found that paying for completion of a complete instance of a task overall leads to more work being carried out than incremental payment for sub-tasks, and that greater payment may increase quantity, but not quality of work [21]. Further interesting work on this subject is described in [10].

This problem of workers volunteering for tasks with no intention to complete them properly, is a major concern in crowdsourcing, since not only does the work not get done properly or perhaps not at all, but depending on the nature of the task, it may be difficult for the requester to check this, and the requester wastes their money.

3.4   Detecting Poor Quality Work

As noted above, it is important that workers are actually capable of successfully completing their assigned task. While not all tasks require specific expertise or skills, it is important that the worker should undertake the task to the best of their ability. Workers may sign up for a task to earn money (and even pass a qualifying test if required), and then attempt to get paid without completing the task properly. Detecting so called "spam" work is an important issue in quality control. While some tasks require all work to be checked, for some other tasks checking all work is impractical. For example, it is not possible to check all relevance assessments made in the development of an information retrieval test collection, even if it is practical to check the indicated relevant documents, it is not possible, without repeating the task, to check the reliability of the relevance judgements of all documents marked as non relevant.

One method to combat the problem of dishonest work is for requesters to set up "honey pots" with known answers. The worker completes these as part of their work, but unbeknownst to them, the requester knows the answer to the honey pot questions and can easily check for faked or poor quality work. The requester can then refuse to pay for the work, and bar the worker from undertaking further work for them. The worker's reputation within the crowdsourcing system will also fall since their work has been rejected, making it more difficult for them to get work with other requesters. This is another reason why workers are less likely to request tasks from requesters with a poor payment record, since it affects the worker's overall rating in the crowdsourcing ecosystems, making them less attractive to other requesters. Thus, not only do workers not want to work for requesters who don't pay them if their work is not perfect, they also do not want to work for them because it can make it more difficult to get other work in the future. Honey pots can be used initially in a worker selection phase prior to fully engaging the worker to filter obvious cheating workers, but also continue to be used once the worker has been selected with the honey pots randomly distributed in with the main task assignments. This topic is examined in more detail in [38], and techniques for managing crowdsource workers and data quality are proposed in other studies including [38][34][28].

4   Crowdsourcing in Language and Multimedia Technology Research

A growing number of examples of the use of crowdsourcing methods have appeared in language and multimedia technology research in recent years. This section briefly reviews some of the most notable examples.

4.1   Language Technology Research

One of the most important early studies examining crowdscourcing in language technology research is described in [33], which demonstrated that non-expert workers can produce work of a similar quality to expert workers for natural language annotation tasks. Callison-Burch and Dredze [4] surveys contributions to the NAACL-2010 workshop on creating Speech and Language Data with Amazon's Mechanical Turk, and highlights important factors which should be taken into account when designing effective crowdsourcing tasks.

A survey of research using crowdsourcing for speech research related tasks is contained in [26]. In more detailed studies of individual activities, the use of crowd workers to transcribe speech is explored in [20], while [7] examines the more challenging task of transcribing non-native read speech and spontaneous speech. Further work on non-expert transcription is described in [23]. Focusing more on speed rather than accuracy, a method for real-time captioning of speech is described in [17]. The related task of collecting spoken resources using crowdsourcing methods is explored in [14].

The PodCastle system explores use of crowd based correction of transcription errors and the use of these corrections to improve system training [8][24]. A more complex crowd-based retraining approach for a spoken language system is described in [22].

In information retrieval relevance assessment for queries is a time consuming and human resource expensive activity which involves manual judgement of the relevance of a, potentially very large, number of documents to a user information need expressed in some form of search query. The nature of the relevance assessment tasks make crowdsourcing an attractive option to undertake human assessment of document relevance. This has been explored in a number of studies including [1]. The very large number of document viewed for short periods by crowdsource workers means that it is not possible to manually check all the assigned relevance labels, which means that issues of worker behaviour including motivation and reward are important, as for example examined in [9].

Crowdsourcing has also been studied in the context of evaluation of machine translation in [3], which showed a similar level of performance to gold standard judgements of translation quality. The training of statistical machine translation systems is reliant on the availability of parallel or at least comparable corpora in the languages for which the translation system is to be developed. The amount of such content suitable for the training of a statistical machine translation system is thus an important issue. This can present a significant problem for language pairs for which sufficient amounts of naturally occurring training data are not available. The use of crowdsourcing for the development of machine translation training data is presented in [13]. Another exploration of this topic incorporating an active learning method is described in [2]. Even when well trained, the output of machine translation systems is not ideal. In some applications manual correction of machine translation output forms part of a practical workflow. The use of crowdsourcing in correction of machine translation output is investigated in [18].

Another important area of language technology research is summarization. An investigation into use of crowdscouring in summarization research is reported in [19], which concludes that while crowdsourcing was not effective for generating gold standard summaries for use in research, it is suggested that it is useful for studying patterns of human behaviour when creating in summaries.

4.2   Multimedia Technology Research

In the area of multimedia research one of the consistently expensive activities is manual labelling of training and test data. Labelling of images using a game-based approach was explored in [37][36]. Further work in image annotation is reported in [35] and [28].

Image labelling using crowdsourcing can be noisy if workers are accidentally careless or deliberately do not attempt to do the work properly, or if correct labelling is simply difficult, for example, if the image is unclear or assignment of the label uncertain for some other reason. Methods to improve label quality are proposed in [31][11][29].

The use of crowdsourcing to improve, extend and share automatically detected concepts in video fragments is examined in [32]. A crowdsourced human validation of image search results is described in [41]. Exploring the area of summarization in video access, [40] describes a method for rapid generation of video summaries incorporating the viewer's preference.

In the emerging area of affect in multimedia, [34] describes a novel method of affective annotation of video using crowdsourcing. An initial investigation into the topic of crowdsourcing for user studies is reported in [12].

Beyond these subjects. other interesting topics to which crowdsourcing is being applied include social data analysis [39].

5   Crowdsourcing Platforms

Although Amazon Mechanical Turk (AMT) is generally the most popular crowdsourcing platform, a number of others are available which offer crowdsourcing functionality; these include: Crowdflower[2], CloudCrowd[3], DoMyStuff[4], Clickworker[5], Smartsheet[6], uTest[7], Elance[8], oDesk[9], and Freelancer [10]. Many of these are more concerned with flexible commercial recruitment services which appear less useful for scientific research. At present, the main alternative to AMT for the type of research examined in this paper is CrowdFlower.

A good way to get started with crowdsourcing is sign up as a worker on one of the these platforms and do some tasks, and to understand the practical issues which arise by monitoring discussion forums.

While other services are available, the remainder of this paper focuses on the use of AMT, however the principles are general and can be applied to any similar crowdsourcing platform. AMT has been online since 2005 with an on-demand, scalable, and real-time workforce. It can be accessed via a "dashboard" GUI or using a programmers' API. A requestor wanting to recruit workers to undertake a task creates a Human Intelligence Task (HIT), which is a web form composed of a number of instructions. AMT HITs are undertaken by workers referred to for AMT as "turkers." The requestor specifies the reward which is available for completing the HIT.

---

[2] http://crowdflower.com/
[3] http://www.cloudcrowd.com/
[4] http://www.domystuff.com/
[5] http://www.clickworker.com/en/
[6] http://www.smartsheet.com/
[7] http://www.utest.com/
[8] https://www.elance.com/
[9] https://www.odesk.com/
[10] http://www.freelancer.com/

6   Implementation of an AMT HIT

This section outlines a suggested procedure for the development and usage of an effective AMT HIT. This is based partially on principles of user-centered design for interaction systems and practical experience working with AMT HITs.

When building a completely new HIT, it can be useful to build a mock up which could be as simple as a list of the instructions to be completed by the worker, and test it locally with your research team. Feedback from these tests can then be incorporated to refine the task. Subsequently a limited test run can be implemented on AMT with a very small dataset. Key questions to be considered include:

- What is the time for completion of the HIT? If replicated by other workers, how long would it take to complete the overall task with a set of HITs?
- Do people understand the task?
- Consider needs for quality control:
  - Is a qualification test needed?
  - Adjust qualification passing grade and/or acceptable approval rate of workers if necessary.
- Check suitability or correctness of the output.
- Look for spammers.
  - Are gold answers (honey pots) needed to catch spam workers?
- Look at comments from workers: are they happy / unhappy?, would they work for you again?, is the HIT too easy / too hard?
- Is the payment rate for work - too high / too low? Do people sign up or not? Do they complain after doing the task that the payment is too small? Is there evidence of poor workers attracted by apparently high payment for the work?
- Address feedback, e.g. poor guidelines, payments, passing grade, etc. - email exchange. Everything counts! The HIT is only as good as the weakest part!
- Run another experiment with new settings and the same data to make sure that everything is now working as expected, it not, iterate again.
- If all is in order, launch a full batch of the HIT.

There are many tasks active on AMT with corresponding HITs on offer at any point. If you want to attract the best workers, you need to grab their attention! Make the HIT look attractive in some way, make it sound interesting, but be honest, workers accepting and completing HITs which are not accurately represented in the description are prone to post complaints, which may affect your ability as a requester to attract more workers in the future.

Split a large crowdsourcing activity into batches of HITs; only have one batch in the system at a time. There are only a limited number of workers available at any time, having multiple batches of the same HIT available in parallel is unlikely to complete the overall activity any faster since it will divide the available effort. Also, running batches of HITs sequentially means that you can review feedback from batch n before running batch $n+1$, allowing you to make small adjustments to the HIT if needed.

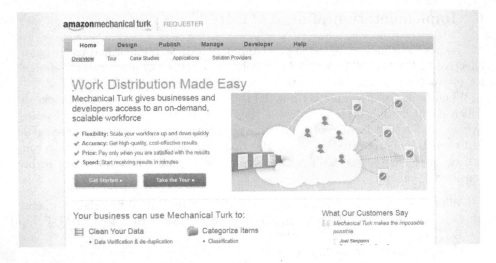

Fig. 1. AMT Requester Entry Point

7   Crowdsourcing Example

This section describes the development and use of an AMT HIT for collection of a query set for the MediaEval 2011 Rich Speech Retrieval (RSR) task [15]. RSR was offered as a benchmark task as part of the MediaEval multimedia evaluation benchmark[11]. Registered task participants were required to try to identify a single video known to be relevant to a searcher's information need in a known-item search task, and to locate the optimal point to start playback within the video, referred to as a jump-in point. This task models a user trying to re-find a previously viewed segment of video. The RSR task wished to explore five different functions of speech, represented as illocutionary speech acts: 'apology', 'definition', 'opinion', 'promise' and 'warning'. The document set consisted of 1974 episodes (247 dev, 1727 test) 350 hours of semi-professional video harvested from blip.tv [16], available for download under a creative commons licence.

An AMT HIT was used to develop the RSR test collection by locating a number of interesting jump-in points in the video collection, describing them and forming a search topic statement for each one. The evaluation task was then to use the topic statement to try to locate the jump-in point. This section gives more details of the task and the AMT HIT used to develop the test collection.

7.1   Setting Up an AMT HIT

The first step is for the requester to enter the AMT system, as shown in Figure 1. Once in the system, the requester selects a category of task which they wish to undertake, see Figure 2.

---

[11] http://www.multimediaeval.org

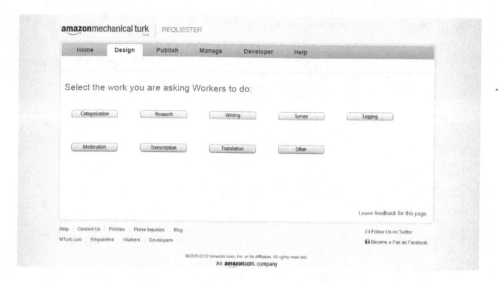

Fig. 2. AMT Options for Design of a HIT

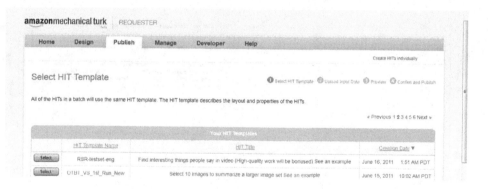

Fig. 3. AMT List of available HIT designs

An AMT HIT is constructed on an HTML form. Several options are available to the requester to develop their HIT:

– Use one of the templates provided within AMT.
– Download one of the templates from AMT, edit it and upload the edited HIT to AMT.
– Write their own, and upload it to AMT.
– Select an existing template that they uploaded previously.

Figure 3 shows the HITs designs available to the requester.

The MediaEval 2011 RSR HIT was written from scratch and uploaded to AMT. Once uploaded the requester can preview the HIT as it will be seen by the worker, see Figure 4. When the requester is satisfied with the HIT, they can publish it to make it available to the workers, see Figure 5. Note that for

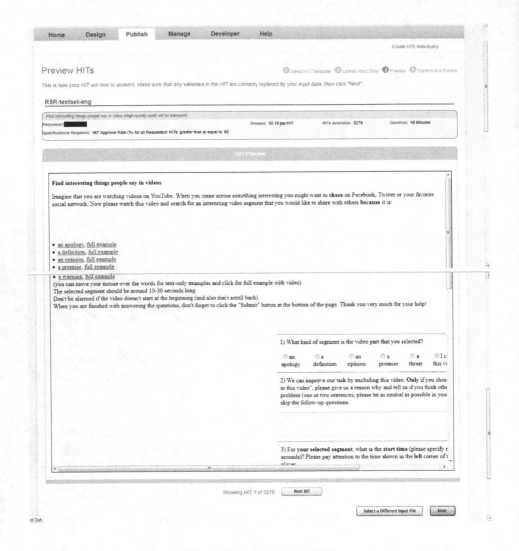

Fig. 4. Previewing the HIT

AMT, the requester must have sufficient credit registered in the system to pay for completion of the batch before it can be made available to workers.

Once a HIT has been selected and made available to workers, the requester can monitor the progress of the current batch of the instance of the HIT. Figure 6 shows the percentage of the requested task completed so far by the workers. This also shows the average time to complete a HIT and the average rate of pay for the work. This information is useful to the requester in assessing the effectiveness of the HIT and to potential workers to decide whether to apply for the HIT.

Completion of the overall RSR query construction task required multiple workers to complete the HIT by viewing different video files. Operation of the

Fig. 5. Publishing HIT to be available to Workers

HIT required input variables to to specify the video to be viewed in this instance of the HIT. The variables gave details of the path to the server where the video to be viewed in the HIT was stored. The code also specified the video player to be used and the video to be played.

A set of HITs to be completed in a single batch are defined in a csv file uploaded by the requester. The values of the variables (the names of the videos in this case) are specified in the file. The csv file to be used in this batch of the HIT is selected using the interface shown in Figure 9. During execution of the batch AMT keeps track of which HITs have been completed. Workers are assigned HITs until either the batch has been completed, or the requester stops execution of further HITs in this batch.

Fig. 6. AMT progress of the current batch of the HIT

7.2   Details of the MediaEval 2011 RSR HIT

This section gives details of the MediaEval 2011 RSR HIT. The version of the HIT shown here was used for collection of the experimental dataset, and was developed iteratively using batch trial runs. The development and use of the HIT had a research element to it. The examples of crowdsourcing in language and multimedia technology research outlined earlier are generally simple tasks where workers are asked to objectively label linguistic or visual content. By contrast, the RSR HIT was exploring the behaviour and effectiveness of untrained crowdsource workers in a creative process, in this case the generation of the search queries to look for the known-item. The ability of carry out research activities requiring creative input potentially greatly increases the scope for use of crowdsourcing in research.

MediaEval 2011 RSR HIT

Find interesting things people say in videos.

Imagine that you are watching videos on YouTube, when you come across something interesting you might want to share it on Facebook, Twitter or your favourite social network.

Now please watch this video and search for an interesting video segment that you would like to share with others because it is:

an apology, full example
a definition, full example
an opinion, full example
a promise, full example
a warning, full example

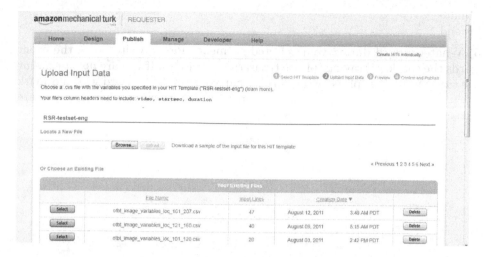

Fig. 7. Selecting a csv file for a batch of HIT runs

(you can move your mouse over the words for text-only examples and click for full example with video)

The selected segment should be around 10-30 seconds long. Don't be alarmed if the video doesn't start at the beginning (and also don't scroll back).

When you are finished with answering the questions, don't forget to click the "Submit" button at the bottom of the page. Thank you very much for your help!

1) What kind of segment is the video part that you selected?
- an apology
- a definition
- an opinion
- a promise
- a warning
- I can't find anything like this in this video

2) We can improve our task by excluding this video. Only if you chose "I can't find anything like this in this video", please give us a reason why and tell us if you think other people will have the same problem (one or two sentences, please be as neutral as possible in your description), and you should skip the follow-up questions.

3) For your selected segment (in 1) above, what is the start time (please specify exactly in minutes and seconds)? Please pay attention to the time shown in the left corner of the bottom line of the video player.
Minute _
Second _

4) For your selected segment (in 1) above, what is the end time (please specify exactly in minutes and seconds)? Please pay attention to the time shown in the left corner of the bottom line of the video player.

Minute _

Second _

5) What was said during your selected segment? Please write down the exact words the speaker is saying (please transcribe precisely). If you are not sure what the exact word was, please write down what your think the word was and mark it with a star (for example, 'French president *Sarkosie was saying ...' if you are not sure how to spell the name 'Sarkozy' properly)

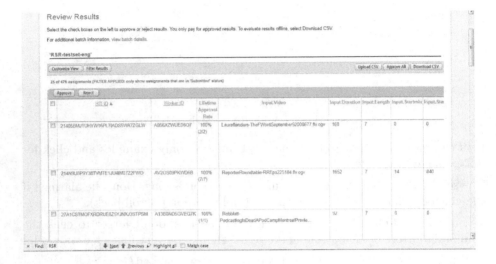

Fig. 8. Requester Results

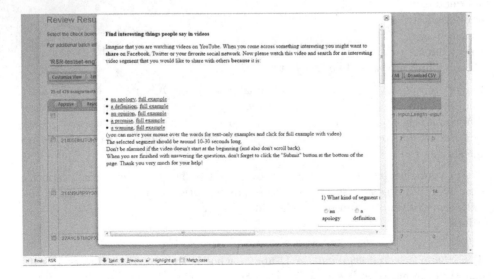

Fig. 9. Requester's view of the HIT as seen by the Worker

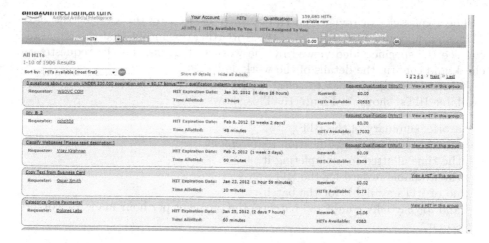

Fig. 10. List of currently available HITs

6) When sharing this particular part of the video (your selected segment) on a social network, what comment would you add to the video to make sure that your friends have an idea what the video segment is about?

Please do not use informal internet language (such as '4 u' instead of 'for you').

Be as objective as possible when describing the video segment and do not express your personal opinion/attitude, either positive or negative.

7) Imagine you would like to search for similar video segments using a search engine (such as Google, Bing, Yahoo) what would you put in the search box?

We understand that this work requires a lot of your time and concentration, so we would like to bonus the high-quality of your results.

Please tell us your opinion about the size of bonus you deserve. Choose and justify your choice. Please keep in mind that we are carrying out non-profit university research (we can afford a maximum of 21 cents bonus, but only for really excellent responses).

When making our decision on your bonus level we create a compromise between our budget and your request.

0 cents

7 cents

11 cents

21 cents

7.3   Details of Completed HITs

The requester can view a summary of the workers who have selected and completed the HIT and their activities, shown in Figure 8. A more detailed version can be downloaded in a csv file.

The requester can review the HIT exactly as seen by the worker, the next slide, shown Figure 9. In the case of the RSR HIT, this means that the requester can see the specific video viewed by the worker. This enables the requester to check and confirm the details of the work delivered.

When deciding whether to select a HIT, a worker can view the currently available HITs, shown in Figure 10. This shows:

- a brief summary of the HIT,
- whether there is a qualification requirement,
- the time allotted for completing it,
- the available reward for the HIT,
- no of HITs available for the batch,
- and for partially completed batches, the payment per hour made to workers so far.

Requesters may also provide potential workers with a sample HIT so that they know what they will need to do.

7.4   Notes on the MediaEval 2011 RSR HIT

There was no qualification requirement for the HIT. However, workers had to have a 90% acceptance rate by requesters for their previous work. A small scale initial run received negative feedback because the reward payment was judged to be too low for the work required. Increasing the reward for a subsequent batch of HITs fixed this problem. Also, indicating that the work was being carried out for a non profit organisation (a university) meant that workers were more willing to accept the level of payment on offer.

Workers were allowed to select their own bonus from several available to reflect the quality of their work. Workers were generally found to be honest and good judges of the bonus their work deserved, interestingly many did not request the maximum available bonus payment.

Some problems were encountered due to the need to play an external video. these included:

- issues with the worker's browser.
- issues with their equipment, e.g. audio playback.
- issues with bandwidth required to play the video.

Workers were allowed to indicate if they were unable to find one of the target speech acts in the video they were given: In which case they did not need to complete the HIT form. Subsequent checking showed that they were generally correct in their judgement. However, some spamming of the HIT was found. In these cases workers were clearly not attempting to complete the HIT properly, and they were not paid in these cases. In some cases workers had completed the HIT, but their work was not found to be useable in the RSR task. In these cases, since they had clearly honestly attempted to complete the task, payment was made. Overall the use of this HIT for development of the MediaEval 2011 RSR was found to be successful, with a general conclusion being that AMT workers are able to untake carefully designed creative tasks. A mode detailed description of the design of the MediaEval 2011 RSR test collection is contained in [6].

8   Resources Available to Support Use of Crowdsourcing

A large number of resources are available from the Crowdsourcing News, Events, and Resources website maintained by Matt Lease at: `http://ir.ischool.utexas.edu/crowd`. This includes slides from conference and workshop tutorials and keynotes, lists of recommended readings, etc. The CrowdScope wiki providing links useful links to crowdsourcing resources is available at `http://crowdscope.org/`.

Acknowledgements. Some of the background material on crowdsourcing for information retrieval draws on presentations by Matt Lease and Omar Alonso, and is used with permission. Thanks to Matt Lease and Martha Larson for invaluable discussions on the topic of crowdsourcing. Many thanks to Maria Eskevich for providing the screen shots for the MediaEval 2011 Rich Speech Retrieval task crowdsourcing example. This work was supported by Science Foundation Ireland (Grant 08/RFP/CMS1677) Research Frontiers Programme 2008 and (Grant 07/CE/I1142) as part of the Centre for Next Generation Localisation (CNGL) project at DCU.

References

1. Alonso, O., Rose, D.E., Stewart, B.: Crowdsourcing for relevance evaluation. SIGIR Forum 42(2), 9–15 (2008)
2. Ambati, V., Vogel, S., Carbonell, J.: Active learning and crowd-sourcing for machine translation. In: Proceedings of the Seventh International Conference on Language Resources and Evaluation (LREC 2012), pp. 2169–2174 (2010)
3. Callison-Burch, C.: Fast, cheap, and creative: Evaluating translation quality using Amazon's Mechanical Turk. In: Proceedings of the 2009 Conference on Empirical Methods in Natural Language Processing (EMNLP 2009), pp. 286–295 (2009)
4. Callison-Burch, C., Dredze, M.: Creating speech and language data with Amazon's Mechanical Turk. In: Proceedings of the NAACL HLT 2010 Workshop on Creating Speech and Language Data with Amazon's Mechanical Turk (CSLDAMT 2010), pp. 1–12. Association for Computational Linguistics, Stroudsburg (2010)
5. Doan, A., Ramakrishnan, R., Halevy, A.Y.: Crowdsourcing systems on the World-Wide Web. Communications of the ACM 54(4), 86–96 (2011)
6. Eskevich, M., Jones, G.J.F., Larson, M., Ordelman, R.: Creating a Data Collection for Evaluating Rich Speech Retrieval. In: Proceedings of the Eighth International Conference on Language Resources and Evaluation (LREC 2012), Istanbul, Turkey (2012)
7. Evanini, K., Higgins, D., Zechner, K.: Using Amazon Mechanical Turk for transcription of non-native speech. In: Proceedings of the NAACL HLT 2010 Workshop on Creating Speech and Language Data with Amazon's Mechanical Turk (CSLDAMT 2010), pp. 53–56. Association for Computational Linguistics (2010)

8. Goto, M., Ogata, J.: Podcastle: Recent advances of a spoken document retrieval service improved by anonymous user contributions. In: Proceedings of Interspeech 2011 (2011)
9. Grady, C., Lease, M.: Crowdsourcing document relevance assessment with Mechanical Turk. In: Proceedings of the NAACL HLT 2010 Workshop on Creating Speech and Language Data with Amazon's Mechanical Turk (CSLDAMT 2010), pp. 172–179. Association for Computational Linguistics (2010)
10. Horton, J.J.: Employer expectations, peer effects and productivity: Evidence from a series of field experiments. CoRR, abs/1008.2437 (2010)
11. Ipeirotis, P.G., Provost, F., Sheng, V., Wang, J.: Repeated Labeling Using Multiple Noisy Labelers. SSRN eLibrary (2010)
12. Kittur, A., Chi, E.H., Suh, B.: Crowdsourcing user studies with Mechanical Turk. In: Proceedings of the 2008 Conference on Human Factors in Computing Systems (CHI 2008), pp. 453–456. ACM (2008)
13. Kunchukuttan, A., Roy, S., Patel, P., Ladha, K., Gupta, S., Khapra, M.M., Bhattacharyya, P.: Experiences in resource generation for machine translation through crowdsourcing. In: Proceedings of the Eighth International Conference on Language Resources and Evaluation (LREC 2012), Istanbul, Turkey (2012)
14. Lane, I., Waibel, A., Eck, M., Rottmann, K.: Tools for collecting speech corpora via Mechanical-Turk. In: Proceedings of the NAACL HLT 2010 Workshop on Creating Speech and Language Data with Amazon's Mechanical Turk (CSLDAMT 2010), pp. 184–187. Association for Computational Linguistics (2010)
15. Larson, M., Eskevich, M., Ordelman, R., Kofler, C., Schmiedeke, S., Jones, G.J.F.: Overview of Mediaeval 2011 Rich Speech Retrieval Task and Genre Tagging Task. In: MediaEval 2011 Workshop Notes Proceedings, vol. 807. CEUR-WS.org (2011)
16. Larson, M., Soleymani, M., Eskevich, M., Serdyukov, P., Ordelman, R., Jones, G.J.F.: The Community and the Crowd: Multimedia Benchmark Dataset Development. IEEE Multimedia 19(3), 15–23 (2012)
17. Lasecki, W.S., Miller, C.D., Sadilek, A., Abumoussa, A., Borrello, D., Kushalnagar, R., Bigham, J.P.: Real-time captioning by groups of non-experts. In: Proceedings of 25th ACM Symposium on User Interface Software and Technology (UIST 2012), pp. 23–34. ACM, Cambridge (2012)
18. Liao, S., Wu, C., Huerta, J.M.: Evaluating human correction quality for machine translation from crowdsourcing. In: Recent Advances in Natural Language Processing (RANLP 2011), pp. 598–603 (2011)
19. Lloret, E., Plaza, L., Aker, A.: Analyzing the capabilities of crowdsourcing services for text summarization. In: Language Resources and Evaluation (LRE) (2012)
20. Marge, M., Banerjee, S., Rudnicky, A.I.: Using the Amazon Mechanical Turk for transcription of spoken language. In: Proceedings of the IEEE International Conference on Acoustics, Speech, and Signal Processing (ICASSP 2010), pp. 5270–5273. IEEE (2010)
21. Mason, W., Watts, D.J.: Financial incentives and the "performance of crowds". In: Proceedings of the ACM SIGKDD Workshop on Human Computation (HCOMP 2009), pp. 77–85. ACM, New York (2009)
22. McGraw, I., Cyphers, S., Pasupat, P., Liu, J., Glass, J.: Automating crowd-supervised learning for spoken language systems. In: Proceedings of Interspeech 2012 (2012)

23. Novotney, S., Callison-Burch, C.: Cheap, fast and good enough: automatic speech recognition with non-expert transcription. In: The 2010 Annual Conference of the North American Chapter of the Association for Computational Linguistics: Human Language Technologies (HLT 2010), pp. 207–215. Association for Computational Linguistics, Stroudsburg (2010)
24. Ogata, J., Goto, M.: PodCastle: Collaborative training of language models on the basis of the wisdom of crowds. In: Proceedings of Interspeech 2012 (2012)
25. Paolacci, G., Chandler, J., Ipeirotis, P.G.: Running Experiments on Amazon Mechanical Turk. Judgment and Decision Making 5(5), 411–419 (2010)
26. Parent, G., Eskenazi, M.: Speaking to the Crowd: looking at past achievements in using crowdsourcing for speech and predicting future challenges. In: Proceedings of Interspeech 2011, pp. 3037–3040 (2011)
27. Pickard, G., Pan, W., Rahwan, I., Cebrian, M., Crane, R., Madan, A., Pentland, A.: Time-critical social mobilization. Science 334(6055), 509–512 (2011)
28. Rashtchian, C., Young, P., Hodosh, M., Hockenmaier, J.: Collecting image annotations using Amazon's Mechanical Turk. In: Proceedings of the NAACL HLT 2010 Workshop on Creating Speech and Language Data with Amazon's Mechanical Turk (CSLDAMT 2010), pp. 139–147. Association for Computational Linguistics, Stroudsburg (2010)
29. Rayker, V.C., Yu, S., Zhao, L.H., Hermosillo Valadez, G., Floring, C., Bogoni, L., May, L.: Learning from crowds. Journal of Machine Learning Research 11, 1297–1322 (2010)
30. Ross, J., Irani, L., Silberman, M.S., Zaldivar, A., Tomlinson, B.: Who are the crowdworkers?: shifting demographics in Mechanical Turk. In: Proceedings of the 28th of the International Conference Extended Abstracts on Human Factors in Computing Systems (CHI EA 2010), pp. 2863–2872. ACM, New York (2010)
31. Sheng, V.S., Provost, F., Ipeirotis, P.G.: Get another label? improving data quality and data mining using multiple, noisy labelers. In: Proceedings of the 14th ACM SIGKDD International Conference on Knowledge Discovery and Data Mining (KDD 2008), pp. 614–622. ACM, New York (2008)
32. Snoek, C.G., Freiburg, B., Oomen, J., Ordelman, R.: Crowdsourcing rock n' roll multimedia retrieval. In: Proceedings of the 18th ACM International Conference on Multimedia (ACM MM 2010), pp. 1535–1538. ACM (2010)
33. Snow, R., O'Connor, B., Jurafsky, D., Ng, A.Y.: Cheap and fast — but is it good?: Evaluating non-expert annotations for natural language tasks. In: Proceedings of the Conference on Empirical Methods in Natural Language Processing (EMNLP 2008), pp. 254–263. Association for Computational Linguistics, Stroudsburg (2008)
34. Soleymani, M., Larson, M.: Crowdsourcing for Affective Annotation of Video: Development of a Viewer-reported Boredom Corpus. In: Carvalho, V., Lease, M., Yilmaz (eds.) Proceedings of the SIGIR 2010 Workshop on Crowdsourcing for Search Evaluation (CSE 2010). ACM (2010)
35. Sorokin, A., Forsyth, D.: Utility data annotation with Amazon Mechanical Turk. In: Proceedings of the First IEEE Workshop on Internet Vision at CVPR 2008, pp. 1–8. IEEE (2008)
36. von Ahn, L.: Games with a Purpose. Computer 39(6), 92–94 (2006)
37. von Ahn, L., Dabbish, L.: Labeling images with a computer game. In: Proceedings of the SIGCHI Conference on Human Factors in Computing Systems (CHI 2004), pp. 319–326. ACM, New York (2004)
38. Wang, J., Ipeirotis, P.G., Provost, F.: Managing crowdsourcing workers. In: Proceedings of the Winter Conference on Business Intelligence (2011)

39. Willett, W., Heer, J., Agrawala, M.: Strategies for crowdsourcing social data analysis. In: Proceedings of the 2012 ACM Annual Conference on Human Factors in Computing Systems (CHI 2012), pp. 227–236. ACM, New York (2012)
40. Wu, S.-Y., Thawonmas, R., Chen, K.-T.: Video summarization via crowdsourcing. In: Extended Abstracts on Human Factors in Computing Systems (CHI 2011), pp. 1531–1536. ACM (2011)
41. Yan, T., Kumar, V., Ganesan, D.: Crowdsearch: exploiting crowds for accurate real-time image search on mobile phones. In: Proceedings of the 8th International Conference on Mobile Systems, Applications, and Services (MobiSys 2010), pp. 77–90. ACM, New York (2010)

Medical (Visual) Information Retrieval

Henning Müller[1,2]

[1] University of Applied Sciences Western Switzerland (HES–SO),
[2] University and University Hospitals of Geneva (HUG), Switzerland
henning.mueller@hevs.ch

Abstract. This text gives a broad overview of the domain of visual medical information retrieval and medical information analysis/search in general. The goal is to describe the specifics of medical information analysis and more specifically of medical visual information retrieval in this book of the PROMISE winter school. The text is meant to deliver an annotated bibliography of important papers and tendencies in the domain that can then guide the reader to find more detailed information on this quickly developing research domain. This text is by no means a systematic review in the field, so some citations might be subjective but should lead the reader to further publications. The given references will provide a solid starting point for exploring the domain of medical visual information retrieval.

Keywords: Medical information retrieval, content–based image retrieval, medical visual information retrieval.

1 Introduction

Medical practice relies on data available on patients and usually tries to find evidence for or against specific diagnosis leading to further examinations or treatment [1, 2]. Decisions are thus often taken based on probabilities for or against a specific diagnosis. The more medical knowledge becomes available the more complex the relationships between the data and a potential outcome become. Modern medicine is thus increasingly producing data that can be treated by computers and the types of tests also change quickly over time. The amount of data produced per patient in modern hospitals has increased strongly over the past 30 years as has the amount of medical knowledge published in the scientific literature [3]. Medical imaging is in large part responsible for the data growth as modern tomographic devices produce ever thinner slices and also temporal sequences leading to an explosion of visual data produced. It is estimated that around 30% of world storage capacity is dedicated to medical imaging and that mammography in the United States alone accounted for over 2 Petabytes in 2009 [4]. Analyzing such large amounts of data now requires computerized tools to remain efficient and particularly good processing infrastructures for computation [5]. Currently most use of the data is per patient but it has become clear that reusing the data to find connections and help solving cases with data of

M. Agosti et al. (Eds.): PROMISE Winter School 2012, LNCS 7757, pp. 155–166, 2013.

other past cases can improve current care. Secondary use of medical data has thus been discussed many times [6, 7].

This article has the aim to introduce medical information retrieval in general as a domain but with a clear focus on retrieving visual information. Also for the retrieval of visual information many techniques from text retrieval are used and thus a general introduction is given and references to medical text retrieval. Then, the more detailed analysis is on the search for visual medical data.

Medical information retrieval has always been an active domain of information retrieval research [8] and many studies have been performed on the information searching behavior of physicians [9–11] showing that there are many information needs in clinical practice but that time is often too short for detailed search. Many physicians have regular information needs during clinical work, teaching preparation and research activities [9, 12]. Studies showed that the time for answering an information need with MedLine is around 30 minutes [11], while clinicians state to have approximately five minutes available [10]. Besides clear information needs there is also often a need to find similar cases, for differential diagnosis and also for cases–based reasoning [13].

Existing medical retrieval engines include the health on the net web page[1] for professional and also public access to health information. Professional access to the literature is given with the PubMed[2] search system that offers many access possibilities to the scientific biomedical literature including manual annotation of the articles with MeSH terms oragnized by the American National Library of Medicine. Medical search engines targeting radiologists but relying on text for research are Goldminer[3] [14] and Yottalook[4]

Section 2 describes basic tools used to analyze medical texts, Section 3 details the main visual search techniques and approaches and finally Section 4 discusses the text critically with its main findings and ideas for future directions.

2   Medical Information Analysis and Retrieval

As said in the introduction, textual medical information retrieval is a mature domain with many techniques and applications available [8]. This domain deals with the analysis of medical texts in general and very often with extracting information from medical texts for further analysis. Natural language processing has for many years resulted in extracting information from medical texts [3, 15, 16] and sometimes mapping this information onto medical ontologies [17] to increase the value of extracted information. In general, medical ontologies have been created for many years to allow for higher quality coding of diagnoses, acts, and events of clinical practice. MeSH (Medical Subject Headings) is a terminology used to annotate PubMed scientific articles, UMLS (Unified Medical Language System) is a metathesaurus containing a large number of terminologies and in

---

[1] http://www.hon.ch/

[2] http://www.pubmed.gov/

[3] http://goldminer.arrs.org/

[4] http://www.yottalook.com/

radiology RadLex is a standard terminoly for use in radiology reports [18]. All these terminologies have links between the items and allow for exploiting semantic analysis. The LinkedLifeData[5] combines these terminologies and several others in a semantic repository that can also be used for extracting information from medical texts. Medical interoperability for data exchange can then rely on the many existing standards [19] to make sure that all partners in a particular health system actually understand the same standards and units when comparing information that has been shared. The National Library of Medicine in the United States is one of the largest actors in health data analysis and retrieval and much research is performed here. This includes text search engines [20] as well as approaches for the retrieval of images [21].

Many parts of medical information retrieval actually use the same principals as general text retrieval [22, 23]. The main particularities are really linked to a detailed analysis of terminologies and the sometimes big differences of medical language in several countries. This means that non–standard abbreviations are frequently used and in some languages latin forms are used, sometimes in combination or to replace normal language forms.

3   Medical Visual Information Retrieval

Several review articles give a much more complete view of the domain and the current tendencies than this somewhat subjective annotated bibliography [24–26]. Early articles mentioning content–based medical image retrieval are [27–29].

3.1   Techniques

The basis for most visual retrieval applications are components for describing the images, or visual features, indexing and storage methods that allow for fast data access also with large databases, distance measures to compare two images or cases and then user interface components that allow presenting results to the user and interacting to optimize the shown results based on feedback obtained from users. Figure 1 shows this basic system layout with its components. Several of these components can include machine learning approaches such as the visual features or the distance measures that strongly depend on the type of data, and there are also many pre–processing steps that can be used to normalize the images for better comparison.

Most of the techniques used in medical image retrieval are broadly similar to techniques employed in non–medical systems. Detailed description of non–medical content–based image retrieval systems can be found in [30, 31]. One of the differences is clearly that medical text processing is quite advanced and that medical images can not really be analyzed without having their textual context. General images can often be analyzed with respect to simple objects or what is *in* the image whereas the context is also require to better integrate what the image is *about* or even what a picture invokes in people [32].

---

[5] http://www.linkedlifedata.com/

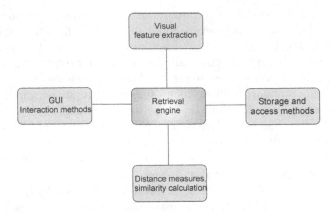

Fig. 1. Overview of the principal components of content–based image retrieval systems

3.2   Applications

Visual medical information retrieval has remained for a long time a purely academic domain with most systems not even tested in clinical routine. One notable example for a small user test in a real clinical setting is [33] that used image retrieval for radiologists in diagnosing interstitial lung diseases showing that particularly inexperienced users gain from getting additional images through visual information retrieval. There are a few retrieval systems that are rather made for browsing in broad databases but these systems offer generally only a low quality [29]. On the other hand many systems were developed for specific applications such as interstitial lung diseases [33, 34], spine images [35] or the liver [36]. A detailed overview of applications and also interfaces of medical image retrieval is given in [37]. A typical screenshot of a medical content–based image retrieval system can be seen in 2, showing the retrieved images to a visual query in a grid layout sorted by similarity.

Another screenshot can be seen in Figure 3 showing the Goldminer radiology search system. Here the images are shown in connection with the articles in which they appear highlighting the need for context and also the fact that most often cases are search for in clinical settings and not really single images without this context.

3.3   Evaluation of Visual and Textual Medical Information Retrieval

Within the Cross Language Evaluation Forum (CLEF[6]) an image retrieval task started in 2003 and a medical image retrieval task was added for 2004 [38]. This contest evaluates the quality of textual and visual information retrieval systems for medical texts with a focus on images and on multilingual retrieval. Varying data sets have been used over the ten years of its existence, starting with teaching files [39], then radiology journal articles and finally articles of the medical open

---

[6] http://www.clef-campaign.org/

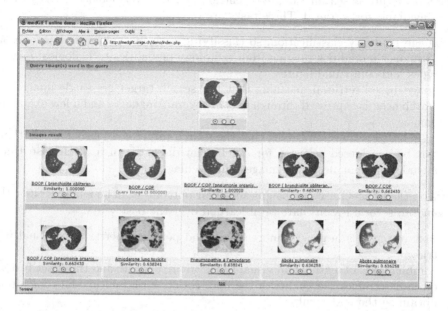

Fig. 2. A screenshot of a typical medical image retrieval system showing the image results in a matrix ordered by similarity score and the diagnosis of the cases, including a link towards the case and the image in full resolution

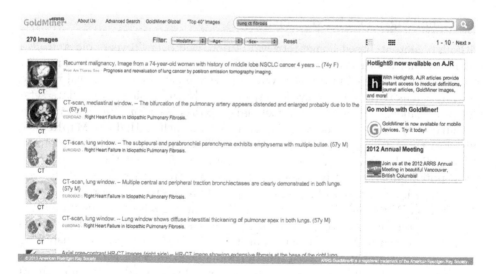

Fig. 3. Screenshot of the Goldminer radiology search engine with a list of images found for a textual search term in connection with the article in which they appear; visual search is not possible in this system

access literature based on PubMed Central. In 2012 over 300'000 images were made available for retrieval. Three tasks are offered:

- image modality classification, so classifying each journal figure into one of 38 images modalities ranging from radiology modalities to biological image types and compound figures;
- image–based retrieval, meaning that the search target are single images; a search need is expressed through text in several languages and a few example images;
- case–based retrieval, meaning that the search target is a journal article that can be considered relevant for differential diagnosis of a given case that includes an anamnesis and images but no diagnosis.

More on the ImageCLEF campaigns and their outcomes can be found in [40, 41]. In general, several lessons have been learned over the past years:

- text retrieval is in general more stable and performs better than visual retrieval;
- combinations of textual and visual retrieval are delicate and the exact fusion often determines the quality of the final results with multimodal runs often obtaining the best results;
- approaches based on various types of visual words most often outperform all other approaches for visual retrieval;
- modality information and other classification–based outcomes can be used well to improve the retrieval results.

3.4   Challenges and Next Steps

Although content–based image retrieval is now well over 20 years old and also medical visual information retrieval over 15 years, still many challenges remain or have been uncovered in the past years as system get closer to clinical routine and physicians request new ways to navigate in the increasingly large data sets. One real challenge are clearly extremely large data sets or *big data* as very few of the current approaches scale well [42]. Approaches such as Hadoop/MapReduce exist but then still need to be adapted to the Terabytes produced in hospitals. What makes things worse in medical imaging is the fact that the *regions of interest* potentially relevant for a specific disease are often extremely small. Search by region of interest is one of the most frequently requested functionality of radiologists [43]. Ways to find out more about potential regions of interest in images can be eye tracking as seen in Figure 4. The images show clearly that the regions actually observed in detail are small and for most imaging types and suspected diseases we can probably create probability maps on whether it can potentially be a region of interest or not. This could potentially also reduce the amount of data to be treated and also transmitted to ease the burden of big data.

Another area that has been touched in ImageCLEF but will require much further research is *case–based retrieval* that also includes images in addition to free text and structured data. Case descriptions or journal articles often include

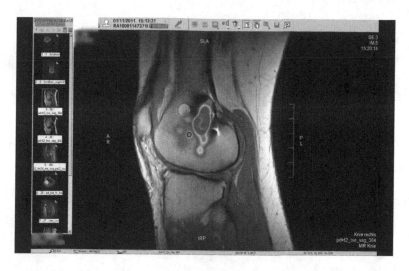

Fig. 4. A screenshot of a test with eye tracking equipment, show that regions of interest or volumes of interest are often rather small

incomplete data and images taken for similar cases might vary between hospitals. The interactions and dependencies between images and clinical data are equally important and much has still to be learned. First publications on case–based retrieval exist in [44–46]. Something that could well help in this respect is a good annotation or coding of images that would allow the use of semantics. In radiology the RadLex standard [18] is an important step into this direction, and this plus the automatic extraction of semantic features can help much for the future. This would also allow to check data consistency and also contradictions using the large body of knowledge of the LinkedLifeData[7].

Currently the by far strongest increase in medical imaging are *multidimensional tomographic* series, including a variety of modalities from CT (Computed Tomography), to MRI (Magnetic Resonance Imaging) and PET (Photon Emission Tomography) and combinations of these such as PET/CT. The increasingly thin slices create more detail and make viewing more difficult but offer many new possibilities for real 3D information retrieval [45, 47, 48]. Such solid 3D texture analysis can help to highlight regions of interest for physicians in volumes and make viewing easier. In the case of 4D data even the simple viewing becomes hard and so there is a read added value in making the data accessible in an easier way [49] 4D data sets can be 3D series with a time component or in the case of dual energy CT that creates 10 volumes of a body region imaged with varying energy levels that can potentially be useful in clinical application but go well beyond human vision.

Figure 5 shows an example of a 3D texture classification system that can be used as diagnosis aid. The different tissue types of the lung are shown in colored regions and can then be visualized in 3D allowing to explore the model or via a

---

[7] http://www.linkedlifedata.com/

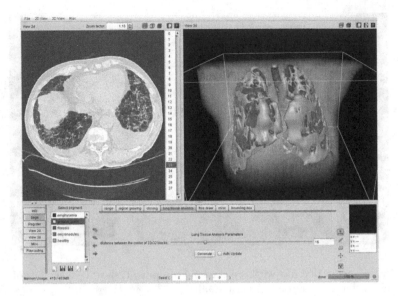

Fig. 5. A web–based interface of a system for diagnosis aid on lung diseases; the texture is classified into different classes and then shown in various 3D views

standard color overlay in a grey scale slice view. This can help physicians viewing images quicker. In general visualization is an extremely hot topic and important in radiology to be able to analyze images quickly. The Osirix[8] viewer is another important example allowing various views on the data and many plugins or tools for specific applications.

4   Discussion and Conclusions

This text gives a broad overview of medical information retrieval with a clear focus on the retrieval of visual information. The idea is to present an annotated bibliography and help getting a quick access to current developments in this field. This text is not a systematic review and thus some of the citations may be arbitrary but they do present current developments in the field and several classical review articles as well. Medical information retrieval has been a busy field for over 40 years and for medical visual information retrieval this has also been the case for 15 years. The way in which medicine moves towards an increasingly information rich field will make it necessary to develop new tools to make stored knowledge accessible and usable by physicians. Before images and their metadata will be fully integrated into information retrieval and clinical decision support I still expect several research rich years.

---

[8] http://www.osirix-viewer.com/

Acknowledgments. This work was funded by the European Union in the context of the KHRESMOI (257528) and PROMISE (258191) FP7 projects. The PROMISE winter school was also funded by the ELIAS (ESF) project making this document possible.

References

1. Simel, D., Drummond, R.: The rational clinical examination: evidence–based clinical diagnosis. McGraw-Hill (August 2008)
2. Bui, A.A.T., Taira, R.K., Dionision, J.D.N., Aberle, D.R., El-Saden, S., Kangarloo, H.: Evidence–based radiology. Academic Radiology 9(6), 662–669 (2002)
3. Hunter, L., Cohen, K.B.: Biomedical language processing: What's beyond pubmed? Molecular Cell 21(5), 589–594 (2006)
4. Riding the wave: How europe can gain from the rising tide of scientific data. Submission to the European Comission (October 2010), http://cordis.europa.eu/fp7/ict/e-infrastructure/docs/hlg-sdi-report.pdf
5. Zhang, C., De Sterck, H., Aboulnaga, A., Djambazian, H., Sladek, R.: Case Study of Scientific Data Processing on a Cloud Using Hadoop. In: Mewhort, D.J.K., Cann, N.M., Slater, G.W., Naughton, T.J. (eds.) HPCS 2009. LNCS, vol. 5976, pp. 400–415. Springer, Heidelberg (2010)
6. Safran, C., Bloomrosen, M., Hammond, W.E., Labkoff, S., Markel-Fox, S., Tang, P.C., Detmer, D.E.: Toward a national framework for the secondary use of health data: An american medical informatics association white paper. MIM 14, 1–9 (2007)
7. Elger, B., Iavindrasana, J., Iacono, L.L., Müller, H., Roduit, N., Summers, P., Wright, J.: Strategies for health data exchange for secondary, cross–institutional clinical research. Computer Methods and Programs in Biomedicine 99(3), 230–251 (2010)
8. Hersh, W.: Information Retrieval — A health and Biomedical Perspective, 2nd edn. Springer (2003)
9. Hersh, W., Jensen, J., Müller, H., Gorman, P., Ruch, P.: A qualitative task analysis for developing an image retrieval test collection. In: ImageCLEF/MUSCLE Workshop on Image Retrieval Evaluation, Vienna, Austria, pp. 11–16 (2005)
10. Hoogendam, A., de Vries Robbé, P.F., Overbeke, A.J.: Answers to questions posed during daily patient care are more likely to be answered by uptodate than pubmed. Journal of Medical Internet Research 10(4) (2008)
11. Hersh, W.R., Hickam, D.H.: How well do physicians use electronic information retrieval systems? Journal of the American Medical Association 280(15), 1347–1352 (1998)
12. Müller, H., Despont-Gros, C., Hersh, W., Jensen, J., Lovis, C., Geissbuhler, A.: Health care professionals' image use and search behaviour. In: Proceedings of the Medical Informatics Europe Conference (MIE 2006), pp. 24–32. IOS Press, Studies in Health Technology and Informatics, Maastricht, The Netherlands (2006)
13. Glasgow, J., Jurisica, I.: Integration of case–based and image–based reasoning. In: AAAI Workshop on Case–Based Reasoning Integrations, pp. 67 74. AAAI Press, Menlo Park (1998)
14. Kahn Jr., C., Thao, C.: Goldminer: A radiology image search engine. American Journal of Roentgenology 188, 1475–1478 (2008)

15. Ruch, P., Baud, R., Geissbuhler, A.: Using lexical disambiguation and named–entity recognition to improve spelling correction in the electronique patient record. AIM 29, 169–184 (2003)

16. Franz, P., Zaiss, A., Hahn, U., Schulz, S., Klar, R.: Automated coding of diagnoses – three methods compared. In: Proceedings of the Annual Symposium of the American Society for Medical Informatics (AMIA), Los Angeles, CA, USA (November 2000)

17. Gobeill, J., Theodoro, D., Patsche, E., Ruch, P.: Taking benefit of query and document expansion using MeSH descriptors in medical ImageCLEF 2009. Working Notes of the 2009 CLEF Workshop, Corfu, Greece (September 2009)

18. Lanlotz, C.P.: Radlex: A new method for indexing online educational materials. Radiographics 26, 1595–1597 (2006)

19. Müller, H., Schumacher, M., Godel, D., Khaled, O.A., Mooser, F., Ding, S.: Medicoordination: A practical approach to interoperability in the swiss health system. In: The Medical Informatics Europe Conference (MIE 2009), Sarajevo, Bosnia–Herzegovina, pp. 210–214 (August 2009)

20. Ide, N.C., Loane, R.F., Demner-Fushman, D.: Application of information technology: Essie: A concept–based search engine for structured biomedical text. Journal of the American Medical Informatics Association 14(3), 253–263 (2007)

21. Demner-Fushman, D., Antani, S., Siadat, M.R., Soltanian-Zadeh, H., Fotouhi, F., Elisevich, K.: Automatically finding images for clinical decision support. In: Proceedings of the Seventh IEEE International Conference on Data Mining Workshops, ICDMW 2007, pp. 139–144. IEEE Computer Society, Washington, DC (2007)

22. Salton, G., Buckley, C.: Term weighting approaches in automatic text retrieval. IPM 24(5), 513–523 (1988)

23. van Rijsbergen, C.J.: Information Retrieval. Prentice Hall, Englewood Cliffs (1979)

24. Müller, H., Michoux, N., Bandon, D., Geissbuhler, A.: A review of content–based image retrieval systems in medicine–clinical benefits and future directions. International Journal of Medical Informatics 73(1), 1–23 (2004)

25. Akgül, C., Rubin, D., Napel, S., Beaulieu, C., Greenspan, H., Acar, B.: Content–based image retrieval in radiology: Current status and future directions. Journal of Digital Imaging 24(2), 208–222 (2011)

26. Tang, L.H.Y., Hanka, R., Ip, H.H.S.: A review of intelligent content–based indexing and browsing of medical images. HIJ 5, 40–49 (1999)

27. Lowe, H.J., Antipov, I., Hersh, W., Smith, C.A.: Towards knowledge–based retrieval of medical images. The role of semantic indexing, image content representation and knowledge–based retrieval. In: Proceedings of the Annual Symposium of the American Society for Medical Informatics (AMIA), Nashville, TN, USA, pp. 882–886 (October 1998)

28. Tagare, H.D., Jaffe, C., Duncan, J.: Medical image databases: A content–based retrieval approach. Journal of the American Medical Informatics Association 4(3), 184–198 (1997)

29. Dahmen, J., Theiner, T., Keysers, D., Ney, H., Lehmann, T., Wein, B.: Classification of radiographs in the 'image retrieval in medical applications' — system (IRMA). In: 6th International RIAO Conference on Content-Based Multimedia Information Access, Paris, France, pp. 551–566 (April 2000)

30. Smeulders, A.W.M., Worring, M., Santini, S., Gupta, A., Jain, R.: Content–based image retrieval at the end of the early years. IEEE Transactions on Pattern Analysis and Machine Intelligence 22(12), 1349–1380 (2000)

31. Datta, R., Joshi, D., Li, J., Wang, J.Z.: Image retrieval: Ideas, influences, and trends of the new age. ACM Computing Surveys 40(2), 1–60 (2008)

32. Jörgensen, C.: Retrieving the unretrievable in electronic imaging systems: emotions, themes and stories. In: Rogowitz, B., Pappas, T.N. (eds.) Human Vision and Electronic Imaging IV, San Jose, California, USA, January 23-29. SPIE Proc., vol. 3644. SPIE Photonics West Conference (1999)

33. Aisen, A.M., Broderick, L.S., Winer-Muram, H., Brodley, C.E., Kak, A.C., Pavlopoulou, C., Dy, J., Shyu, C.R., Marchiori, A.: Automated storage and retrieval of thin–section CT images to assist diagnosis: System description and preliminary assessment. Radiology 228(1), 265–270 (2003)

34. Depeursinge, A., Sage, D., Hidki, A., Platon, A., Poletti, P.A., Unser, M., Müller, H.: Lung tissue classification using Wavelet frames. In: 29th Annual International Conference of the IEEE Engineering in Medicine and Biology Society, EMBS 2007, Lyon, France, pp. 6259–6262. IEEE Computer Society (2007)

35. Hsu, W., Antani, S., Long, L.R., Neve, L., Thoma, G.R.: Spirs: A web-based image retrieval system for large biomedical databases. International Journal of Medical Informatics 78(suppl. 1), S13–S24 (2009); MedInfo 2007

36. Costa, M.J., Tsymbal, A., Hammon, M., Cavallaro, A., Sühling, M., Seifert, S., Comaniciu, D.: A Discriminative Distance Learning–Based CBIR Framework for Characterization of Indeterminate Liver Lesions. In: Müller, H., Greenspan, H., Syeda-Mahmood, T. (eds.) MCBR-CDS 2011. LNCS, vol. 7075, pp. 92–104. Springer, Heidelberg (2012)

37. Depeursinge, A., Fischer, B., Müller, H., Deserno, T.M.: Prototypes for content–based image retrieval in clinical practice. The Open Medical Informatics Journal 5, 58–72 (2011)

38. Clough, P., Müller, H., Sanderson, M.: The CLEF 2004 Cross-Language Image Retrieval Track. In: Peters, C., Clough, P., Gonzalo, J., Jones, G.J.F., Kluck, M., Magnini, B. (eds.) CLEF 2004. LNCS, vol. 3491, pp. 597–613. Springer, Heidelberg (2005)

39. Hersh, W., Müller, H., Kalpathy-Cramer, J., Kim, E., Zhou, X.: The consolidated ImageCLEFmed medical image retrieval task test collection. Journal of Digital Imaging 22(6), 648–655 (2009)

40. Müller, H., Clough, P., Deselaers, T., Caputo, B. (eds.): ImageCLEF – Experimental Evaluation in Visual Information Retrieval. The Springer International Series on Information Retrieval, vol. 32. Springer, Heidelberg (2010)

41. Kalpathy-Cramer, J., Müller, H., Bedrick, S., Eggel, I., García Seco de Herrera, A., Tsikrika, T.: The CLEF 2011 medical image retrieval and classification tasks. Working Notes of CLEF 2011 (Cross Language Evaluation Forum) (September 2011)

42. Dean, J., Ghemawat, S.: Mapreduce: simplified data processing on large clusters. In: Proceedings of the 6th Conference on Symposium on Opearting Systems Design & Implementation, OSDI 2004, vol. 6, p. 10. USENIX Association, Berkeley (2004)

43. Markonis, D., Holzer, M., Dung, S., Vargas, A., Langs, G., Kriewel, S., Müller, H.: A survey on visual information search behavior and requirements of radiologists. Methods of Information in Medicine (forthcoming 2012)

44. Quellec, G., Lamard, M., Cazuguel, G., Roux, C., Cochener, B.: Case retrieval in medical databases by fusing heterogeneous information. IEEE Transactions on Medical Imaging 30(1), 108–118 (2011)

45. Depeursinge, A., Vargas, A., Platon, A., Geissbuhler, A., Poletti, P.–A., Müller, H.: 3D Case–Based Retrieval for Interstitial Lung Diseases. In: Caputo, B., Müller, H., Syeda-Mahmood, T., Duncan, J.S., Wang, F., Kalpathy-Cramer, J. (eds.) MCBR-CDS 2009. LNCS, vol. 5853, pp. 39–48. Springer, Heidelberg (2010)

46. Zhou, X., Depeursinge, A., Stern, R., Lovis, C., Müller, H.: Case–based visual retrieval of fractures. International Journal of Computer Assisted Radiology and Surgery 5(suppl. 1), 11548/S162–11548/S163 (2010)
47. Depeursinge, A., Zrimec, T., Busayarat, S., Müller, H.: 3D lung image retrieval using localized features. In: Medical Imaging 2011: Computer–Aided Diagnosis. SPIE, vol. 7963, p. 79632E (2011)
48. Funkhouser, T., Min, P., Kazhdan, M., Chen, J., Halderman, A., Dobkin, D., Jacobs, D.: A search engine for 3d models. ACM Transactions on Graphics 22(1), 83–105 (2003)
49. Johnson, T.R.C., Krauß, B., Sedlmair, M., Grasruck, M., Bruder, H., Morhard, D., Fink, C., Weckbach, S., Lenhard, M., Schmidt, B., Flohr, T., Reiser, M.F., Becker, C.R.: Material differentiation by dual energy CT: initial experience. European Radiology 17(6), 1510–1517 (2007)

Is Visualization Usable for Displaying Web Search Results in an Exploratory Search Context?

Aline Crédeville and Dominic Forest

École de bibliothéconomie et des sciences de l'information, Université de Montréal, Canada
{aline.credeville,dominic.forest}@umontreal.ca

Abstract. Information visualization is defined as an interactive and graphic amplifying cognition. Moreover, the field of information retrieval is the original scope of information visualization. Nevertheless, many problems remain. The exploratory research information is presented as a task context conducive to the use of visualization. The research aims to identify the dynamic and interactive graphics that use a search visual interface (versus text), and the gain in terms of usability compared to strategic and tactical requirements of the task of exploratory search on the Web exploratory type. The theoretical, conceptual and methodological framework is presented.

Keywords: information visualization, exploratory search, clustering, usability.

1 Introduction

The search engine has established itself as an almost exclusive means of searching and browsing the web, and its technical and algorithmic performance is widely recognized. However, the "query-result" paradigm has several interactivity limitations and is only appropriate for a limited spectrum of search taxonomies [1]. Indeed, Google's search interface is considered adequate only for 17% of the searches it performs [2]. Considering the broad spectrum of information search taxonomies [2], [3] and information behaviours [4], a new current in scientific research has emerged in the past years that focuses on the interaction between the user and the system rather than the individual analysis of those entities [5], [6]. Indeed, the searching interface has become a focal point for researchers [7]–[10]. For exploratory searching in particular [11], new interfaces are being developed for the benefit of relevant exploratory tactics and strategies [9]. In this respect, visualization of search results appears as a promising device for the information seeking process.

Due to the double interactive and visual-perceptual process it entails [12], [13], visualization is characterized by its tendency to amplify the cognitive faculties deployed by the user for knowledge building, analysis and learning processes [14]. Nevertheless, in the field of information retrieval, the evidence of cognitive amplification is yet to be demonstrated within the exploratory search context.

Thus, our research stands on the crossroads of several challenges. Firstly, although it is known that visualising information aids memorisation and analysis of information

M. Agosti et al. (Eds.): PROMISE Winter School 2012, LNCS 7757, pp. 167–176, 2013.

in general, the means of implementing visually structured search results remains to be determined. Secondly, the new interactive modalities required by the exploratory research process introduce additional dimensions which extend beyond the reach of typical recall and precision metrics. Thirdly, it has not yet been verified that, when compared to other interfaces designed for exploratory search, visual and interactive presentation of results leads to a clear gain over a textual list-based presentation, based on the same clustering algorithm.

The goal of this research is to assess the gain in terms of usability, from the user's point of view, of exploring search results through a visual layout (as opposed to a textual layout) when performing exploratory searches on the Web. Increasing usability of an interface means reducing the cognitive load associated with its use and simplifying the cognitive, affective and physical processes related to the final task of the user.

Because we believe that interactive visualization reduces cognitive load associated with information treatment processes required by cognitive strategies and research tactics in the context of exploratory information search, we assert that it can benefit the user's investigation and discovery processes beyond the known positive effects of clustered results [15].

Our research aims to evaluate the usability of visualization in the context of exploratory information search on the web. To accomplish this, we wish, through heuristic analysis and controlled experimentation by simulating tasks related to exploratory information search, to:

- Identify the graphical and interactive functional factors of visualization that have an impact on the process of exploratory information searching
- Correlate visualization and exploratory information searching in terms of usability on the basis of identifiable search strategies and interactive views, according to either the user's proficiency in a particular field of knowledge or his expertise in information searching
- Through interaction between the user and the context-related visualization device, define what represents a gain or an obstacle in the process of exploratory information search, in particular with respect to the user's own strategies and tactics

2   Litterature Review

2.1   Exploratory Search

Marchionini [11] and White and Roth [16] have modeled the exploratory search process by providing perspective on the iterative and non-linear dynamics between different cognitive strategies and associated search tactics.

This model highlights interactions between different strategies and their associated tactics. Among exploratory search tactics, several behavioural information search models, such as the « berry-picking model » by Bates [17], the « sense-making model» by Dervin [18], and « information foraging » by Pirolli et Card [19] can be recognized.

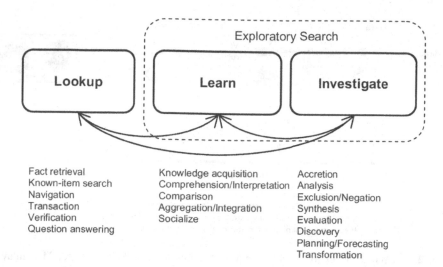

Fact retrieval
Known-item search
Navigation
Transaction
Verification
Question answering

Knowledge acquisition
Comprehension/Interpretation
Comparison
Aggregation/Integration
Socialize

Accretion
Analysis
Exclusion/Negation
Synthesis
Evaluation
Discovery
Planning/Forecasting
Transformation

Fig. 1. Exploratory search model based on Marchionini [11] (Source: White and Roth [16] p. 14, reprinted with permission)

The main learning strategy partly reminds us of Kulthau's more general process [20], [21] which consists in reducing cognitive and affective uncertainties by providing new information to address a gap or a weakness in the state of knowledge.

The process of exploratory information, aimed explicitly at the acquisition of new knowledge, is a typical example of this type of process [1]. Thus, with respect to these cognitive challenges, the « query-response » paradigm that dominates the search engine environment is considered inefficient, if not detrimental.

Since 2006, an increasing number of scientific meetings (EESS2006 ; ESI2007; HCIR2010; WISI2010) are being organized to discuss the main challenges associated with exploratory information search: interactivity and evaluation. Two types of interface are emerging to support exploratory information search: faceted interfaces such as mSpace [22] and visual interfaces such as Carrot2Search [23].

2.2   Search Results Visualization

The visualization of search results is a device for visualising information that consists in displaying the results that match a user's query in a graphical and dynamic manner, and proposing a device that facilitates navigation within these results through interactive views.

The visualization of information (fig 2) is an interactive device acting as an external cognitive aid [24]. Graphical and interactive representation of results aims at revealing dominant themes or informational motives that characterize the results, in the same manner that performing a mathematical calculation in writing relieves the cognitive load of mental calculation on the memory.

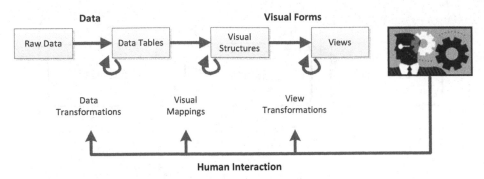

Fig. 2. Reference model for information visualization process (Source: Card, Mackinlay et Shneiderman [14] p. 17 reprinted with permission)

To accomplish this, visualization of search results is designed with the aid of clustering algorithms originating from the field of text searching. The web has and will continue to bring numerous challenges regarding the structuring of search results [23]. To this day, unsupervised clustering algorithms (Suffix Tree Clustering, k-means) can be adapted to the dynamics, the heterogeneity and the size of the web. Moreover, this structuring process, with or without downstream visualization, is known to facilitate investigation and discovery within large masses of textual material. As a result of these properties, visualization helps the knowledge crystallization process.

This crystallization process (fig 3) calls for tactics and strategies that are similar to those of exploratory information search. Interactive viewing allows direct manipulation of the graphic representation in order to enable analytical and investigatory processing of results, thus providing an insight into the state of knowledge available on the web on a particular subject.

However, beneath the surface of visualization's generic principles, the application of visualization in the environment of search results remains problematic. Some openly criticize the use of this device on search results given the textual nature of information [8]. In the commercial sector, two important players have been forced to cease their operations as visual meta-search engines: Kartoo and Grokker. On several occasions, in a general context or with reference to information search, researchers [25]–[27] report similar findings concerning visualization: challenges include a lack of understanding of the cognitive processes involved, scalability issues associated with the variable size of the information mass to be processed, and difficulties related to categorization and labelling of search results [23].

On a more fundamental level, a major obstacle to the establishment of this device is the absence of an authoritative evaluation method [28]. Although the theoretical principle of cognitive amplification is agreed upon, its application is based on a multidimensional analysis, where a deep understanding of the interaction between the user and the system is essential. The question is then: how to evaluate the impact of interactive views on the user experience of information seeking process?

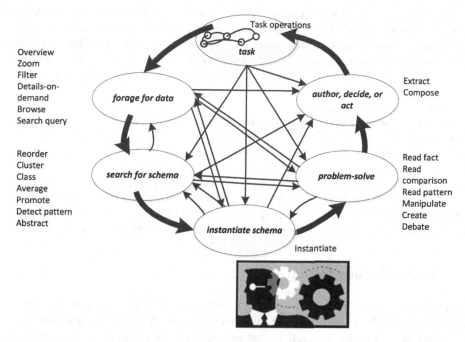

Overview
Zoom
Filter
Details-on-
demand
Browse
Search query

Reorder
Cluster
Class
Average
Promote
Detect pattern
Abstract

Extract
Compose

Read fact
Read
comparison
Read pattern
Manipulate
Create
Debate

Instantiate

Fig. 3. Knowledge crystallization during information visualization process (Source: Card, Mackinlay et Shneiderman [14] reprinted with permission)

2.3   Evaluation of Search Results Visualization

The evaluation of a system aims to assess its capacity to satisfy a user according to chosen criteria [29]. In the fields of both scientific research and innovation, evaluation serves the role of a barometer that is able to validate the quality of a system with respect to different criteria, such as performance, satisfaction, usefulness or usability. The objective, the context, the task at hand and the stage of maturity of the system are all relevant criteria for selecting a scenario and an evaluative approach [30]. Traditionally, information retrieval systems were evaluated through performance, a system-centered criterion, by measuring the system's recall and precision rates [31]. The interdependency between the interactions generated by the system's use and the information seeking process performed by the user makes placing the user at the core of the evaluation process essential.

Evaluating the visualization of search results will address the requirements of the task at hand as well as those of the exploratory search and of the visualization process. To perform this assessment, we aim to take advantage of the shared nature of visualization and information seeking processes, as summarized by Zhang [32], and to gauge the added value of the visualization device. Several evaluation methods are in use, although none have earned general recognition [33]. To evaluate the user experience with respect to a given task, it is recommended to assess device usability [30]

In practice, it appears that few usability studies have been conducted to this date [25], [34], [35] and that controlled, user-centric experiments are currently the preferred approach. The latter offer the advantage of precise and generalizable results [28]. Most are focused on method evaluation and measuring the impacts of individual characteristics (gender, spatial abilities, cognitive style, associative memory). However, the heterogeneity of chosen measures, tasks and visualizations thwarts the process of comparing results [36]. In addition, some case studies and longitudinal studies have been performed; their results are very detailed but remain hardly generalizable. Moreover, although not pertaining specifically to the evaluation of visualization of search results, the usability evaluation framework designed by Wilson [37] establishes measures that allow the assessment of interactive features according to the strategies of exploratory research. The last method for evaluating user experience considered in this research focuses on the insight gained by the user from the visualization of the presented information, rather than on the device and its components. North [38] mentions that these two evaluations are not in opposition but that they are, on the contrary, rather complementary. Indeed, Rester and Pohl's [39] study on the evaluation of a visualization device designed to facilitate exploratory research processes confirms this statement.

3   General Study Design

Our research seeks to evaluate, in terms of usability, the added value of the visualization of search results in the context of exploratory information search on the web. The main hypothesis of this research is that interactive views support the tactics and strategies related to information searching.

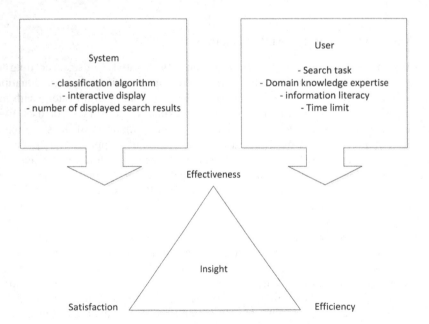

Fig. 4. Design of the usability evaluation of search results visualization

The evaluation framework (fig 4) covers two phases and calls for two experimental exercises. The first phase aims to evaluate the usability of the device through a two-stage process. During the first stage, the interface is inspected for a first time according to heuristics [40]. The second stage implies controlled testing of the interface by two types of users (experts in information search or experts in a field of knowledge) by simulating an exploratory information research task.

In practice, the objective of evaluating the usability of a visualization device for search results is to demonstrate that the different system components (indexing, organization, interactive display) are processing the information required to accomplish the user's task in an efficient, effective and satisfactory manner. Thus, an interface with a high degree of usability is a system that helps reduce the user's cognitive load to a minimum. Several objectives are pursued by evaluating the relative usability of a visualization device. Firstly, the limitations and weaknesses associated with the visualization device within and outside of the information search context will be identified. Secondly, the interface features that are used to support research strategies and tactics will be compared in terms of usability.

The second phase is of a qualitative and investigatory nature. Its aim is to assess the insights the user receives through the use of a visualization device, according to the chosen tactics and strategies of exploratory information search.

The system selected for this experiment is the Carrot2Search engine (fig 5). This system features a textual as well as a visual interface, is based on high-performance automatic classification algorithms and defines itself as open software for academic purposes.

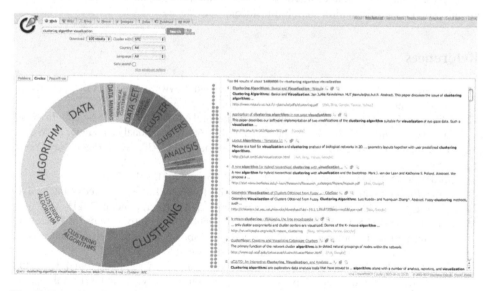

Fig. 5. Example of visual clustered search results interface with the STC algorithm from Carrot2search engine

Several types of expertise are tested simultaneously to shed light on the various factors known to have an impact on the skills required for the use of information visualization and exploratory information search on the web. Thus, the proposed heuristic analysis will be performed by information visualization experts. The experimental phase calls for two types of users: 15 volunteer users that have demonstrated their proficiency in information handling by successfully completing the Information Search coursework at the Library Sciences School of the University of Montreal, as well as 15 users that have proven skills in a field of knowledge related to the task of information search.

4   Conclusion

In theory, visualization constitutes an external cognitive aid. It supports memorisation and the processes of analysis and investigation by highlighting patterns and relationships between various pieces of information. These cognitive properties appear to assist the strategies and tactics required by exploratory information search. This research aims to evaluate, in terms of usability, the added value of a device designed for the visualization of search results within an appropriate context. We hope this work will make three types of contribution to evolving knowledge. Theoretically, we seek empirical evidence confirming the cognitive benefits of visualization in the context of exploratory information search. Methodologically, we aspire to devise effective qualitative metrics for evaluating the visual interface for exploratory information search. Lastly, we wish to formulate practical recommendations for successfully integrating visualization into information search interfaces.

References

1. schraefel, m.c: Building Knowledge: What's beyond Keyword Search? Computer 42(3), 52–59 (2009)
2. White, R.W., Drucker, S.M.: Investigating Behavioral Variability in Web Search. In: Williamson, C., Zurko, M.E. (eds.) Proceedings of the 16th International Conference on World Wide Web (WWW 2007), Banff, Alberta, Canada, pp. 21–30. ACM Press, New York (2007)
3. Broder, A.: A Taxonomy of Web Search. SIGIR Forum 36(2), 3–10 (2002)
4. Wang, P.: Information Behaviour and Seeking. In: Ruthven, I., Kelly, D. (eds.) Interactive Information Seeking, Behaviour and Retrieval, pp. 15–41. Facet, London (2011)
5. Cool, C., Belkin, N.J.: A Classification of Interactions with Information. In: Bruce, H. (ed.) International Conference on Conceptions of Library and Information Science No4 (CoLIS 2004), pp. 1–16. Libraries Unlimited, Greenwood Village (2002)
6. Cool, C., Belkin, N.J.: Interactive information retrieval: history and background. In: Ruthven, I., Kelly, D. (eds.) Interactive Information Seeking, Behaviour and Retrieval, pp. 1–14. Facet, London (2011)
7. Marchionini, G.: Toward Human-Computer Information Retrieval. Bulletin of the American Society for Information Science and Technology 32(5), 20–22 (2006)
8. Hearst, M.A.: Search User Interfaces. Cambridge University Press, New York (2009)

9. Wilson, M.L., Kules, B., Schraefel, m.c, Shneiderman, B.: From Keyword Search to Exploration: Designing Future Search Interfaces for the Web. Foundations and Trends® in Web Science 2(1), 1–97 (2010)

10. Jansen, B.J., Rieh, S.Y.: The Seventeen Theoretical Constructs of Information Searching and Information Retrieval. Journal of the American Society for Information Science and Technology 61(8), 1517–1534 (2010)

11. Marchionini, G.: Exploratory Search: from Finding to Understanding. Communications of the ACM - Supporting Exploratory Search 49(4), 41–46 (2006)

12. Bederson, B., Shneiderman, B.: The Craft of Information Visualization: Readings and Reflections. Morgan Kaufmann Publishers, San Diego (2003)

13. Ware, C.: Information Visualization Perception for Design. Morgan Kaufmann Publishers, San Francisco (2000)

14. Card, S.K., Mackinlay, J.D., Shneiderman, B.: Readings in Information Visualization: Using Vision to Think. Morgan Kaufmann Publishers, San Francisco (1999)

15. Kules, B., Shneiderman, B.: Users Can Change their Web Search Tactics: Design Guidelines for Categorized Overviews. Information Processing and Management 44(2), 463–484 (2008)

16. White, R.W., Roth, R.A.: Exploratory Search: Beyond the Query-Response Paradigm. Morgan & Claypool Publishers, San Rafael (2009)

17. Bates, M.J.: The Design of Browsing and Berrypicking Techniques for the Online Search Interface. Online Information Review 13(5), 407–424 (1989)

18. Dervin, B.: From the Mind's Eye of the User the Sense-making Qualitative-quantitative Methodology. In: Glazier, J.D., Powell, R.D. (eds.) Qualitative Research in Information Management, pp. 61–87. Libraries Unlimited, Englewood (1992)

19. Pirolli, P., Card, S.: Information Foraging. Psychological Review 106, 643–675 (1999)

20. Kuhlthau, C.C.: A Principle of Uncertainty for Information Seeking. Journal of Documentation 49(4), 339–355 (1993)

21. Kuhlthau, C.C., Heinström, J., Todd, R.J.: The 'Information Search Process' Revisited: Is the Model still Useful? Information Research 13(4) (2008), http://informationr.net/ir/13-4/paper355.html (accessed October 29, 2012)

22. Smith, D.A., Russell, A., Wilson, M.L., Owens, A., Schraefel, m.c: mSpace.fm (2005), http://mspace.fm/ (accessed October 29, 2012)

23. Carpineto, C., Osiński, S., Romano, G., Weiss, D.: A Survey of Web Clustering Engines. ACM Computing Surveys 41(3), 17:1–17:38 (2009)

24. Norman, D.A.: Things that make us smart. Addison Wesley, Don Mills (1993)

25. Chen, C.: Top 10 Unsolved Information Visualization Problems. IEEE Computer Graphics and Applications, 12–16 (2005)

26. Burkhard, R.A., Andrienko, G., Andrienko, N., Dykes, J., Koutamanis, A., Kienreich, W., Phaal, R., Blackwell, A., Eppler, M., Huang, J., Meagher, M., Grun, A., Lang, S., Perrin, D., Weber, W., Moere, A.V., Herr, B., Börner, K., Fekete, J.-D., Brodbeck, D.: Visualization Summit 2007: ten research goals for 2010. Information Visualization 6(3), 169–188 (2007)

27. Kerren, A., Stasko, J.T., Fekete, J.-D., North, C.: Workshop Report: Information Visualization-Human-Centered Issues in Visual Representation, Interaction, and Evaluation. Information Visualization 6(3), 189–196 (2007)

28. Carpendale, S.: Evaluating Information Visualizations. In: Kerren, A., Stasko, J.T., Fekete, J.-D., North, C. (eds.) Information Visualization. LNCS, vol. 4950, pp. 19–45. Springer, Heidelberg (2008)

29. Al-Maskari, A., Sanderson, M.: A review of factors influencing user satisfaction in information retrieval. Journal of the American Society for Information Science and Technology 61(5), 859–868 (2010)
30. Lam, H., Bertini, E., Isenberg, P., Plaisant, C., Carpendale, S.: Seven Guiding Scenarios for Information Visualization Evaluation. TechReport 2011-992-04. University of Calgary, Calgary (2011)
31. Harman, D.K., Voorhees, E.M.: TREC: An Overview. Annual Review of Information Science and Technology 40, 113–155 (2006)
32. Zhang, J.: Benchmarks and Evaluation Criteria for Information Retrieval Visualization. In: Zhang, J. (ed.) Visualization for Information Retrieval, pp. 239–254. Springer, Heidelberg (2008)
33. Plaisant, C.: The Challenge of Information Visualization Evaluation. In: Costabile, M.F. (ed.) Proceedings of the Working Conference on Advanced Visual Interfaces (AVI 2004), Gallipoli, Italy, pp. 109–116. ACM Press, New York (2004)
34. Freitas, C.M.D.S., Luzzardi, P.R.G., Cava, R.A., Winckler, M., Pimenta, M.S., Nedel, L.P.: On Evaluating Information Visualization Techniques. In: De Marsico, M., Levialdi, S., Panizzi, E. (eds.) Proceedings of the Working Conference on Advanced Visual Interfaces (AVI 2002), Trento, Italy, pp. 373–374. ACM Press, New York (2002)
35. Valiati, E.R.A., Freitas, C.M.D.S., Pimenta, M.S.: Using Multi-dimensional in-depth Long-term Case Studies for Information Visualization Evaluation. In: Bertini, E., Perer, A., Plaisant, C., Santucci, G. (eds.) B Proceedings of the 2008 AVI Workshop on BEyond Time and Errors: Novel Evaluation Methods for Information Visualization (BELIV 2008), Florence, Italy, pp. 1–7. ACM press, New York (2008)
36. Julien, C.-A., Leide, J.E., Bouthillier, F.: Controlled User Evaluations of Information Visualization Interfaces for Text Retrieval: Literature Review and Meta-analysis. Journal of the American Society for Information Science and Technology 59(6), 1012–1024 (2008)
37. Wilson, M.L.: An Analytical Inspection Framework for Evaluating the Search Tactics and User Profiles Supported by Information Seeking Interfaces. Ph.D., University of Southampton, Southampton, United Kingdom (2009)
38. North, C.: Toward Measuring Visualization Insight. IEEE Computer Graphics and Applications 26(3), 6–9 (2006)
39. Rester, M., Pohl, M.: Methods for the evaluation of an interactive InfoVis tool supporting exploratory reasoning processes. In: Bertini, E., Plaisant, C., Santucci, G. (eds.) Proceedings of the 2006 AVI workshop on BEyond Time and Errors: Novel Evaluation Methods for Information Visualization, pp. 1–6. ACM Press, New York (2006)
40. Zuk, T., Schlesier, L., Neumann, P., Hancock, M.S., Carpendale, S.: Heuristics for information visualization evaluation. In: Bertini, E., Plaisant, C., Santucci, G. (eds.) Proceedings of the 2006 AVI workshop on BEyond Time and Errors: Novel Evaluation Methods for Information Visualization, pp. 1–6. ACM Press, New York (2006)

Author Index